W9-CPF-834

REVOLUTION

Take Charge Strategies for Business Success

JIM TOMPKINS

Library of Congress Cataloging-in-Publication Data

Revolution: take charge strategies for business success.

Includes index.
I. Leadership II. Success in Business I. Tompkins, James A.
HD31.T636 1998 658.4—dc20 98-96796
ISBN: 0-9658659-4-0

I dedicate this book to the many Revolutionary clients of Tompkins Associates, Inc. who have provided me the opportunity to grow, to participate in their Revolutions, and to become a Revolutionary Leader.

Jim Tompkins
October, 1998
Raleigh, North Carolina

Contents

PART I
Foundations

Preface

Peak performance doesn't necessarily lead to success. In fact, peak performance often leads to failure. This is true both for individuals and for organizations, and due to today's turbulent times, the definition of peak performance changes daily. What was yesterday's peak performance is merely good performance today, average performance next week, and poor performance next month. Once an individual or organization has achieved peak performance, the tendency is to stop getting better. Thus begins the journey to failure.

Therefore the key to long-term success is not the achievement of peak performance, but rather the continuous process of beginning anew and climbing to a new peak, and the next peak, and the next peak. A Revolutionary Leader is one who is able to continuously climb to one new peak after another. A Revolutionary Organization is an organization that is able to continuously climb to new peak after new peak by creating a culture that continuously improves relationships with its employees and partners.

This book is a guide for you as an individual and for you as a member of an organization as you seek to achieve Peak-to-Peak Performance. This book is based upon my experiences and my observations. As an individual, I have gone from success to failure, from failure to success, and from success to success. As a consultant to some of the world's largest organizations, smallest organizations, and everything else in between, I have watched and actively participated as these organizations have gone from success to failure, from failure to success, and from success to success. I have been down headed up, up headed down, and up heading higher. Personally and professionally I have learned many lessons from these experiences. This book presents my discoveries, as well as a roadmap for you to follow to become a Revolutionary Organization and to achieve Peak-to-Peak performance.

I have consciously been learning the principles of Organizational Revolution for over 20 years, and I can track my subconscious awareness of the Revolution principles to more than 40 years ago. We all have been successful at something, and then subsequently been unsuccessful at the same thing. That's life. The success of life has a lot to do with our ability to learn from our successes as well as failures, and to use this knowledge to travel to new levels of success. This process of Peak-to-Peak evolution has always been at the core of every successful individual and organization.

For your organization to become a Revolutionary Organization, you must learn the principles that make any Revolution successful and then apply them to your Organizational Revolution. By observing the principles of Revolution, we find that businesses wishing to become Revolutionary must pursue Revolution in four key areas: *Foundations, Leadership, Collaboration*, and *Rewards*. This book unveils for you seventeen principles of Revolution grouped into these four key areas, each followed by a thorough application of the principle to Organizational Revolution. I believe you are about to discover what you have been searching for to turn your organization toward continuous success, and in a format that is going to have immediate application.

This books combines science, which is the discovery, testing, and documentationof data, with engineering, which is the application of science. I have done all I can to present both the science and application of Organizational Revolution to you in a reader-friendly, interesting, and compelling way. My goal for this book is to supply you with more actual, usable, take-away information than you have ever found in a book before.

Many organizations have allowed Tompkins Associates, Inc., to help them become Revolutionary Organizations. I am indebted to these clients because it is through their confidence that the Revolutionary process has evolved and continues to evolve. It is these clients that deserve the credit for this book.

The last three words of the conclusion of this book are, *Go, Go, Go*. In concert with this ending, allow me to strongly encourage you now, at the outset, to *Begin, Begin, Begin*.

Part I

Foundations

Organizations are not truly successful when they achieve peak performance, as their achievement of peak performance is often the beginning of failure. More often than not, success leads not to success, but to failure. True organizational success occurs when the organization understands that today's peak performance is tomorrow's good performance, next week's average performance, and next month's poor performance. True organizational success occurs only when an organization understands that it must continuously evolve from one level of peak performance to a higher level, to a higher level, and still higher. This process of continuously creating Peak-to-Peak Performance requires a commitment to continuous improvement, harnessing the energy of change, motivational leadership, Revolutionizing corporate culture, and alignment. These five requirements are the foundations of Organizational Revolution and true success.

This first section develops these foundations of Organizational Revolution in detail. If you are genuinely wanting to Revolutionize your organization and achieve Peak-to-Peak Performance, this is where you must begin, and where you must continuously return. As you begin your journey toward Revolution, keep in mind that the present valley you may be in does not have to be a permanent position. Success can be attained. But I don't want you to see this book merely as a way out of your present valley. I want this book to lead you from peak, to peak, to peak. . .; and from success, to success, to success. . . . It is the repetition of success that defines true success. This is what I want for your organization, and I am certain it is what you want as well. Let's begin the journey.

1

Continuous Process

Revolution Principle #1:

Revolution is never a spur-of-the-moment decision. It is a process, and in a true revolutionary scenerio, a continuous process.

"Success has ruined many a man."

—Benjamin Franklin

"Each success only buys an admission ticket to a more difficult problem."

—Henry Kissinger

"We cannot solve today's problems with the same level of thinking that created the problems in the first place."

—Albert Einstein

Revolution must be a process. In any context, attempting to initiate change in a thoughtless, cavalier manner is bound to backfire and fail. Successful Revolution is the end result of a long, thoughtful, and persistent process. The Revolution process usually follows this pattern:

- *Irritation.* An uncomfortable problem becomes apparent.
- *Motivation.* Someone, usually a charismatic leader, calls attention to the problem and holds out the vision of solving the problem.
- *Education.* Those who suffer under the problem seek to understand its complex nature.
- *Collaboration.* Those who understand the problem and are still convinced they can solve it, bind together to develop a powerful force. They collectively plan their strategy for solving the problem.
- *Action.* The motivated, educated group carries out its plan to solve the problem.

A Revolution which fails to pursue any part of this pattern will be unsuccessful because each element is integral to the others and represents a crucial part of the total process.

Further, a Revolution which ceases its revolutionary process becomes subject to a counterrevolution, leading to chaos rather than improvement. We have seen this far too often in third world politics, with its numerous subsequent attempts at para-military take-overs. Sure, you can force the president into exile and become the new dictator, but the moment you get comfortable a new coup is forming to kick you out. The continuous process principle is the foundational principle for successful Revolution.

How does this continuous process principle apply to business? Revolution in the business environment must be seen not as improvement, but as continuous improvement—a continuous process. Whatever business you're in, as you celebrate your climb to the top of the mountain, many are planning to topple you. There is no lasting solution to the business problems you face. In fact, every solution brings with it more problems. There is no paradigm shift that will make us whole for the long term. There is no magic, no quick fix, and no solution to stop the flow of problems. Sure, implementing new programs may change the problems, but the problems themselves will never go away. There will always be more. In fact, this is the fundamental premise upon which the business of the future must operate: The more success you have, the more problems you have. You fight and fight and fight to get to the top, to achieve peak performance. Then, just as you start to celebrate, you begin your subtle but sure decline. Why? Because when you get to the top you are no longer the underdog, some other organization now has that role. And it is in part a result of your success that these other underdogs believe they too can climb the mountain and knock you off. So the question is not have you reached peak performance; it is have you learned to travel from one peak to another peak? And is your organization poised to thrive on the problems, changes, and threats each new peak brings?

To increase their responsiveness to change and its related problems, business leaders must realize that they do not need another program, but rather a fundamental shift in the way they do business. We don't need a solution to the immediate problems, but a new way of doing business which realistically faces the fact that there is no solution and that problems are continuous. We need a solution that recognizes that the only way to win is to change our approach to business, one which installs a process that anticipates and solves problems before they are problems, and one which continuously transforms theirs into an organization with strong, prosperous longevity. These basic characteristics are what define business success today, and even more so tomorrow. Even further, they are the first step toward Organizational Revolution.

Why is Success so Dangerous?

Success and failure are both a part of life. No matter what you do, you will need to learn to deal with both success and failure. Here are the four patterns of success and failure you must understand:

1. FAIL/FAIL: You fail and you fail some more. You have not been successful, you lose confidence, and so you fail again. The result? An even further lack of confidence, more failure, and a resignation to failing. You stop trying. You fail.
2. FAIL/SUCCEED: You fail, you learn, and you succeed. You have not been successful, but you learn from your lack of success. You enjoy and are motivated by the underdog role. Your motivation to be successful uses the failures as building blocks to your becoming successful. You succeed.
3. SUCCEED/FAIL: You're successful, you become content with your success, and you stop getting better. Your dreams come true, and you don't replace them with new dreams. You become invincible in your own mind, you protect what you have instead of pushing forward, your decline accelerates, you blame others, and you fail.

4. SUCCEED/SUCCEED: You're successful, but you realize that since you are no longer the underdog that you *are* in fact the underdog. You are dedicated to getting better, you define new dreams, and you focus all your energies on getting better. In fact, you no longer want to be the best of the best, you want to be better than the best, in a category all by yourself. You continue to succeed. You believe in creating Peak-to-Peak Performance.

Why is success so dangerous? Because most organizations cycle through time alternating between the Fail/Succeed and Succeed/Fail modes. They begin with a surge of entrepreneurial energy and climb the mountain to success; the organization achieves peak performance. They become smug, stop being entrepreneurial, protect their success, decline, and fail. Their performance falls and they find themselves in a valley. They bring in new leadership, reorganize, reignite the entrepreneurial fires, and once again climb the mountain to success—peak performance. Unfortunately, they again become smug, again stop being entrepreneurial, and again return to the valley. This cycle goes on and on.

An outsider may not see these cycles at work in many big organizations because different portions of the organizations are at different phases of their Fail/Succeed or Succeed/Fail cycles. In the aggregate they appear to be stable. But they are *not* stable. They are merely cycling out of a phase and giving the appearance of stability. This Fail/Succeed or Succeed/Fail cycling will generally continue over time until an organization loses touch with its own mortality and cycles from a Succeed/Fail into a Fail/Fail. Then everyone asks, "What happened?" and "How could such a great company go out of business?"

There is another way! Not many have found this way, but it is captured in these quotations from a few people who are the Succeed/Succeed pioneers. These individuals truly understood how to create Peak-to-Peak Performance. Consider John Wooden, the greatest college basketball coach of all times who said:

"It's what you learn after you know it all that counts."[1]

Or consider the words of Jerry Garcia, leader of the most successful concert rock group of all times, the Grateful Dead:

"You don't just want to be considered the best of the best. You want to be considered the only one who does what you do."[2]

Or, from Oliver Cromwell:

"He who stops being better, stops being good."[3]

My Personal Story

Let's take my case as an example. My career can be summarized as having built a successful engineering-based consulting firm while having two major detours, one in diversification and one in real estate. I have been to the peak, to the valley, back to the peak, back to the valley, and once again to the peak. Upon arriving at the peak for the third time, I made a pledge to never again travel to the valley.

Having made this pledge, I began pursuing the science of individual and organizational peak performance. I have learned a lot, and some of what I've learned may shake some of your beliefs. Nevertheless, the natural order of individual and organizational life is clear: Success does not breed success.

So what is the science of peak performance? It is this science that defines the process of harnessing the energy of change. It is my hope that you are able to apply this science, both individually and corporately, to stay out of your valleys. Take it from one who has been there: The peaks are a lot more fun!

As I began my understanding of peak performance, I discovered that many before me had wrestled with the issues I was trying to understand. Particularly useful were quotations from Benjamin Franklin and Winston Churchill who said, respectively, "Success has ruined many a man,"[4] and "Success is rarely final."[5]

These quotes allowed me to understand that the natural order of life is not "success breeds success." The statements by Franklin and Churchill expressed their understanding that success is not a permanent state and is often the beginning of failure. But why does this happen? Henry Kissinger lays the groundwork with the quotation, "Each success only buys an admission ticket to a more difficult problem."[6]

Success Leads to More Challenges

Let's use a metaphor of life as a series of rooms. Each of us, individually and collectively as organizations, needs an admission ticket to travel from room to room. At any given point, you and your organization may find yourselves in a room full of challenges. You work hard, you overcome these challenges, and you achieve peak performance.

While you're basking in your success in the first room, you receive an admission ticket to the next room with a new set of challenges. In fact, these challenges, if not conquered, could become major problems that will send you to a valley instead of a peak. These new problems are difficult because they are different from the problems in the previous rooms. Albert Einstein referred to this when he said, "We cannot solve today's problems with the same level of thinking that created the problem in the first place." We obtain admission to a new room because of our success, but if we think like we did in the old rooms, we will never maintain peak performance.

Business is difficult, and it will become even more difficult as economics become more globalized, but what are you going to do about it? You have two choices: You can choose to cycle through the Success/Failure routine which, with the barrage of downsizing, rightsizing, delayering, restructuring, repositioning, demassing, and reengineering, is clearly the dominant pattern of business today. Or you can decide to Revolutionize the fundamental way you do business and move from one level of peak-performance to yet higher levels of peak-performance confidently carrying your success into the future. After all, why not become better than the best? Why not grow? Why not be successful today, tomorrow, and into the future? Each organization has the opportunity of becoming the best, then better than the best; of achieving peak performance, then ascending to new peaks. But their leaders must decide to make the journey. As numerous Nike ads have said, "You can do it."

IT ISN'T MAGIC

If it isn't magic, what makes corporations disappear? The caption to a figure in the *Fortune* article, "Dinosaurs," was "Some Leaders in Market Value Do a Disappearing Act."[7] In 1972 the company with the world's highest stock market valuation was IBM, with a value of $47 billion. Again in 1982, IBM led the world with a value of $57 billion. However, in 1992 IBM did not even make the top 25, and had a value of only $29 billion. Similarly, General Motors was in fourth place in 1972 with a value of $23 billion, fifth place in 1982 with a value of $19 billion, but in 1992 fell all the way to 40th place with a value of $22 billion. Also, Sears Roebuck was in sixth place with a value of $18 billion in 1972, 13th place at $10 billion in 1982, and in 81st place in 1992 with a value below $16 billion.

The key to keep in mind here is that during these same twenty years (1972–1992) the Standard and Poors 500 was up 269 percent. What happened? How could these three giants all fall? At GM the most common explanation is "inability to execute;" at IBM "When a company gets to the top, the process of how decisions are made becomes all-consuming. The focus is on how decisions are made rather than what you decide." At Sears they created a "whole library of bulletins that spell out procedures for dealing with almost any problem." Lots of procedures, but no action. Will these giant companies disappear? It isn't clear. It *is* clear that they went from success to failure in a big way; the next phase is up to the present leadership. They can cycle from failure back to success or to their ultimate failure. The choice is theirs. If they pursue Revolution they certainly can go from failure to success, to success, to success, and so on. Or they may totally disappear. Either way, it will not be magic.

Where Are We Today?

In some ways it's almost scary to pick up a newspaper or watch the news; so much is happening. Business is crazy, the world is crazy. The dismantling of the Berlin Wall in 1989 marked the beginning of a change campaign. Absolutely nothing is stable; everything is in transition. In the business world, we have been shocked by layoff after layoff, bankruptcy after bankruptcy, and merger after merger, to the point that we aren't shocked any longer. In the political arena we have been shaken by unstable currencies, public debt, and political unrest, so much so that we are no longer fazed by any of it. We have become calloused and deadened to the neverending change in which we live. The only constant today and into the future is an ever-increasing rate of change. Change is occurring so rapidly that before an organization has adapted to the last change, a new one occurs. There is no steady state. Organizations must not only learn to live with constant change, but also to embrace change and harness its energy to become better and better. Successful organizations use the energy of change to continuously move to new peaks of performance, evolving into the future at a record-setting pace.

CHANGE–CHANGE–CHANGE–CHANGE–CHANGE

- In 1956 there were 7000 periodicals published in the United States. Today there are over 22,000.
- In 1989 the average supermarket stocked 25,000 items. Today there are over 30,000 items.
- From 1892 to 1982 there was only one Coke. Today there are seven varieties.
- In today's automobile there are more dollars in its microelectronics than its steel.
- When I was a boy you could either buy tennis shoes or basketball shoes. By 1980 you could buy tennis, basketball, running, walking, aerobic, and cross-training styles. Today one company sells ten versions of their walking shoes, including one to only walk uphill.

In the early 1990s, the philosophy of paradigm-shifting became popular as a way to keep up with change. Now we must realize that when you shift from one paradigm, you go on to another. We don't need just a shift in paradigms, but a realization that we must continuously shift from paradigm to paradigm. Today's rate of change demands a process for continuous paradigm-shifting and a continuous escalation to new levels of peak performance. It is the paradigm-shift mentality that has caused businesses to shift from one program to another. Many of these programs were valid, but since they were viewed as programs they were destined to fail. It is interesting to view the life of a program as it travels through its phases:

Phase I: Skepticism
Phase II: Excitement
Phase III: Acceptance
Phase IV: Questioning
Phase V: Disillusion
Phase VI: Dismissal

It doesn't matter which program it is (Malcolm Baldrige National Quality Award, Just-In-Time, Total Quality Management, Reengineering, Efficient Consumer Response, etc.); it will succumb to these phases because programs aren't miraculous. Although this is hard for fad-chasers to accept, there is no one program which possesses the hidden secret to your success. These programs can be beneficial, but they can't be viewed as independent pieces of a puzzle which, when implemented, will miraculously usher in an organization's long-term success. The problem lies in the Success/Fail evolution of organizations as they move from program to program. It's okay to pursue these programs, but only within the context of an ongoing, continuous *process* of discovery, learning, growing, evolving, improving, and performing. It is the adoption of this process that defines true success, not the adoption of the latest program.

NO MORE MIRACULOUS RECOVERIES

Robert Eaton, as the new chairman of Chrysler, was very upbeat as he read to his management team a *Wall Street Journal* article about the "miraculous recovery" of Chrysler in the early 1990s. He shocked his managers, however, when he reminded them that the same Chrysler miraculous recovery story had been written in 1956, then again in 1965, 1976, and again in 1983. Eaton told his managers, "I've got a better idea. Let's stop getting sick. My personal ambition is to be the first chairman never to lead a Chrysler comeback."

Call to Action

A successful organization understands the process of continuous renewal, of Success/Success – Success/Success – Success/Success, of being the underdog *because* you are on top, and of non-stop ascension to higher levels of peak performance. A successful organization is one that is dedicated to growing, to prospering, to being successful, and to building more success. To accomplish these patterns of genuine success, you must pursue Revolution! What will be your next performance destination, a peak or a valley?

2

The Science of Change

Revolution Principle #2:

Genuine revolution seeks to change for the sake of improvement.

"If you always do what you've always done, the future will look a lot like the past."

—Unknown

"Let us not mistake change for progress."

—Abraham Lincoln

Revolution and change are synonymous. Revolution is simply premeditated change. However, genuine Revolution is change for the sake of improvement, never change for the sake of change. Revolution requires far too much energy and far too much unease not to operate for the sake of improvement. To maintain motivation and commitment, a Revolution must promise a higher level of existence at the end. Life must have the potential of becoming better, easier, or more profitable, or those involved will abandon the cause.

There is no virtue in change outside of improvement. Change does not imply better unless better means change. When the motive for change is power, personal advancement, or forced authority, change is trouble. But when the motive for change is to meet new challenges, to advance the well-being of the group, to increase effectiveness or freedom, or to force out corrupt leadership, change is virtuous and should be welcomed. This is how one must judge the validity of any Revolution.

In business, change is shaded by the same principles. It can be either a welcomed, though uncomfortable, ally, or a deadly foe, all depending on the motive and the goal. I want to talk about change in the positive sense and argue that if its energy is harnessed and if its motive is to improve the well-being of the entire organization, then it should be embraced and used, as opposed to simply tolerated and managed.

Assumptions Can Kill You

The quotation, "If you always do what you've always done, the future will look a lot like the past," is true only if everything else (not just what *you* do) stays the same. When the environment changes, doing what you always do will result in a future even worse than the past!

Extending this thought further, one can see a paradigm that is often an invisible portion of a company's business plan: The past is a good indicator of the future. Unfortunately, for many organizations, this is not true. In most organizations today, the future is not based upon the past but rather upon the present. This radical idea can help us reevaluate our thinking about harnessing the energy of change.

The traditional process of managing change indicates that we used to be at Point A (past, present) and need to manage the process to get to Point B (future). Realistically, though, yesterday's performance will not be acceptable tomorrow. If we are basing the future on the past instead of the present, we will always be behind. In addition, change brings discontinuities that interrupt the smooth flow of a simple line. For instance, when a new technology comes to market, it makes projecting from the present impossible.

Don't Manage Change, Use It

We must realize that the phrase "manage change" is inconsistent. In fact, I believe the phrase is an oxymoron. To manage means to control. In today's dynamic environment, do you believe any person has the ability to control change? None of us can control change, so any attempt to "manage" change will be futile.

What we need to do is not try to manage change, but rather to understand how to harness the energy of change. To do this we must understand the science of change.

The Science of Change

Success today is based upon our ability to harness the energy of change. Unfortunately, many resist change because it often requires pain. By resisting change, we are subconsciously resisting success.

Begin understanding the science of change by understanding the relationship between change and pain. The creation of pain to accompany change is a natural function. Pain is our body's way of telling us we are harming ourselves. In a similar way, pain is an organization's signal that it is harming itself. This organizational pain may occur in quality problems, competitiveness, customer satisfaction, turnover, and so on. For your organization to prosper, you will have pain. So the challenge is not *if* this pain occurs but *how* your organization responds.

The Opportunity in Change

The challenge is not the pain, the negative event. The challenge, and in fact the opportunity, is how we respond to this pain. We must not resist change and flee from pain. We need to find a process to harness change and eliminate pain. We need a Revolution in the way we deal with change.

Resilience and Change

The pain of change is affected by an individual's and an organization's resilience, along with the speed of change. Resilience is an individual's or an organization's ability to absorb change or the ability to bounce back after setbacks.

If the speed of change is less than our resilience, we are able to deal with the pain. As a result, we are able to harness the energy of change and become successful. If the speed of change is greater than our resilience, the pain of change is too much. As a result we feel stress, disorientation, and we gradually grind to a halt as we fail. Since we cannot control the speed of change, it is vital that we build up our resilience and the ability to manage our resilience capacity.

Individual resilience depends on our individual perceptions of our certainty and control levels. The higher our certainty of a change and the higher our control over a change, the less energy we need to allocate to a change.

This is why we all respond differently to change. Have you noticed that two individuals faced with the exact same event will react differently? The person with low resilience, a high level of uncertainty, or perceived low control is going to experience more pain and will resist change. The person with higher resilience and a high level of certainty or control will deal with the pain and harness the energy of change.

The Total System

Interestingly, our personal resilience has a lot to do with our personal lives, our careers, and our social consciousness. Our personal lives often control our resilience capacity. For example, if your personal life occupies all your energy for change and you are under major stress, you have very little capacity to deal with change in your professional life. Thus if a person has car trouble, a parking ticket, a sick child, a sore knee, a big credit card bill, and a broken garage door opener, it is not surprising that they would resist professional change. This person is taxed to their capacity and resists change in an attempt to expend as little energy as possible in their profession.

An interesting conclusion drawn from this is that an organization has no choice but to be interested in the entire person, since resilience comes from the person's entire life. Thus, organizations that are concerned with their employees' total quality of life and promote balance between work and home lives are on target to better harness the energy of change.

Building Your Capacity

Maybe you have overlooked the fact that managing your resilience also involves raising your resilience capacity. Guidelines that will prove useful in managing your resilience capacity include:

1. *Raising your resilience capacity comes from both increased pain management and remedy management.* Pain management is an ability that pushes us from the present to the future. Remedy management requires an understanding of the benefits that result from embracing change. This understanding provides the motivation to deal with the pain of change and wholeheartedly embrace the tasks needed to achieve growth. Remedy management pulls us from the present to the future. For prolonged change (and thus prolonged success), organizations must excel at both pain management and remedy management.
2. *Lowering the effort needed to harness the energy of change requires an organization to deal with the perceived levels of certainty and control.* Certainty results from clear expectations, no surprises, and continuity of organizational purpose. Control comes from participation, involvement, appropriate empowerment, and the timeliness of the information flowing in the organization. When certainty and control are high, individuals require less effort to harness the energy of change. Thus, they are more able to handle an increased speed of change and a correspondingly accelerated rate of success.
3. *The energy to deal with change comes from having a balanced life.* Just as tightrope walkers must have everything in balance before they can confidently move forward with a minimal risk of falling, so too individuals must have balance in their lives so that they may confidently move forward. Organizations must be interested in all aspects of an employee's life since things done in one's personal life play a major role in how successful one is in one's professional life.

Boomerang Principles

In order to become a successful organization that truly harnesses the energy of change, you must consider the four "Boomerang Principles":

1. *What comes back is exactly what is put forth.* When you throw a boomerang, you don't get some other boomerang back; you get the same one. As an organization pursues becoming a Revolutionary peak-to-peak organization, the reactions, responses, and commitment received will mirror the feelings, thoughts, and commitment you put forth. In both words and actions, your dedication to creating Peak-to-Peak Performance will be mirrored in the words and actions of others.
2. *What comes back is always more than what was put forth.* A boomerang gains momentum and returns at a faster speed. As an organization pursues becoming a Revolutionary peak-to-peak organization, the synergy that evolves acts as a multiplier for the evolution of renewal progress, improvement, growth, and success.
3. *Results are always obtained after the investment is made.* A boomerang never comes back until after it is thrown. How long it takes to return depends upon many complex factors and is very difficult to predict. The same is true with the process of becoming a Revolutionary, peak-to-peak enterprise—it takes time.
4. *Benefits will be positive only if the peak-to-peak leader knows the path.* Sometimes a boomerang is thrown and comes back. Sometimes it doesn't. It takes practice to know how to throw a boomerang. The same is true for a Revolutionary organization. The leader needs to know how to nurture the process and overcome difficulties. To ensure success, the leader must have an in-depth understanding of the peak-to-peak process. Only then will Peak-to-Peak Performance result.

Call to Action

Unfortunately, there is no seven-step plan to help every organization harness the energy of change. The path to success is to take action. The most important thing you can achieve is to decide to harness the energy of change and use it for your organizational good, rather than being run over by it. Here are four actions to begin the change process:

1. Analyze "pain" symptoms to see what they're telling you.
2. Balance your life to increase your personal resilience.
3. Use the energy of changing situations to achieve new goals.
4. When you're successful, expect new challenges.

The key to success is to take action. Starting quickly and continuing to accelerate will create a sense of momentum, which pulls people into the process.

3

Follow the Leader

Revolution Principle #3:

Although Revolution is a grassroots effort, it is characterized by its leaders.

The most important element of a Revolution is its leaders. Even if the ranks of a revolution number a million constituents, without proper leadership there will not be an effective Revolution, but rather only a chaotic uprising; and we have seen plenty of those.

Both elements of a Revolution are vital—the grassroots element and the leadership element. Leaders without grassroots support and voluntary infrastructure become dictators. Grassroots energy without proper leadership, or with poor or corrupt leadership, becomes merely a fringe element. But grassroots energy channeled by solid, integrity-laden leadership becomes a movement with permanent, lasting results.

The role of leaders of Revolutions is primarily to motivate. They are the individuals who hold up the vision, who remind people of the benefits, who set the course, and who reward faithfulness and courage. Leaders either make or break a Revolution.

The application of this Revolution principle to business is so direct, it's almost frightening. A successful organization, particularly one pursuing Revolution, is characterized by people who exhibit a high level of energy, intensity, passion, and determination to continuously aspire in the direction of their vision. Revolution leaders must exhibit those same characteristics and aspirations, but even more so. They must surpass their employees in energy, intensity, passion, and determination in order to motivate. Even more, they must channel the energy of everyone else in the following ways:

1. How they think
2. How they communicate
3. How they work
4. How they treat people

Leaders Motivate by How They Think

Leadership is not a set of personality traits. However, all genuine leaders do have six key qualities which represent the essence of a leader. These qualities define the inner character of the leader, whereas the other three leadership characteristics (how they communicate, work, and treat people) define the outer character. These are vital to the integrity of a Revolution, because they are what characterize the action. The six key qualities are:

- **Integrity**
  Integrity means that the leader tells and lives the truth. Integrity means that the leader deals in a straightforward, sincere fashion with people and situations, and that they do not compromise on that which they believe to be true. Integrity demands the specification of ethical behavior and the elimination of Mickey Mouse rules and regulations that induce game-playing and cheating. Integrity demands honesty in all dealings, where honesty is measured by the consistency between word and deed, by leaders doing what they say they will do. It is from this honesty that trust and loyalty spring.

No organization can be successful without a trust of leadership, and a loyalty from subordinate to leader and from leader to subordinate. The similarity of the following two quotations from two well-known leaders keynotes how essential integrity is to a leader. First, Margaret Thatcher, the dynamic leader of England, having served more than 11 years as Prime Minister, speaks about her upbringing:

> "We were Methodists, and Methodist means method. We were taught what was right and wrong in considerable detail. There were certain things you just didn't do and that was that."[1]

Secondly, from Senator Sam J. Ervin, Jr., who, during the nationally televised Watergate hearings, gave clear evidence of his loyalty to the truth when he said:

> "What's right is right, and what's wrong is wrong, and you can't compromise with integrity."[2]

- **Credibility**

Credibility is related to integrity but is more than integrity, in that it includes being *accountable*, being *genuine*, and being *open*. Credibility is one of the most difficult qualities for a leader to maintain, as there exists today a cynicism, a skepticism, and a level of scrutiny that often results in the wrongful loss of credibility.

Unfortunately, credibility is earned minute by minute, hour by hour, day by day, and week by week, but may be lost in a moment by a misspoken remark, a slip of the tongue, a careless act, or even just the *appearance* of one of these minor transgressions. If leaders aren't genuine and open with themselves, they will lose credibility. But even if they *are* genuine and open with themselves, they stand a real risk of wrongfully losing credibility.

The leader's path to credibility, then, is not an easy one. They must take care in all their interactions that they are clear, precise, accurate, and cannot be misunderstood or misrepresented. It is only after a tremendous level of credibility has been established between a leader and an ally that one's guard may be relaxed. Even then, the leader who wishes to maintain a high level of credibility must work hard at being responsive, accountable, sensitive, sincere, and genuine.

- **Enthusiasm**

For many years, managers have been taught that their feelings and emotions should not be brought to work. This is wrong! In fact, as Ralph Waldo Emerson has said, "Nothing great was ever accomplished without enthusiasm."[3] Revolution and Peak-to-Peak Performance is most easily achieved when people's feelings and emotions are unleashed. Many managers have believed that an outward display of emotion indicates weakness; that to be enthusiastic about something was to demonstrate a lack of maturity and a loss of professionalism. We all have been in companies where smiling was frowned upon. This is so unfortunate!

The truth is, if you want people to get excited about something, you must first get excited yourself. Leaders must be excited about, and demonstrate an enthusiasm for, the future. They must exhibit energy, have a bounce in their step about what's happening and what will be happening. Have you ever noticed that they call the persons doing cheers on the sidelines "cheer*leaders*" and not cheer-*managers*? Leaders must be cheerleaders for their organizations, not in a plastic or phony manner, but in a sincere, genuine manner. It is a fact that enthusiasm is contagious, even for oneself; if you desire to be enthusiastic, you must simply act enthusiastic. It is as basic as planting apple seeds to get apple trees, planting acorns to get great oaks. So we plant enthusiasm to get enthusiasm. Leaders must be inspirational, and from their inspiration will flow an enthusiasm for Revolution and Peak-to-Peak Performance in the following hours, days, weeks, months, and years.

- **Optimism**

From enthusiasm comes optimism. Optimism is an incurable condition of people who focus on success. Optimism comes from an inner confidence in what you are doing and the course you are pursuing. It is the confidence in oneself that keeps an optimist from getting hung up by minor setbacks and always focusing on the path forward.

Perhaps the best way to define the power of optimism is to look at a situation in which there was a loss of optimism. Think about Karl Wallenda, one of the greatest tightrope aerialists of all times. Shortly after Wallenda fell to his death during a performance in Puerto Rico, his wife described Wallenda's loss of confidence. She recalled: "All Karl thought about for three straight months, prior to the Puerto Rico performance, was falling. It was the first time he'd ever thought about that, and it seemed to me that he put all his energies into not falling rather than walking the tightrope. The great Wallenda lost his confidence and fell to his death because of it."[4]

By way of contrast, consider Lee Trevino, one of the all-time money winners on both the PGA Tour and the PGA Seniors Tour. Prior to a U.S. Open Lee had consulted a doctor, seeking relief from the flu. The doctor told Lee not to play, as his flu might get worse. His reply was "Might get better . . . might even win!" He came in second. Another time, he was asked how he thought he would do in the Canadian Open. He responded, "Are you kidding, that's my tournament!" The next week he won his third Canadian Open in four years. Lee Trevino is an optimist. All genuine leaders must be optimists.

- **Urgency**

Leaders cannot change the past. They can impact the future, but only based upon what they do *today*, what they do *now*! Leaders must act with a sense of urgency so that their organization will act with a sense of urgency. They must help their people understand that Peak-to-Peak Performance is continuous, that it is never ending, and that the time for action is *now*. They must help their people prepare for the next battle, rather than savoring the win from the last battle.

A successful organization truly understands the challenge of time compression and demonstrates true hustle. An approach which I adopted more than ten years ago is a salutation I use on most memos. This salutation has become sort of a trademark, and has now been embossed on a plaque, a tee-shirt, and a hat. This salutation summarizes my desire for action, my encouragement to do something, and my belief that anything that is worth doing is worth doing now. My salutation is "*Go, Go, Go!*"

- **Determination**

The leader demonstrates determination by courageously stepping forward, by facing doubts and uncertainties, accepting risk, and moving forward. In short, leaders act.

Leaders have the courage to pioneer, to step out into the unknown. This is not to say that they never have doubts, uncertainties, or concerns. To the contrary, they do have these feelings, but they put up a good front. They do not burden others with their concerns and they push themselves out of the comfort zone and keep on going. The leader is brave enough to fail and has created a work environment where it is okay to fail.

Leaders are driven and results-oriented. They are known for their "take-charge" personalities and because of their determination are self-starting and change-oriented. Their determination results in them being both friendly and firm. Leaders who are too firm bulldoze their people and do not inspire them to great performance. Leaders who are too friendly do not challenge their people, so little is accomplished. Leaders must balance the friendly aspects of being pleasant, personable, likable, and interesting with the firm aspects of competitiveness, aggressiveness, and high expectations. It is this balance that creates the determination required to pull an organization forward to Peak-to-Peak Performance.

Leaders Motivate by How They Communicate

Leaders don't think of communication as something *they* do, but view it from the receiver's end. That's to say, for them communication is not the generation of a message, but rather the *receipt* of the message by the receiver. It is only after a receiver gets a message (either correctly or incorrectly) that a message can be said to have been communicated (this applies to either good or bad communication). This receiver-oriented way of viewing communication, therefore, includes not only what a leader may say, but everything that has an impact on how the receiver may receive the message.

While discussing the fact that communication consists of a great deal more than what leaders say, A.J. Zaremba presents the following examples of organizational communication problems in his book, *Management In A New Key: Communication in the Modern Organization*:

1. The inappropriate use of print communication. An overabundance of memos, bulletins, and internal letters.
2. A hyperactive grapevine. An unusually active 'informal' communication network, which spreads inaccurate information.
3. A defensive communication climate which intimidates employees and keeps them from expressing themselves without fear of retribution.

4. A credibility problem within the organization that makes employees wonder about the veracity of the messages they do receive.
5. A weak interoffice mail system which results in correspondence being received late.
6. An ineffective method of notifying employees of how well or how poorly they are performing. This often results in fear, mistrust, and sometimes anger toward the organization.
7. Employee perceptions that no one is concerned with their suggestions and input. This results in employee reluctance to communicate to management regarding important issues that management needs to know about.
8. A heavy and inappropriate reliance on committees and meetings. Meetings are not the panacea for all organizational problems and sometimes create communication problems because of overuse and/or meeting mismanagement.
9. Informational briefings/presentations that are neither informational nor brief and are perceived as time wasters by subordinates.[5]

Zaremba goes on to present the elements necessary for leaders to communicate effectively:

1. Use various methods of sending information in order to facilitate accurate receipt.
2. Cultivate and maintain viable networks that permit the flow of organizational information.
3. Cultivate a supportive organizational climate that is conducive to sending and receiving information.
4. Recognize the importance of nonverbal factors in determining communication success.
5. Be capable of making presentations consistent with specific organizational needs.
6. Be capable of interacting with employees on a comfortable, one-to-one level.
7. Intelligently participate in and manage conferences and meetings consistent with specific organizational needs.[6]

The overall responsibility of communications, then, is shared between the organization and the leader.

What is the communication role of the leader? Communication is not just what leaders say. Communication is also what leaders don't say, how they say what they say, and how they act in general. There is nothing more important to a leader's communication ability than their ability to "walk in the other person's moccasins." Empathy is critical to quality communications, but it is not just feeling *for* another person, it is feeling *with* them. My wife always laughs at me because when I watch a boxing match on television, I "bob and weave." When I watch the movie *Rocky*, it's as if I am in the ring with him. I feel the punches, I throw my punches, I feel the thrill of victory. This is empathy. It is truly being in the other person's shoes.

Being "other person–focused" is the key to being successful at receiver-oriented communication. This empathy requires leaders to be open and sensitive to others, to realize all people are unique, and to recognize that everyone has the potential to receive the same message differently. Leaders need to understand that it is possible for twenty people to hear the same presentation, but have twenty different understandings of what was said. For this reason, leaders must communicate in simple words, with conviction and certainty. The objective is to ensure the receivers get the message the leader is sending. All chances for ambiguity must be eliminated.

Models of Great Communication

Consider Margaret Thatcher's speech to a group of business leaders in which she stated:

> "I came to office with one deliberate intent: To change Britain from a dependent to a self-reliant society; from a give-it-to-me to a do-it-yourself nation; a get-up and-go instead of sit-back-and-wait Britain."

What clarity! What empathy! What effective communication! You may agree or disagree with Mrs. Thatcher, but you clearly received her message; you understood her.

One great American communicator was Ronald Reagan. President Reagan had the special talent of helping the listener receive his message by telling stories. Former Speaker of the United States House of Representatives, Tip O'Neil, said of President Reagan:

> He's always got a disarming story. I don't know where he gets them, but he's always got them. He calls up: 'Tip, you and I are political enemies only until six o'clock. It's four o'clock, now, can we pretend it's six o'clock?' How can you dislike a guy like that?

President Reagan had a mastery of his voice. He could make his voice quiver and sometimes even break while telling an emotional story, forming a tear in the corner of the eye of thousands of listeners. In addition to his ability to tell a story, Reagan was a master at the simplicity of communication. In the book *Superachievers* by Gschwandtner, Reagan's mastery of simple communication was presented as follows:

1. *Simple language*: He stays clear of complex words or phrases. His audience does not need a dictionary to understand his thoughts. Like a good sales representative, he knows that life is too short to waste time with complicated language.
2. *Simple mini-memos*: As governor of California, he developed a highly successful system for handing down decisions. After hearing out his subordinate's detailed recommendations, he would draft a concise one-page, four-paragraph summary of a problem with clear recommendations on how to solve it. His style initially drew criticism but got better results than that of the previous governor.
3. *Simple techniques of persuasion*: In his presidential campaign, he scored points with highly persuasive statements such as, "Recession is when your neighbor loses his job. Depression is when you lose yours. And recovery is when Jimmy Carter loses his." Some of his simple but profound one-liners have created tremendous impact. For example, "How can we love our country and not love our countrymen?' Or, concerning the Panama Canal, "We built it, we paid for it, it's ours, and we are going to keep it.'
4. *Simple life philosophies*: Son of a shoe salesman, Ronald Reagan exudes an air of simple virtues. Haynes Jackson, a *Washington Post* writer, commented in a front-page editorial, "He lacks the arrogance or insecurities of some presidents. The presidency does not own him: he's not uptight in the job. Those who have known him for years say he has changed hardly at all since entering the White House."[7]

In conjunction with this simplicity of communication, consider the following conversation between President Woodrow Wilson and a reporter:

REPORTER: "How long would it take you to prepare for a simple ten minute speech?"

WILSON: "Two weeks."

REPORTER: "How long for an hour speech?"

WILSON: "One week."

REPORTER: "How long for a two-hour speech?"

WILSON: "I'm ready now."

In addition to effective communication being clear and simple, it requires an endless repetition of the same message. They must continue to present the same message over and over again via several different communication mediums. It is this frequent, consistent repetition that will result in the message being received.

ABRAHAM LINCOLN: COMMUNICATOR SUPREME

Although President Reagan ranks among the greatest communicators of the twentieth century, probably the greatest communicator of all time was Abraham Lincoln. In the book *Lincoln on Leadership*, Donald Phillips, the author, dedicates the last unit of the book to communication. The three chapters in this unit are:

1. Master the Art of Public Speaking
2. Influence People Through Conversation and Story Telling
3. Preach a Vision and Continually Reaffirm It

Included in the "Lincoln Principles" at the end of these chapters are the following thoughts that are certainly critical for today's leaders:

- Be your organization's best speaker.
- Use humor and body language.
- Prepare thoroughly for every presentation.
- A speech is not done, nor an article complete, until it is delivered/published.
- Reinforce what you say in writing.
- Be pleasant in all dealings.
- Speak in simple terms. Be friendly.
- A good laugh is good for you.
- A good story will often influence people and soften disagreements.
- Loyalty flows from private conversations.
- Everywhere you go, at every conceivable opportunity, reaffirm, reassert, and remind everyone of your vision.

(continued)

- Do not force your vision on others; persuade them to your way of thinking.
- Live your vision in your own personal leadership style.
- When implementing change, call on the past, relate to the present, and use both the past and present as a link to the future.

Abraham Lincoln was certainly a leader who could communicate.[8]

Leaders Motivate by How They Work

There is an interesting paradox when it comes to elevating people's quality of work. The paradox goes like this: People enjoy their work because they get good results, but they get good results because they work hard and smart. They work hard and smart because they have high energy, but they have high energy because they enjoy their work. People cannot begin to improve their work by enjoying their work, because enjoying their work is a result of the good results obtained by their working hard and smart. Work is improved by working hard and smart. But they can't really start working hard and smart because working hard and smart is a result of the high energy that results from enjoying their work . . . Get the picture?

Leaders who wish to improve the quality and quantity of work within their organization must model work excellence themselves. There are two vital rules pertaining to work that leaders must practice: First, work hard and smart, and second, enjoy work.

Work Hard and Smart

If all you do is work hard, you will not be successful. Interestingly, if all you do is work smart, you will also not be successful. Mike Ditka, the Hall of Fame football player and former Super Bowl champion coach of the Chicago Bears, says it like this:

> "Know the value and definition of hard work. You work hard not just by sweating, but by applying your physical and mental capacities to perform a job thoroughly and properly. Brains always beat brawn. Work hard, but work smart."[9]

The leader's ability to work hard and smart sets the pace of an organization. As a leader, people are watching you. Where you choose to spend your time will become the organization's focus. I believe that every leader should live by these five personal work policies:

1. *Make the right decisions.* Making the right decision means making the right *decision* at the right *time* and communicating the decision to the right *people.* Always focus on all *three* rights to make right decisions.
2. *Don't become a time-management nut.* Defining one's day in 30-minute increments and only working on high-priority items is an obsolete concept of hard work. Interruptions are an important part of a leader's day, and provide the leader with the much-needed picture of what's really happening.
3. *Pay attention to the right details.* It's easy to get buried in details. Deal only with those details relevant to the decision you need to make. Delegate to others the handling of those details relevant to their level of decision making.
4. *Go the extra mile.* Exceed expectations in everything you do. Really listen to people. Ask questions. Be friendly. Be real. Provide higher quality and greater responsiveness than people thought possible. Impress everyone you touch. Treat every interaction and assignment as if your credibility was at stake—it probably is.
5. *Think loose.* Realize that change is inevitable. Accept change. Anticipate change. Don't let change control you. Know when to cut your losses. Don't be afraid to admit a mistake; learn from it and move on.

These five personal work policies will model for others the Revolution you are leading.

Enjoy Work

Happiness flows from the satisfaction and the recognition of a job well done. There are four things that a leader should do to personally enjoy work, and to ensure employee satisfaction and recognition of a job well done:

1. *Grow as a person.* The issue here is not organizational learning but individual learning, individual growth. The growth of the leader is important to an organization for three reasons. First, the leader derives personal satisfaction from learning, and thus enjoys work. Second, the leader's learning sets the pace for the rest of the organization's learning. And, third, when the leader recognizes this, it ignites new ideas and thinking throughout the organization. A leader's learning may occur in any of the following areas:
   - Enhanced understanding of a company's operations, industry, competition, and/or customers.
   - Learning from a mistake that was made.
   - Enhanced understanding of the future of their business by learning about other companies or industries and/or the economy in general.
   - Increased awareness and/or skills in dealing with people, communicating, growing, measuring, and so on.
   - Enhanced education in some business-related or business-unrelated aspect. This could include anything from reading a good book, to taking a college course in marketing, to learning how to fly an airplane.
2. *Be a realist.* A leader must be realistic. Realism is a form of intellectual honesty, and demands looking at things as they truly are. A leader's realism is critical to employees achieving satisfaction, because they don't have to deal with or attempt to overcome mental games or self-delusion on the part of the leader. By being realistic, the leader not only sets realistic expectations that can be met, but also encourages others to be realistic. This will result in job satisfaction for both the leader and for the organization.
3. *Be natural.* There is little job satisfaction or enjoyment when the leader is a phony. Leaders must be themselves, be accessible, and be predictable. For this to occur, you as a leader must get to know your employees and the employees must get to know you. You will gain commitment and respect from your employees by spending time with them, listening to them, showing compassion, and caring.
4. *Have fun.* Leaders must be committed to having fun. To do this, they must be positive. Some practical ways leaders can be positive are:

- *Celebrate success.* Have a party. Don't be so serious. Loosen up. Buy pizza for the company. Clap.
- *Say thank you.* Show genuine appreciation for the work people have done. Nothing is a substitute for sincere, public praise for a job well done.
- *Laugh.* Maintain your sense of humor. Find some humor in yourself and in your mistakes. Unleash the child within.

There are always plenty of obstacles to optimism, but none of them can be allowed to steal it away. The most common obstacle to optimism is criticism. Leaders will be criticized and will be the recipients of cheap shots. But slander comes with the territory. The faster a leader can learn that, the more optimistic they will be. The second most common obstacle to optimism is disappointment. People will let you down. They will miss deadlines, perform poorly, and fail to communicate. If a leader realizes that up front, they will possess the optimism necessary to help people meet their expectations. If a leader loses their optimism because of disappointment, they only breed further disappointment.

Leaders determine the relevance of criticism and disappointment. There is no question that you will be criticised and disappointed; the only question is how will you respond? If you respond to criticism with a counter attack, or respond to disappointment with an outburst, there is little likelihood that people will enjoy their work.

How should a leader respond to criticism? Here are the two methods that I use:

Response 1. Write a letter responding to the criticism. This letter should set the record straight, allow you to vent your anger—and should never be mailed. Throw this letter away after it is written and take no further action.

Response 2. If the criticism will really have an impact on the performance of the organization, you need to respond. But don't respond to the criticism. Instead, write a memo presenting the truth and explaining the facts of the situation. Present this memo in a positive manner via a "for your information" format.

Similarly, there are two courses of action a leader could take to address a disappointment.

Response 1. The preferred approach is a chat. This chat should not focus on punishment but rather on gaining a better understanding of expectations, roadblocks, and barriers. The focus of the chat should be "What can I (the leader) do to help the person meet future expectations."

Response 2. If the chat hasn't been effective, the second course of action is a more formal interaction which, although it won't be an enjoyable discussion, shouldn't be personal and should focus not on the individual, but rather on the individual's performance. In this discussion, a formal, time-phased path for corrective action should be established.

Both courses of action dealing with disappointment should be ended on a positive note, with the anticipation of positive results in the future.

Leaders Motivate by How They Treat People

The Golden Rule states: "Do unto others as you would have them do to you." Another translation of Luke 6:31 says "Treat others as you want them to treat you." It would seem clear, then, that if leaders treat people in the same way they want people to treat them, all will be fine. However, it isn't that easy. Although most commonly interpreted that way, the Golden Rule doesn't say that you should treat others the same way you like to be treated. The Golden Rule says that since you want others to treat you the way you like to be treated, you should treat others as *they* would like to be treated. Or more simply, treat others the way they would like to be treated. This is the definition of how a genuine leader treats people—how they want to be treated.

Treating people how they want to be treated has much to do with compassion, politeness, courteousness, trust, dignity, respect, and fairness. Obviously, these topics could easily fill this entire book. Since my purpose isn't to produce a treatise on business manners, I will not address the many aspects of business etiquette and the many challenges of dealing with people. Instead, I offer these ten principles of a leader's treatment of people. They are simple, but in a Revolutionary environment they are often forgotten.

1. *Like yourself.* You must have a positive self-image before you can have a positive image of others.
2. *Accept others.* Accept people as they are, not as you would like them to be. Accept differences in people, and love diversity.
3. *Respect others.* Every person is unique and no matter if friend or stranger, merits your appreciation, honor, and respect.
4. *Trust others.* Demonstrating your trust in other people not only makes the people trustworthy, but it also encourages them to trust you.

5. *Think "we.* Great performance is the result not of an "I" but a "we" mentality.
6. *Be real.* You are a real person and, like all people, you have feelings, concerns, and interests. You should socialize, participate in small talk, be seen, and be involved.
7. *Say "thank you."* Truly appreciate people helping you. Say thank you many, many times every day.
8. *Anger slowly, or not at all.* You may or may not have a temper. However, if you do, it should be seen only very rarely.
9. *Encourage others.* Know when to give someone a pat on the back and a pep talk. Be available when people need your support.
10. *Be a nice person.* You should be liked by many because you are gentle, kind, and considerate.

Call to Action

What kind of leader are you? As you read this chapter, could my description of leadership be substituted by a description of you? Are there things in your leadership style which can be improved? Remember, you set the tone of the organizational revolution you are trying to lead. This day, make yourself a student of the science of leadership and apply what you have learned. The results will be beyond your wildest dreams.

4

Cultural Revolution

Revolution Principle #4:

Revolution involves more than simply reorganizing existing fortresses. It involves transforming the culture within which those fortresses reside.

Anyone who has read Charles Dickens' novels is keenly aware of the cultural changes that took place in England during the industrial revolution. The use of automation and mass production in manufacturing literally changed the way people lived. It was far more than simply building some new buildings and manufacturing products a little quicker. Women and children entered the work place. Large portions of the work force moved to the city. Products were not sold from a stand in the front yard anymore, but were merchandised in retail stores. More people could have quality products at lower prices. And international trade became a viable method of boosting the economy. As a result,

England and the rest of the world were irreversibly changed (just ask Charles Dickens).

This is the essence of Revolution: The changes wrought transform the culture of the social structure. If all we do is rearrange the centers of power, or maybe even erect a few new ones, there has not been a Revolution. If we simply recreate the external appearance, there has not been a Revolution. If we join forces with ally fortresses, there has not been a Revolution. If we hoist up massive armaments to protect us from enemy fortresses, there has not been a Revolution. Only when the reality of the populace is altered, and the actual life experience of the common people is different—only when the culture has been transformed—is there a Revolution.

The world of business has seen many attempts to change without transforming culture. For example, when sales decline, many assume the answer is to change the person who heads the sales force. Or when company morale is low, many choose to throw a company picnic. Or when a competitor goes up for sale, many choose to buy and merge. Each of these can be valid expressions of business strategy. But rarely do such moves affect the inner-workings of the organization, the elements that fuel the daily success—the organization's culture. This Revolution principle is vital to business. Organizational Revolution requires cultural transformation. Leaders of Revolutions must understand the dynamics of corporate culture and how to change it if they ever wish to be successful.

What is Organizational Culture?

Culture is the foundation upon which organizations are built. It permeates every organizational activity and event, and allows one to interpret all that occurs. Each organization has a unique culture that plays an important role in its success.

An organization's culture is the perception of the people within the organization of how things work. It is intangible, unseen, and hard to define. To the contrary, the manifestations of culture are tangible, visible, and often well-defined. Cultural *manifestations* include:

- Company cars
- Time clocks
- Neckties

- Starched white shirts
- Executive lunch rooms
- Windows in offices
- Reserved parking
- Founder's picture in the hall
- Seating arrangements

Culture may also be perceived in an organization's language, jargon, stories, expectations, rewards, ceremonies, and titles.

YOU CAN'T SEE IT, BUT YOU CAN HEAR IT

My name is James A. Tompkins, Ph.D. This is the name that appears on my business card and is typed at the bottom of my letters. However, I always introduce myself to everyone as Jim Tompkins. Nevertheless, in various organizations where I work, I am called by various people Jim, Mr. Tompkins, Dr. Tompkins, Dr. Jim, Mr. T., Dr. T, and Jimbo. I receive correspondence addressed to all of these handles plus JAT, Dr. James A. Tompkins, Dr. J.A. Tompkins, and Mr. Jim Tompkins. Interestingly, even what we are called is a result of culture.

How is Organizational Culture Formed?

An organization's culture is initially created in the minds of the organization's founders. Their homes, families, friends, schools, churches, and business experiences are what shape the essence of this early culture. The culture of a start-up organization of three surfers in California will be different from a start-up organization of three Harvard MBAs in New York, as well as a start-up organization of three Ph.D. scientists in Japan. These differences have to do with the differences between the surfer, the Harvard MBAs, and the Japanese Ph.D. scientists themselves. From these individual differences, the organization's cultural differences evolve.

The organization's founders and the culture they create will be the standard in screening employees (see Figure 4.1). Those not conforming to the culture will be rejected; their behavior will be at odds with the culture. Employees who do conform to the culture will be accepted;

they will behave in accordance with the culture. This conformed behavior determines the organization's performance—for better or worse.

All aspects of the organization are impacted by the continuing Revolution of its culture. A leader seeking a cultural Revolution within their organization, must transform the rules, habits, procedures, standards, norms, rewards, language, jargon, stories, expectations, ceremonies, and titles that impact the screening of employees, the cultural conformance, the organization's behavior, and, thus, the organization's performance.

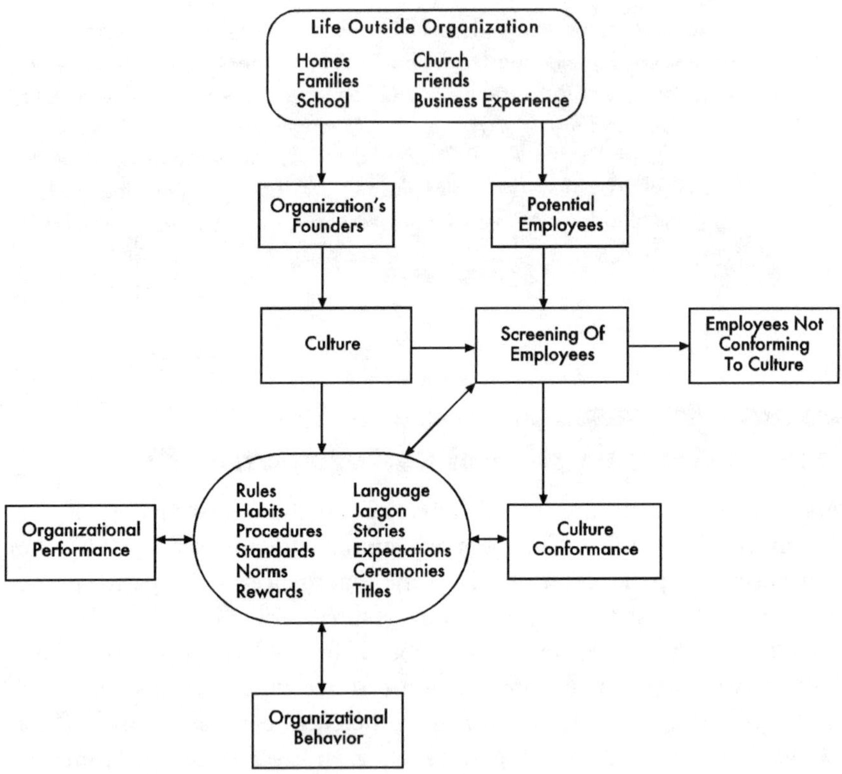

Figure 4.1 An Organization's Cultural Evolution

Old Culture...New Culture

A leader must realize that an organization's existing culture will work to stifle the introduction of a new one. Existing cultures work to maintain existing cultures. There are many examples of ambitious leaders who desired to transform an organization, but due to the routine of the existing culture, were not successful in achieving Revolution. A leader must understand that existing cultures will always work to maintain the status quo, to resist change. Without a cultural Revolution, the leader will be consumed. A corporate cultural Revolution must go beyond simple changes in the cultural manifestations and perceptions, and transform the organization's culture. This is the only way to shape corporate performance.

LEE IACOCCA AND THE CULTURAL REVOLUTION AT CHRYSLER

In Lee Iacocca's autobiography, he entitles the chapter of him joining Chrysler "Aboard a Sinking Ship." In this chapter, Iacocca describes what he found when he arrived at Chrysler: "Not a company but 35 'mini-empires.' The problems were not just with the executives but 'nobody was doing anything right.'" The organization had adopted a Chrysler culture that did not work and could not be made to work. Iacocca states:

> "There was so much to do and so little time! I had to eliminate thirty-five little duchies. I had to bring some cohesion and unity into the company. I had to get rid of the many people who didn't know what they were doing. I had to replace them by finding guys with experience who could move fast."[1]

Chrysler had engineering, financial, manufacturing, quality, marketing, and public relations problems. However, at the heart of all these problems was the culture of Chrysler. Iacocca had to transform the rules, habits, procedures, standards, norms, expectations, ceremonies, and titles of Chrysler, and then and only then was he in a position to begin the recovery. Five years later, after an unbelievable chain of events, Chrysler had a whole new culture and a whole new way of doing business. After all he had been through, he writes, "Now that we were out of danger, it was time to think about having fun again."[2] What an exciting story! What an unbelievable turnaround! This is Corporate Cultural Revolution.

Is Your Corporate Culture Dynamic or Dying?

The following two questions must be asked by leaders seeking cultural Revolution:

1. What does a dynamic culture look like?
2. How can you shape your organization so as to create a dynamic culture?

Although these questions are fair and good, they cannot be answered. In fact, these questions are directly related to the following leadership questions, which also cannot be answered:

1. What is good leadership?
2. How can you shape your personality to establish good leadership?

The difficulty is that neither leadership nor culture is a set of personality traits. Good leaders are comprised of many different personality types. Organizational traits of almost every variety can be found in dynamic business cultures. In the book *Corporate Culture and Performance*, the authors conclude:

> "The single most visible factor that distinguishes major cultural changes that succeed from those that fail is competent leadership at the top."[3]

This, obviously, takes us right back to the unanswerable "What is good leadership?" question.

Although we cannot define a dynamic culture, we can describe some characteristics that are found in them, as opposed to those that are dying. A symbol for the culture of a dying organization is a dinosaur. Dinosaurs, although once very powerful and rulers of all the earth, aren't alive anymore; they're dead. Crocodiles, however, existed before dinosaurs, and still exist today. Crocodiles are survivors. Crocodiles know how to adapt to new circumstances; they are dynamic. So then, whereas the dinosaur is a symbol of an obsolete, failing culture, the crocodile is a symbol of a surviving, winning, prospering culture—a dynamic culture.

The objective of a dinosaur is to know what's happening, to make all the decisions, to be in control. Control is comfort for a dinosaur. Control is less important to a crocodile; its objective is growth. For a crocodile, growth is comfort. A crocodile is driven by stretching, pushing, pulling, and improving.

The foundation of a dinosaur organization is analysis. Dinosaur organizations have task force after task force, analyzing every possible alternative. And even after every alternative has been analyzed, there is always one more meeting with one more set of alternatives that need to be scrutinized. Thus, the decision process in dinosaur organizations is excruciatingly slow. In a crocodile organization, the foundation is a shared, consistent vision of where the organization is headed. The rightness of a path is measured more by its consistency with the overall vision than by analysis. Dinosaur organizations often have analysis paralysis, but crocodile organizations are able to make decisions and make progress because everyone within the organization shares the vision of where they're headed. And where dinosaur organizations wish to implement a solution next year, crocodile organizations want to do something today in order to be better tomorrow.

The process a dinosaur organization pursues is one of optimization—to maximize or minimize some objective. They seek to define the ultimate solution so that the problem may be resolved once and for all, never having to be addressed again. The crocodile organization understands that this does not work. The crocodile organization has a total focus on Continuous Revolution and peak-to-peak performance. It understands that today's optimal solution is next month's okay solution, and next year's mediocre solution. In fact, the reason crocodile organizations don't get hung up with excessive analysis is because they know that today's solution will be continuously improved. Today's solution will be replaced by tomorrow's solution which will be replaced by the solution after the next one. Crocodile organizations spend more time focusing on the solution after the next one than they do on the next solution, as they truly understand the process of continuous, never-ending Revolution and Peak-To-Peak Performance.

The result of a overly-controlled, highly-analytical, optimization-seeking dinosaur organization is a culture of authoritarian bureaucracy. This bureaucracy has a life of its own; in fact, we often find that "the system," not individuals, makes decisions. In a crocodile organization, the result is not a culture of authoritarian bureaucracy, but a culture of learning, where the daily mandate is to continuously do better, learning from both successes and failures. Political nonsense is minimized and every opportunity is viewed as a way to learn, to improve, become better prepared to face tomorrow, and to strive for a new level of peak performance. In short, where dinosaurs seek authoritarian bureaucracy, crocodiles seek learning.

Dinosaurs have control as an objective, using analysis to pursue optimization, and the result is a culture of authoritarian bureaucracy. Crocodiles, however, seek the process of Revolution and peak-to-peak performance, and the desired result is a culture of learning. What is the culture of your organization—dinosaur or crocodile? If you really want to create a Revolutionary company, you must be a crocodile.

Another indication of an organization's culture is the attitude the organization exhibits toward Revolution. Three attitudes exist:

Type I: Static Consistency

Type II: Dynamic Inconsistency

Type III: Dynamic Consistency

A Type I attitude indicates a dying culture. Type I organizations resist Revolution. They pride themselves on maintaining the status quo, seldom realizing when there is an opportunity to improve. Within the walls of a Type I organization, you will hear statements such as "We have optimized our operations, and there is no room for improvement," or "If it ain't broken, don't fix it," or "We have always been profitable, so why should we Revolutionize anything?" or "Don't rock the boat."

A Type II attitude is also an indication of a dying culture, but in this case, the dying is occurring with less finesse. Type II organizations realize they are not successful and are actively installing new programs. They are busy organizations. Everyone is on a task force or two, but no one has a chance to work because the entire day is spent in meetings. There is no shared direction of where they are headed. Each person has their own direction. Although there are islands of success, the whole of the organization is not becoming Revolutionary. You will hear these kinds of statement in a Type II organization: "We have been working hard implementing new programs, but everyone is marching to a different drummer. Maybe the next program will work," or "This too will pass. Don't pay attention to all these new programs, our management is a bunch of frogs that keep jumping from program to program."

A Type III attitude is the attitude of an organization that has a dynamic, Revolutionary culture. Type III organizations truly understand the meaning of dynamic consistency. They are driven by a dynamic "improve, improve, improve" mentality, based upon a clear, shared, consistent direction of where the organization is headed. Type III organizations understand the difference between "change, change, change," and "improve, improve, improve." They understand what Abraham Lincoln meant when he said, "Let us not mistake change for progress." Type III organizations are focused on achieving peak-after-peak-after-peak performance. You will hear these kinds of statements in a Type III organization: "Our Revolutionary leadership encourages us to take risks and to either enjoy the success or learn from the mistake," or "We value diversity as it is by listening to and understanding others that we are able to learn, grow, improve, and achieve the next level of peak performance." What kind of statements can one hear inside the walls of your organization? They reveal much about the culture of your organization.

Shaping a Dynamic Culture

As I mentioned earlier, existing cultures work to maintain existing cultures. An organization's culture will evolve, but unless there is a significant external influence, the evolution will be very slow. The most common external influences that facilitate the shaping of a dynamic, Revolutionary culture are:

1. A crisis
2. A pending crisis
3. A new direction

A crisis is the ideal motivator for creating a dynamic culture. During a crisis, it is common for the impossible to be accomplished. We have all seen a six-week job completed in one day in the thick of a crisis. When a crisis surfaces, rules, habits, procedures, standards, and norms are expected to be put aside. In fact, some leaders not currently faced with a crisis try to create one in order to reap the results. This can work for a while, but these types of leaders will quickly become like the boy who cried wolf—their warnings will bring only inaction and disbelief. Therefore, leaders should not create crises. If a crisis truly exists, the leader should shine a light on it and call for action.

What about past crises that are still unresolved? Whereas leaders shouldn't create crises, they should identify, research, and document pending crises. There is no question that in today's hyper-changeable business environment there are pending crises in all organizations. When the pending crisis is indeed valid and believable, the leader should document it, then shine light on it, and and call for action just like they would in a new crisis.

The third external influence that facilitates the shaping of a dynamic culture is when a leader defines a new path, a new direction for an organization. In this case, the leader must wipe the slate clean and begin anew. If too many of the cultural manifestations of the past are allowed to remain, the organization may not see the new direction as one truly new, but rather as the continuation of an old direction. Once a leader actually makes the case for the new direction, they should shine a light on this new direction and create a sense of urgency.

JACK WELCH: THE QUINTESSENTIAL LEADER

In 1981, Jack Welch became the CEO of General Electric. GE did not have a crisis. GE was profitable, had a very strong balance sheet, and to most of the organization, was doing just fine. However, Welch was concerned with the slow-moving GE bureaucracy, slow growth, a lack of innovation, and the fact that GE was a non-global business. Welch didn't have a crisis, but he certainly had a pending crisis. He didn't wait. He went into action. What did he do? According to *Fortune*, Welch pursued a three-stage revolution:

- Stage 1: Awakening. Documenting the pending crisis and shining a light on the pending crisis.
- Stage 2: Envisioning. The GE organization understands the pending crisis and is positioned to be transformers.
- Stage 3: Re-architecting. The transformation process.[4]

Although the words are different, this book sets forth a proven process for awakening, envisioning, and re-architecting. GE, is one of the most successful organizations in the world today. What a leader!

Call to Action

Have your employees got the tragic impression that your organization hops ftom one program to another with very little experienced change? If so, your organization has not experienced cultural transformation. Do you really want to be Revolutionary? If so, then get out of the program-hopping game, and begin to focus on transforming the reality of your organization—its culture.

Part II

There have been many, many pages written and speeches given on the management-versus-leadership challenge. Is management more important or is leadership? Do we need both management and leadership? It must be said at the outset that Revolutionary Organizations must have both outstanding management and outstanding leadership. Today's challenge lies in the fact that we have an abundance of management and a shortage of leadership. To create the required management/leadership balance, a Revolution from management to leadership is required. In this section, I once again look to the science of Revolution for principles that provide us the key leadership tasks that must be addressed if a leader is to position their organization for Organizational Revolution.

By observing the leadership requirements in a Revolution, we discover that on top of the foundational truth that leaders must motivate, leaders must also provide clear vision. They must see leadership as a verb; that is to say leadership is what we do not who we are. I want to explore these additional leadership characteristics with you. May this section be the beginning of your Leadership Revolution.

Leadership

5

The Vision Thing

Revolution Principle #5:

In order to keep Revolutionaries motivated, leaders must clearly communicate where their leaders are taking them.

Most Revolutions are not successful. There are many attempted Revolutions that backfire, fizzle out, or lack the people-power to accomplish its goals. There is no doubt that the main reason why Revolutions fail is because the leaders did not clearly communicate where they were taking the followers.

For example, think of a political Revolution somewhere in South America. A leader convinces a large group of citizens that medical care could be better, there could be less violence and government oppression, and that there could be less taxes. He is a charismatic leader who draws followers to him magnetically. He asks that everyone interested in such improvements show up the next day for special training. A large group respond to his call.

When they arrive, they find that the training is military training, but they are not informed why. They are only told that the training is necessary for the improvements. They soon find themselves marching toward the capital, donning fatigues with guns in hand. They realize that the leader is planning to throw the government out by force, and that probably a majority of them will likely lose their lives. Ninety-five percent of them desert because although they want change, they do not want to die. The Revolution fails.

If the leader had communicated to the citizens why, how, and when he planned to make the changes of which he spoke, those who volunteered would have been aligned and committed. The Revolution may have taken longer to achieve, but abandonment would not have occurred.

In an Organizational Revolution, the same problem exists. If the leaders do not clearly communicate where they are taking the organization, you can count on failure. People need to understand what their efforts are for, where they are headed, how they will get there, and how they may measure if they have been successful.

In this chapter I want to give you the tools you need to communicate to your organization where you and your Revolution are taking them. This is a very practical chapter because if there is only one thing I want you to do well, it is this: Communicate your vision.

Once a person learns what it means to serve as a leader within their organization, they must then seek to lead the organization effectively. This is usually where the breakdown occurs. A person reads a leadership book or attends a leadership seminar where they learn what it means to be a leader in eloquent terms. But how do you actually *do* it? What are the first steps of leadership? Where does a leadership Revolution begin? I want to provide that application element for you, because I want your Revolution to succeed.

The first and most important role of leadership is defining a company's vision and aligning the people in the company behind this vision. Consider the following quotations in support of this definition of leadership:

> "The leader's job is to create a vision."[1]
>
> —Robert Swiggett
> Chairman, Kollmorgen Corporation

"Action without vision is stumbling in the dark, and vision without action is poverty-stricken poetry."[2]

—Warren Bennis
Author, *On Becoming A Leader*

"There is no more powerful engine driving an organization toward excellence and long-range success than an attractive, worthwhile, and achievable vision of the future, widely shared."[3]

—Burt Nanus
Author, *Visionary Leadership*

"Vision is the beginning point for leading the journey. Vision focuses. Vision inspires. Without a vision, people perish. Vision is our alarm clock in the morning, our caffeine in the evening. Vision touches the heart. It becomes the criterion against which all behavior is measured. Vision becomes the glasses that tightly focus all of our sights and actions on that which we want to be tomorrow—not what we were yesterday or what we are today. The focus on vision disciplines us to think strategically. The vision is the framework for leading the journey."[4]

—James Belasco and Ralph Stayer
Authors, *Flight Of The Buffalo*

"Without question, communicating the vision, and the atmosphere around the vision, has been, and is continuing to be, by far, the toughest job we face."[5]

—Jack Welch
Chairman, General Electric

"The first dictionary definition of a 'leader' describes a primary shoot of a plant, the main artery through which the organism lives and thrives. In much the same way, organizations prosper or die as a result of their leader's ability to embody and communicate the company's vision."[6]

—Donald Phillips
Author, *Lincoln On Leadership*

"Many leaders have personal visions that never get translated into shared visions that galvanize an organization. . .What has been lacking is a discipline for translating individual vision into a shared vision."[7]

—Peter Senge
Author, *The Fifth Discipline*

"No matter what it is called—personal agenda, purpose, legacy, dream, goal, or vision—the intent is the same. Leaders must be forward-looking and have a clear sense of direction that they want their organization to take."[8]

—James Kouzes and Barry Posner
Authors, *The Leadership Challenge*

"Vision without action is merely a dream. Action without vision just passes time. Vision with action can change the world."

—Joel Barker
President, Infinity Limited, Inc.

In spite of the ample evidence in support of leadership's role in defining a vision and aligning people with this vision, there still appears to be some debate about the matter. Consider the following quotations:

"Take 'this vision thing' for instance. Leaders are responsible to craft a vision. Leaders are responsible to implement that vision. Leaders are responsible for empowering their people to use the vision. That paradigm of leader responsibility for other people's performance, given today's circumstances, guarantees organizational failure."[9]

—James Belasco and Ralph Stayer
Authors, *Flight Of The Buffalo*

"Being a visionary is trivial."[10]

—Bill Gates
Chairman, Microsoft Corp.

"Vision may not exactly be dead in corporate America, but a surprising number of chief executive officers are casting aside their crystal balls to concentrate on the nuts-and-bolts of running their businesses in these leaner times."[11]

—Douglas Lavin
Reporter, *Wall Street Journal*

> "Internally, we don't use the word vision . . . This is a business of fundamentals. There isn't any magic."[12]
>
> —Robert Eaton
> Chairman, Chrysler Corp

> "One of the more ubiquitous forms of office decor these days is a suitably framed—and generally obtuse—vision statement. It always purports to speak to the driving sense of purpose underlying the organization. It's depressingly easy to point out that most of these statements are anything but visionary. In fact, if you picked 20 employees at random and asked them to recite the thing from memory, let alone make one up from scratch, chances are they wouldn't come anywhere near the happy horror hanging on the wall in your company lobby."[13]
>
> —Dick Schaaf
> Author, *Pursuing Total Quality*

> "A lot of companies see this as a quick fix. These organizations use vision as a public relations' tool, not as something to change the fundamental culture."
>
> —James Shaffer
> Vice President, Towers Perrin

Although there appears to be a debate between the visionaries and the nuts-and-bolts leaders, there really is no debate. It is actually a lack of understanding and a poor use of terminology. If the "vision thing" is done poorly, there will be little positive benefit.

What is This "Vision Thing?"

The apparent "vision thing" debate is not a debate, but a product of combining doubletalk and doublethink. This is unfortunate, for we already understand vision, have personal experience in forming and pursuing a vision, and know the power of a vision. Think back to your childhood. What were your goals, your aspirations? You could daydream about these aspirations for hours, day after day. These aspirations could not be put down in a sentence or two, there were too many different elements to them. That's why it was so easy to lose yourself in your visualization, to play make believe, actually seeing yourself achieving your aspirations. Those aspirations had a powerful impact on your life and functioned as a model of your future success. This is the "vision thing," and it always amounted to more than a one-or-two sentence slogan. I refer to these aspirations, this "vision thing," as the Model of Success. The lack of understanding of the Model of Success has resulted in the vision debate.

WHICH WAY IS IT?

In July of 1993, the new Chairman of IBM, Louis Gerstner, was quoted on the front page of the *Wall Street Journal* as saying, "The last thing IBM needs now is a vision." The cover story of the November 15, 1993 *Fortune* magazine proclaimed "Gerstner's New Vision for IBM." Well, which way is it? In January of 1994, in an article on vision in the *Wall Street Journal*, an IBM spokesman explained:

> "What Lou Gerstner was saying was that a 25- or 30-word sentence is simplistic and not realistic and not his first priority. But since then, Mr. Gerstner has distributed to employees a list of 'IBM Principles' consisting of eight to eighteen words each. The principles pledge 'a minimum of bureaucracy' and sensitivity to staff and others. And the spokesman says Mr. Gerstner does plan to articulate an explicit 'vision' for the company some time in 1994."

The question remains, which way is it?

In 1982, in Tom Peters' book *In Search Of Excellence*, there is no mention of the importance of vision. In his 1988 book, *Thriving On Chaos*, a company's vision is presented as being "essential" for directing the initiative and energy of front-line employees.[14] Then, in his 1992 book, *Liberation Management*, in a portion of the book entitled "The Vision and Values Trap," he sets the record straight when he says, "All good ideas eventually get oversold. The importance of a corporate vision and values is no exception," and then concludes, "Values? Visions? Can't live without 'em. . . Can't live with 'em either."[15] The question remains, which way is it?

The One-Sentence Fallacy

To understand the fallacy of a one-or two-sentence Model of Success, one must consider what result is expected from having a clear Model of Success. In a study done by Kouzes and Posner asking people to explain when people performed at their best, it was found that when a Model of Success was effectively communicated, significantly higher levels of job satisfaction, commitment, loyalty, esprit de corps, clarity about organizational values, pride in the organization, organizational productivity, and encouragement to be productive all resulted. Obviously, this cannot be achieved with a few sentences. Nanus believes that by presenting such a Model of Success:

1. People will be committed and energized.
2. Workers' lives will be more meaningful.
3. A standard of excellence will be established.
4. The present will be bridged with the future.[16]

Further, Nanus believes that a powerful and transforming Model of Success has seven special properties:

1. It is appropriate for the organization and for the times.
2. It sets standards of excellence and reflects high ideals.
3. It clarifies purpose and direction.
4. It inspires enthusiasm and encourages commitment.
5. It is well articulated and easily understood.
6. It reflects the uniqueness of the organization.
7. It is ambitious.[17]

So, if a Model of Success isn't just a few sentences, what is it? That's a question I found I couldn't answer easily. I didn't know how to define a Model of Success. To begin to shed some light on this issue, I read about Ford, Edison, Goodyear, Watson, Toyota, Kroc, Walton, and many others. The question constantly in my mind was, "What is it that these great Revolutionaries gave their organizations? What was their Model of Success that they communicated to their staff to obtain alignment and success?" After much study, it became clear that what these great leaders did for their organizations is answer the following five Model of Success questions. As a Revolution leader, you are the one who needs to answer these same questions for your organization:

1. Where are we headed?
2. How will we get there?
3. What is the science of our business?
4. What values shall be practiced?
5. How will we measure success?

Based on these five questions, when you define your organization's Model of Success the following five elements must be defined:

1. *Vision:* A description of where you are headed.
2. *Mission:* How to accomplish the Vision.
3. *Requirements of Success:* The science of your business.
4. *Guiding Principles:* The values we practice as we pursue our Vision.
5. *Evidence of Success:* Measurable results that will demonstrate when our organization is moving towards their Vision.

A useful communications tool for illustrating the first four of those elements is presented in Figures 5.1a-e. (Note that the Evidence of Success typically are not included on the bull's eye, as different organizational elements may have different Evidences of Success.)

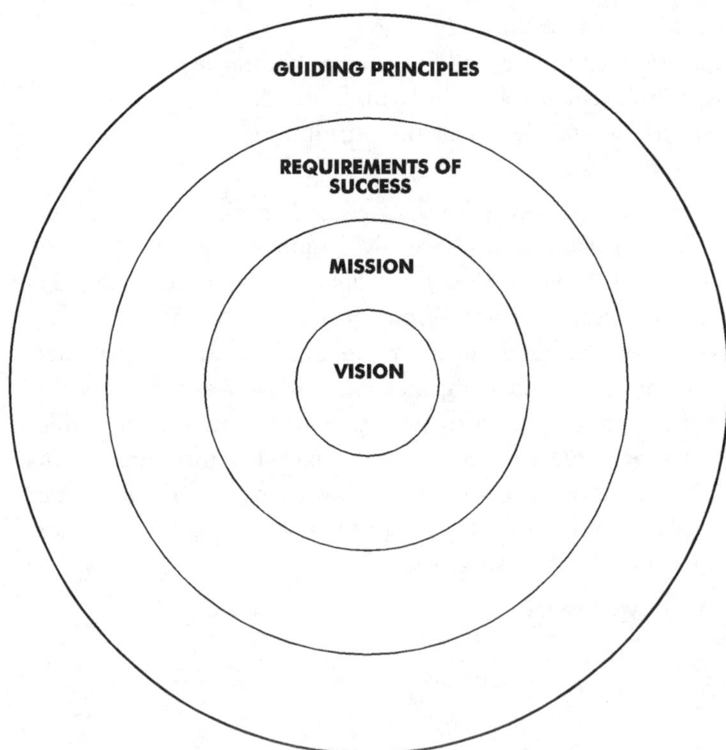

Figure 5.1a Bull's Eye Format

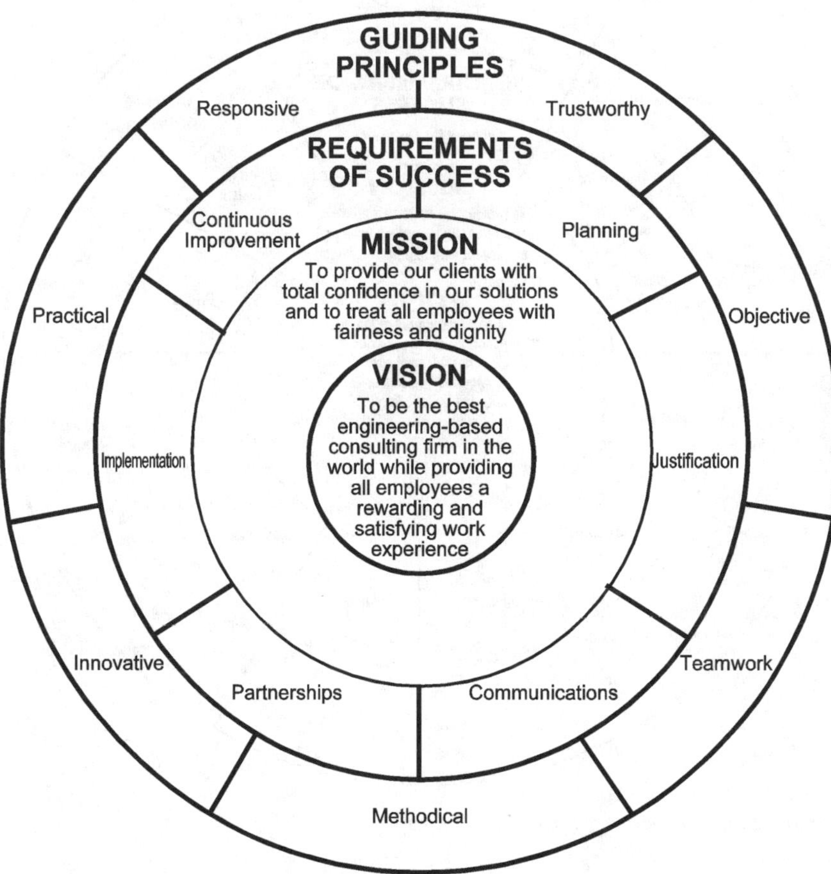

Figure 5.1b Tompkins Associates, Inc. Bull's Eye

Figure 5.1c Trucking Firm Bull's Eye

Figure 5.1d Job Shop Bull's Eye

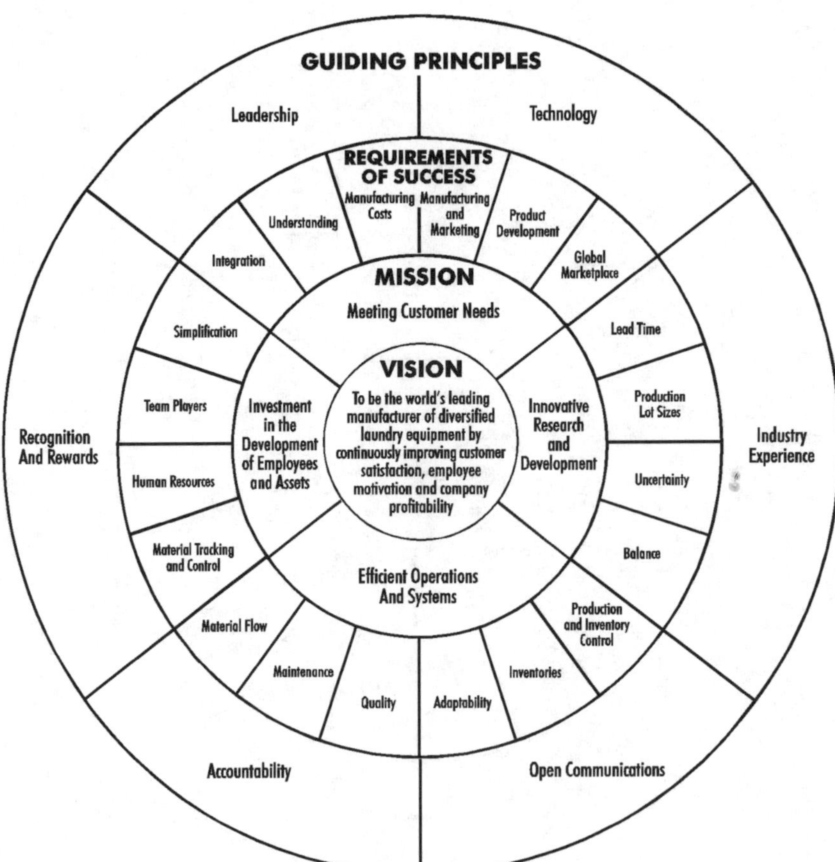

Figure 5.1e. Appliance Manufacture Bull's Eye

Understanding the Elements of the Model of Success

The first two elements of the Model of Success are intimately linked. Often, these two elements are referred to as the Vision/Mission Set. The vision and mission are closely linked; the vision addresses the *where* and the mission the *how.* The vision is a *goal* and the mission is a *strategy.* The word *vision* involves the "seeing" of the future. In his book, *Hey, Wait A Minute: I Wrote A Book,* John Madden writes about a conversation he had with Vince Lombardi about seeing the future and coaching. Lombardi said:

> "The best coaches know what the end result looks like, whether it's an offensive play, a defensive play, a defensive coverage or just some area of the organization. If you don't know what the end result is supposed to look like, you can't get there. All teams basically do the same thing. We all have drafts, we all have training camps, we all have practices. But the bad coaches don't know what the hell they want. The good coaches do."[18]

In the same vein, I recall reading in a sports magazine that Larry Bird and Wayne Gretsky were described as follows:

> "The difference between Larry (Wayne) and all the other players is that most players go to where the ball (puck) is, whereas Larry (Wayne) goes to where the ball (puck) is going to be. They actually see a play develop before it happens."

Leaders must work back from what they see in the future to the present. If instead leaders attempt to project from the present to the future, they will never reach their destination. You reach the future by focusing on where you're headed, not by looking at where you have been. In fact, a vision should be stated such that the present is described as a past condition of the future, not as a future condition of the past. As a mental picture of the future, visions should be expressions of optimism, hope, excellence, ideals, and Revolutionary possibilities for the company of tomorrow. Each company vision must be unique and can only be appropriate for that particular company.

DOES VISION ELECT PRESIDENTS?

George Bush was aware of the comments about him having a problem with "this vision thing," but he was unable to step up to the problem. In fact, it is reported that he did not want to hear about the "V" word. The criticism followed Bush before he was President:

"He does not have a clear, crisp, describable ideal for the country," while he was President.

> "Never has the lack of vision in Washington been more obvious. Ronald Reagan ran for President to do, George Bush to serve. Ronald Reagan knew where he wanted to move America; George Bush is unconceived about where America ends up,"

and when he was defeated for reelection:

> "Did the lack of vision defeat Bush? It certainly contributed to his loss. After the Gulf War, he seemed to be what *Newsweek* called him in its post-election analysis: A man without a mission. Since he failed to articulate and communicate what he stood for, the electorate threw him over for a candidate who did. Bill Clinton convinced voters of at least one thing: The status quo will change."

The mission portion of the Vision/Mission Set presents the strategy that the company should follow as it pursues its vision. For example, the visions of both Tiffany's and Wal-Mart include total customer satisfaction. The methods and strategies employed to achieve this vision, however, are very different. Tiffany's wishes to pamper, gratify, and entertain, whereas Wal-Mart wishes to provide friendly and fast service at the best price. The mission defines the strategic thrust of the company (Rolls Royce or Chevrolet) and serves as a focal point expression of the company's operating principles (McDonald's standardization versus Burger King's "have it your way"). The mission should be helpful to everyone in the company in providing guidance on how to respond to various day-to-day circumstances. For example, at Tompkins Associates, Inc., where our mission is "to provide our clients with total confidence in our solutions and to treat all employees with fairness and dignity," I respond to all of the following questions with the question, "What would give our clients the greatest confidence?"

- Should we fax the report or send it overnight?
- Do we invoice the client so the invoice arrives on the due date or so that it is mailed on the due date?
- Should we have our logo or the client's logo on the bid specification?

- Should we hand out the materials for the meeting before or after the presentation?
- Should we stay at hotel X or hotel Y?
- Who should attend a project update meeting?

In this way, the mission becomes the organization's operating policy, in that it describes how we will be doing business.

The third element of the Model of Success answers these three questions:

1. What is the science of our business?
2. What are the rules of our game?
3. What are the paradigms in which we believe?

All of those questions are answered by an organization's Requirements of Success. It is absolutely critical that everyone in an organization has a clear understanding of the Requirements of Success. This means that, although what appears in the bull's-eye is a single word or a short phrase, there should exist, and be widely shared, an explanation of each Requirement of Success. Unlike the other four elements of the Model of Success, the Requirements of Success are not unique for each company. In fact, in the two industries where Tompkins Associates, Inc. practices most, manufacturing and warehousing, we have established and widely disseminated the Requirements of Success. In the manufacturing area, these Requirements of Success were the topic of the bestselling *Winning Manufacturing* book, the video tape, *Manufacturing: Making A Difference,* and several articles, speeches, and seminars. The 20 manufacturing Requirements of Success, as defined fully in the book *Winning Manufacturing* are:

1. *Manufacturing costs*: Manufacturing costs must be significantly reduced.
2. *Manufacturing and marketing*: Manufacturing and marketing must become integrated and function as a team.
3. *Product development*: Product development must become an integrated, iterative process.
4. *Global marketplace*: All manufacturing decisions must be made within the context of an integrated global strategy.
5. *Lead time*: Significant reductions in lead times must occur.
6. *Production lot sizes*: Production lot sizes and set-up times must be minimized.
7. *Uncertainty*: All uncertainty must be minimized; discipline must be increased.
8. *Balance*: All manufacturing operations must be balanced.

9. *Production and inventory control*: The production and inventory control system must be straightforward and transparent.
10. *Inventories*: Drastic reductions in inventory must occur.
11. *Adaptability*: Manufacturing facilities, operations, and personnel must become more adaptable.
12. *Quality*: Product quality, vendor quality, and information quality must improve.
13. *Maintenance*: Manufacturing process failures must be minimized.
14. *Material Flow*: Material flow must be efficient.
15. *Material tracking and control*: Material tracking and control systems must be upgraded.
16. *Human resources*: Every manager must be dedicated to creating an environment where every employee is motivated and happy.
17. *Team players*: Everyone associated with manufacturing must work together as a team.
18. *Simplification*: All of manufacturing must be simplified.
19. *Integration*: All organizations and operations must be integrated.
20. *Understanding*: Manufacturing management must understand Winning Manufacturing.

In the warehousing area, these Requirements of Success were the topic of the video tape *Warehouse Strategies*, as well as several articles, speeches, and seminars. The 20 warehousing Requirements of Success are:

1. *Professionalism*: Warehousing will be viewed as a critical logistics step and a competitive strength and not as a necessary evil.
2. *Customer Awareness*: Successful warehouse operations will have a high regard for the customer, will know the customer's requirements, and will consistently meet these requirements.
3. *Measurement*: Warehouse standards will be established, performance will be measured against these standards and timely actions will be taken to overcome any deviations.
4. *Operations Planning*: Systems and procedures will be put into effect that allow the warehouse manager to proactively plan the operations as opposed to reactively respond to external circumstances.
5. *Logistics Network*: Warehouses will not be viewed as independent operations, but as elements of the overall, well-planned logistics system.

6. *Third Party*: The reduction of lead times, shorter product lives, and increased inventory turnover will result in an increased use of third parties.
7. *Pace*: The reduction of lead times, shorter product lives, and increased inventory turnover will result in an increase in the pace of the warehouse.
8. *Variety*: More SKUs and more special customer requirements will result in an increase in the variety of tasks performed in the warehouse.
9. *Flexibility*: Due to the increase in warehouse pace and variety, all warehouse systems, equipment and people will be more flexible.
10. *Uncertainty*: All uncertainty will be minimized, discipline will be increased.
11. *Integration*: Activities within the warehouse (receive, store, pick, and ship) will be more integrated and the warehouse will be more integrated within the overall logistics system.
12. *Inventory Management*: Real-time warehouse management systems will utilize cycle counting to manage inventory accuracy, and accuracy above 99 percent will be the norm.
13. *Space Utilization*: Space will be more efficiently and effectively utilized.
14. *Housekeeping*: Quality housekeeping will be a priority and a source of employee pride.
15. *Order Picking*: The criticality of order picking will be understood and procedures and layouts will be designed to maximize picking efficiency and effectiveness.
16. *Team-Based Continuous Improvement*: The power of the people will be unleashed via a methodical team-based process.
17. *Continuous Flow*: There will be a clear focus on pulling product through the logistics system and not on building huge inventories.
18. *Warehouse Management Systems*: A real-time, bar-code based, RF communication WMS (warehouse management system) will be required to meet today's requirements.
19. *Total Cost of Logistics*: The goal will be to minimize the total life cycle costs of logistics, from order submission to product delivery, while providing excellence in customer service.
20. *Leadership*: There must be a balance between the control aspects of management and harnessing the energy of change to create Peak-to-Peak Performance of leadership.

The explanations of the Requirements of Success from the Tompkins Associates, Inc. Model of Success are as follows:

Table 5.2 Explanations of the Requirements of Success (for Tompkins Associates, Inc.)

Action	Description
Planning	Tompkins shall provide their clients with strategic contingency, and detail planning of the highest quality. Internally, Vision, Goals, and Action Plans shall be used to lead and manage the affairs of our business.
Justification	Valid justification is the core of all of our recommendations. Through this technology, Tompkins will ensure wise expenditures of clients' funds. We shall apply the same vigor to the expenditure of our own funds that we do to our clients' funds.
Communication	High quality written and oral communications are a prerequisite to a successful consulting relationship. Quality communications is mandatory for successful planning, justification, and implementation. We believe in open and honest communications. Every effort shall be made to ensure employee involvement and participation through positive, ongoing communications.
Partnership	We are dedicated to the success and growth of our clients. We treat our clients' business with the same dedication and intensity as our own. We are dedicated to the success of our employees. We shall provide an environment in which all employees can enjoy working, develop professionally, be compensated fairly, and participate in company management.
Implementation	We are focused on improving our clients' business by implementing quality recommendations and implementing policies and practices that will result in happy employees, exceptional growth, and increasing profits.
Continuous Improvement	Continuous improvement is the key to success in today's dynamic world. We will address all client and company opportunities not only as opportunities for improvement today, but as a baseline upon which to build continuous improvement.

The Requirements of Success for an organization will most often be a compilation, revision, and/or adaptation of the requirements presented in this chapter. The Requirements of Success should present the basic truths of the company, in the language of the company, so that all company employees gain knowledge of the underpinnings of their company.

The fourth element of the Model of Success, the Guiding Principles, presents a set of standards about how people should be treated. These values are deep-seated, pervasive standards that influence all that we do: our judgments, our opinions, our attitudes, our desires, our fears, our responses, and our actions. These values give direction to the company and define the spirit in which things in the company should be accomplished. As an individual contemplates different actions, they consciously and subconsciously compare the alternatives to these values to define the right path. Successful organizations always demonstrate a set of Guiding Principles that present a strong commitment to the people in the company. This commitment flows from values like trust, fairness, openness, teamwork, development, continuous improvement, respect, participation, pride, dignity, security, accountability, and responsiveness. Because of the company's commitment to their people, the employees, in turn, become committed to the company.

The last element of an organization's Model of Success defines how an organization will measure their movement toward its vision. There is power in defining an organization's measures. And *what* gets measured becomes important. An old leadership principle I learned many years ago is still relevant today: "If you want it, measure it. If you cannot measure it, forget it." Measurement is a tool that leadership should use to help focus their organization on the bull's eye.

Measurement is what provides leaders the information they need to provide organizational feedback, and it is this feedback that serves as the basis for celebration or correction. Without the feedback of these measurements, you don't know if you should redouble your efforts, or if you should change your course.

Unfortunately, in many companies the traditional accounting-based measures used in the 1980s are still being used today. Accounting-based measures drive employees to play games in order to achieve cost and revenue targets, without regard to the actual performance of the business. Accounting-based measures attempt to control how a business functions. This is a real problem, as routine accounting data does not reflect customer satisfaction, market share, quality, employee development, company growth, and hundreds of other measures that are more important than whether Region X achieved its budget. Effective Measures of Success must be real time, meaningful to an organizational entity, based upon the metric of the organizational entity being measured, and accurate. Without effective Measures of Success, an organization will not know if it's moving closer to its vision or not.

WE WILL MEET GOAL THIS MONTH!

At one of the largest beverage manufacturers in the world, achieving corporate accounting-based goals is the norm. Jumping through hoops, internal chaos, and performance suicide is also the norm. The practice of playing ridiculous games with order placement and when these orders are shipped, is widely known within the company. Orders are scheduled to be shipped throughout the month.

However, as the month ends, orders are stolen from the next month to satisfy monthly financial goals. This action causes the next month to be short, so orders are stolen even further out to meet goal. As obvious a problem as this is, the vicious cycle continues. Customers are dissatisfied by receiving unwanted product, production scheduling constantly juggles orders and production, packaging efficiencies and schedule attainment drops, inventories rise, obsolete product is prevalent and employee morale spirals downward. Why? Because the company has decided, "We *WILL* meet goal this month, no matter how much it costs!"

To define the Measures of Success, one must define the organizational entity to be measured, the perspective of measurement, and the performance to be measured. The definition of the organizational entity could be very broad (a whole company or division) or very narrow (a department or a team). The perspective of measurement could be the employees, owners (stockholders), partners (customers and suppliers), community/environment, and/or operations. The performance to be measured could be:

1. Effectiveness
2. Efficiency
3. Quality
4. Relationships
5. Innovation
6. Financial

Performance to be Measured						
Perspective	**Effectiveness**	**Efficiency**	**Quality**	**Relationships**	**Innovation**	**Financial**
Employees	A. 75% of staff pass competency test B. 80% of all employees on improvement teams	A. .2 hours/order B. 98% standard	A. Eliminate order checking B. Achieve 99% rating on corporate packaging audit	A. No time lost accidents B. Reduce turnover 50%	A. 10 Continuous Improvement Teams B. Implement industrial performance tracking	A. $.11 of distribution per dollar shipped B. Pay no detention penalties
Owners	A. 99.2% inventory accuracy B. Allocate 50% of budget savings to continuous improvement	A. Increase throughput 20% B. Respond to all suggestions in 2 weeks	A. Receive Ford A1 rating B. Obtain ISO 9000 certification	A. Participate in local community groups B. Conduct 2 outside tours per quarter	A. Increase market share by 5% B. Establish 10 strategic partnerships	A. 6 inventory turns B. Greater than 25% ROI on all investments
Customers	A. .1% returns B. .4% stockouts	A. Respond to all inquiries in 1 hour or less B. Turn around customer trucks in less than 2 hours	A. .1% errors B. .2% damage in shipment	A. .05% complaints B. 12-hour lead time	A. Visit 10% of all customers each quarter B. Retain 95% of house accounts	A. Reduce freight claims to .2% of dollars shipped B. No price increases for next year
Community/ Environment	A. .2% damage ratio B. Receive good citizen award from city	A. Respond to all Department of Labor inquiries in 2 weeks or less B. Implement checklists to simplify environmental audits	A. No product contamination B. Eliminate need to distribute products	A. Spend 50% of all disposal dollars with handicapped industries B. Zero lawsuits	A. Recycle all corrugated B. Eliminate birds from warehouse	A. Pay no government fines B. Make product recycling a break-even proposition
Operations	A. 98% fill rate B. 99% delivery on time	A. 82% space utilization B. 95% equipment utilization	A. 99.4% housekeeping rating B. Receive 95 rating on customer service cards	A. Report performance to corporate monthly B. Monthly meetings with MIS on distribution priorities	A. Reduce fork truck damage 70% B. Reduce number of trucking firms used to 6	A. Below budget on expenses B. Energy consumption reduced 10% annually

Figure 5.2 Measures of Success for the Distribution Improvement Team

Performance to be Measured						
Perspective	**Effectiveness**	**Efficiency**	**Quality**	**Relationships**	**Innovation**	**Financial**
Employees	A. Implement gainsharing B. 80% of all employees on improvement teams	A. Run plant at 92% efficiency B. 5% absenteeism	A. Achieve 98% first pass quality B. Implement shop floor SPQ	A. No time lost on accid nts B. Reduce 50% turnover	A.Create functional teams for 80% of all production departments B. Cross train 80% of staff in 3 functions	A.Increase total compensation 5% per year B. Reduce rework costs by 10%
Owners	A. Grow volume 10% per year B. Allocate 50% of budget savings to continuous improvement	A. Reduce new product development time to 4 months B. Respond to all suggestions in 2 weeks	A. Be ISO 9000 certified B. Eliminate reinspection prior to ship	A. Reduce warranty claims 10% B. Reduce number of suppliers by 20%	A. Increase marketshare by 5% B. Conform to ADA by end of third quarter	A. Exceed profit goal B. Greater than 25% ROI on all investments
Customers	A. Achieve 95% on on-time delivery B. Ship 98% of all orders complete	A. Bid all specials in 48 hours or less B. All service calls returned within 1 hour	A. .1% customer returns B. .1% damage in shipment	A. 80% of sales to be repeat orders B. .05% complaints	A. Visit 10% of all customers each quarter B. Conduct 4 customer training seminars per year	A. No price increases for next year B. Eliminate charges for freight on back orders
Suppliers	A. Do not change 4 week schedule B. Always order in carton quanities	A. EDI 80% of all purchase orders B. Pay all invoices on time	A. Conduct quarterly improvement meetings with top 10 suppliers B. Eliminate incoming inspection	A. Share 6-month production plans B. Return all special packaging	A. Visit 10% of all suppliers each quarter B. Participate in new product design for manufacture	A. Increase sales by 10% B. Pay for tooling up front and not as a portion of part cost

Figure 5.3 Measures of Success for the Manufacturing Team

(continued)

Performance to be Measured (continued)						
Perspective	**Effectiveness**	**Efficiency**	**Quality**	**Relationships**	**Innovation**	**Financial**
Community/ Environment	A. Receive good citizen award from city B. No layoffs	A. Respond to all Department of Labor inquiries within 2 weeks B. Improve discharge water purity to 98%	A. Receive no EPA citations B. Install back lot drainage system	A. Zero lawsuits B. Spend 50% of all disposal dollars with handicapped industries	A. Obtain 3 patents per year B. Support local athletic leagues	A. Pay no government fines B. Become self-insured
Operations	A. Forecast error less than 10% B. Implement TPM	A. Reduce cycle time to 48 hours B. Reduce schedule variation to 2%	A. 99.4% house-keeping rating B. Reduce SWCP 10%	A. Report performance to corporate monthly B. Work with product engineering from time of product conception	A. Reduce WIP 10% B. Reduce waste by 10%	A. Below budget on expenses B. Increase ROA 10%

Figure 5.3 Measures of Success for the Manufacturing Team

What should exist, then, is a series of Evidences of Success for each organizational entity. Figure 5.2 shows an example of the Evidence of Success for the organizational entity of the Distribution Improvement Team. Figure 5.3 provides an example of the Measures of Success for the organizational entity of the Manufacturing Team.

The Power of the Vision/Mission Set

The power of a Vision/Mission Set could easily be demonstrated by recounting Sam Walton's Wal-Mart/Sam's success. But some may say that this was a one-time success story due more to Mr. Walton than to the alignment of the Wal-Mart organization with the leadership-developed Model of Success. Well then, let's look at other success stories that are today borrowing a page from Mr. Walton's book.

Consider the following somewhat generic Vision/Mission Set:

Vision:

To profitably grow our retail chain of specialty superstores by exceeding the expectations of all stockholders, employees, and customers.

Mission:

1. Close traditional stores and replace with superstores several times larger with several times more stock keeping units.
2. Make shopping in our superstores fun.
3. Implement Every Day Low Prices (EDLP).
4. Sell name brand and premium quality merchandise not supplied by competing vendors but by partners.
5. Maintain the convenience and service of our traditional stores.
6. Finance expansion by selling shares of common stock.
7. Expand both the number of stores as well as the sales per store.
8. Expand into new geographical markets as well as to increase penetration in existing geographical markets.
9. Reduce operating costs through volume purchasing and distribution excellence.
10. Attract and retain highly motivated, well-qualified employees by providing excellent training, development, incentives, and growth opportunities.

Interestingly, the above Vision/Mission Set is not a Vision/Mission Set of any one specific retail organization, but rather an approximation of several chains such as:

Petco: Pet-related products

Pet Depot: Pet-related products

Home Depot: Home improvement products

HQ: Home improvement products

Lowes: Home improvement products

Bed, Bath & Beyond: Linen and bath products

Linens 'n Things: Linen and bath products

Pacific Linens: Linen and bath products

Tops: Consumer electronics

Staples: Office supplies

Office Depot: Office supplies

Baby Superstore: Baby items

Gymboree: Children's clothing

Yet the success of all of these firms in growth, profit, and customer satisfaction has been unbelievable. It is clear, in all of these cases, that the leadership's definition of the Vision/Mission Set played a key role in the success of their organization.

How to Develop a Model of Success for Your Organization

I have seen organizations spend months, and in one case, more than a year, developing a vision. I have heard of companies who have spent over $100,000 to develop a vision. This is ridiculous. The total duration from the beginning of the development of a Model of Success to its completion should be less than a month and should require less than 15 hours of time from each of your organization's top leaders. The six-step process for developing a Model of Success for your organization is as follows:

Step 1. Define who should participate in the Model of Success development.

Step 2. Conduct a Model of Success Orientation Meeting.

Step 3. Complete and compile a Model of Success Development Questionnaire.

Step 4. Conduct a Model of Success Development Retreat.

Step 5. Complete and compile a Model of Success Refinement Questionnaire.

Step 6. Conduct a Model of Success Wrap-up Meeting.

The first step of developing your organization's Model of Success is to define the top leaders in your organization who should participate in the development of the Model of Success. This group will be known as the *Steering Team*, as they will be defining the overall direction of the firm. The Steering Team should consist of the top person and the top person's staff. All significant organizational elements should be represented. The number of people on the Steering Team should be between five and ten. The Steering Team members must have a clear understanding of your business, both good insight and foresight, and a healthy imagination.

The second step of developing your organization's Model of Success is a Model of Success Orientation Meeting. This two-to-three-hour session should be conducted by an outside facilitator and should cover all the material presented in this chapter. This orientation will define:

1. The elements of a Model of Success.
2. Why an organization needs a Model of Success.
3. The use of the Model of Success to drive the process of team-based Revolution and Peak-to-Peak Performance.

The third step is a questionnaire that should be given to the Steering Team a couple of days after the orientation. The Steering Team should be asked to complete this questionnaire and return it to the outside facilitator a few days later. The purposes of this questionnaire are:

1. To confirm an understanding of the Model of Success.
2. To stimulate the Steering Team to begin thinking about their organization's Model of Success.

The outside facilitator should compile the results of the Model of Success Development Questionnaire. This information will be used in the fourth step.

The fourth step is the Model of Success Development Retreat. This half-day session for the Steering Team and the outside facilitator should be conducted in an environment where there will be no interruptions. The retreat should begin with the outside facilitator summarizing the results of the first ten questions of the Model of Success Development Questionnaire and ensuring that the Steering Team has an understanding of the elements of the Model of Success. After this brief review, the outside facilitator should work with the Steering Team to define the first draft of the Vision, Mission, Requirements of Success, and Guiding Principles.

The fifth step is a questionnaire that should be given to the Steering Team a couple of days after the Model of Success Development Retreat. The Steering Team should be asked to complete the questionnaire and return it to the outside facilitator a few days later. The purposes of this questionnaire are:

1. Refine the Vision, Mission, Requirements of Success, and Guiding Principles.
2. Obtain a first draft of the Evidences of Success.

The results of this questionnaire should be compiled for the Model of Success Wrap-up Meeting.

The last step in the definition of the Model of Success is the Model of Success wrap-up meeting. The outside facilitator should present recommendations on all five elements of the Model of Success based upon the input received on the Model of Success refinement questionnaire. This meeting should address all concerns presented in the refinement questionnaire plus the following questions:

1. *Is the Model of Success doable?* Will your employees understand it and will they believe it can be accomplished? Is it realistic? Does the Model of Success uniquely represent your company's future?
2. *Is the Model of Success authentic?* Is the Model of Success an honest attempt at defining a direction or is it just a marketing slogan or a public relations gimmick?
3. *Is the Model of Success compelling?* Can employees get excited about the Model of Success? Is the Model of Success future oriented, challenging, and aggressive? Is the Model of Success too ambitious or not ambitious enough? Will the Model of Success inspire enthusiasm and encourage commitment?
4. *Is the Model of Success personally enriching?* Will employees understand how their life will be improved by pursuing the Model of Success? Will employees understand how they will grow while pursuing the Model of Success? Does the Model of Success set forth a standard of excellence and reflect high ideals?

5. *Is the Model of Success focused yet flexible?* Will the Model of Success provide the framework for the unification of all employees' efforts without restricting the company from pursuing breakthrough opportunities and possibilities?

The result of the Model of Success Wrap-up Meeting should be unanimous acceptance by the Steering Team of the organization's Model of Success.

Achieving Model of Success Alignment

As the importance of organizational vision and goals has become so prominent in recent years, organizational alignment is now becoming even more prominent. This is a logical evolution, for no matter how polished and inspiring an organization's Vision and Model of Success are, unless those within the organization "buy in" to the vision and adopt it as their own, the organization has accomplished very little.

The difference between the successful organization that achieves Peak-to-Peak Performance and the traditional organization that flounders is not the quality of the Model of Success, but the quality of the organization's *alignment* with the Model of Success. There is no greater challenge for the leader than the challenge to obtain organizational alignment with the Model of Success.

In today's complex organizations, no one is autonomous. All organizational elements and all employees are interdependent. This interdependence can be an asset if everyone is focused and working together, but a major liability if people are *not* focused and *not* working together. In fact, in an organization that is aligned, change brings about improvements, progress, success, and a sense of accomplishment. By contrast, in an organization that is not aligned, change brings about confusion, demoralization, failure, and a sense of futility. The interdependence of an organization requires that as change occurs, every person in the organization be aligned.

The Model of Success must be instilled into every person in the company, in much the same way as the DNA code that infuses the architecture of the whole into every cell of your body. Having every person focused on the Model of Success allows the interdependent organization to work as a powerful whole instead of many conflicting elements. This alignment is powerful, for people will be pulling in the same direction, and pulling harder, as they have confidence they are pulling in the right direction. For a leader to define an organization's direction, they must define the Model of Success and obtain their company's alignment with it.

Just What is Alignment?

To clearly define what alignment is, let me quote authors George Labobitz and Victor Rosansky from their book *The Power of Alignment*.

- Imagine working in an organization where every member, from top management to the newly hired employee, shares an understanding of the business, its goals, and its purpose.
- Imagine working in a department where everyone knows how he or she contributes to the company's business strategy.
- Imagine being on a team whose every member can clearly state the needs of the company's customers and how the team contributes to satisfying those needs.[19]

The authors go on to define the process of alignment with the following propositions:

Alignment is when an organization is able to:

- Connect their employees' behavior to the mission of the company, turning intentions into action.
- Link teams and processes to the changing needs of customers.
- Shape business strategy with real-time information from customers.
- Create a culture in which these elements all work together seamlessly.[20]

Therefore alignment is the behavioral and emotional interconnectedness of employees to the vision, mission, and function of an organization. Anyone who has been involved in organizational leadership for any length of time will know that this is extremely difficult. But without a doubt, the establishment and increase of organizational alignment is a fundamental necessity of business today, and should be a primary target for Revolution.

The Path of Alignment

For many, the subject of alignment may be new territory, or territory which is not yet understood. What I want to do here is to chart out what I believe are the ten foundational building blocks of alignment, providing you with a distilled discussion on alignment and a clear usable path forward. I want to give you the eight "P's" of alignment. Alignment must be:

Preceded

Alignment does not occur in a vacuum. It requires many other Revolutions to have taken place first before it can be pursued. In particular, alignment must be preceded by the development of an organization's Model of Success. If I were to boil down in one sentence what alignment is, I would say alignment is the adoption of the organization's Model of Success as one's own. Alignment means the acceptance of the responsibility for making the Model of Success a reality. Alignment is demonstrated commitment to the Model of Success on the part of the employees. Therefore, if you currently do not have a Model of Success, your organization cannot be aligned yet.

Public

As may be seen in Figure 5.4, the next step in achieving alignment is *communication.* Public communication is the conduit of alignment. This is not a one-time meeting where the Model of Success is explained, but rather a publicly pervasive, consistent, on-going, persistent, never-ending focus on the Model of Success. Leaders must accept as their primary task (a cause or a crusade even) their role as champion of the Model of Success. Leaders must promote and, yes, even *sell* the Model of Success. Leaders must publicly breathe life into the Model of Success and make it exciting and fun. The process of Revolution provides a vehicle for the leader to communicate the Model of Success to everyone in their organization and to provide total focus on the Model of Success.

As may be seen in Figure 5.4, the communication of the Model of Success will open up three different paths. The most difficult path results in a resistance to the Model of Success. These people, the resisters, don't believe the Model of Success is relevant; due to their lack of trust in leadership, they cannot be made to understand the Model of

Success. The resisters won't comply with the Model of Success, cannot be made to understand the Model of Success, and will resist efforts to try to force compliance with it. Depending upon the historical culture of an organization, the resisters will be anywhere from 15 to 50 percent of the total work force. These resisters are not bad people. They shouldn't be fired. In fact, the resisters often have valid reasons for their lack of trust in leadership. But persistent communication will not result in the resister becoming aligned. The resisters must be won over with demonstrated performance. To win over the resisters, the leader must not only talk the talk, but also walk the walk.

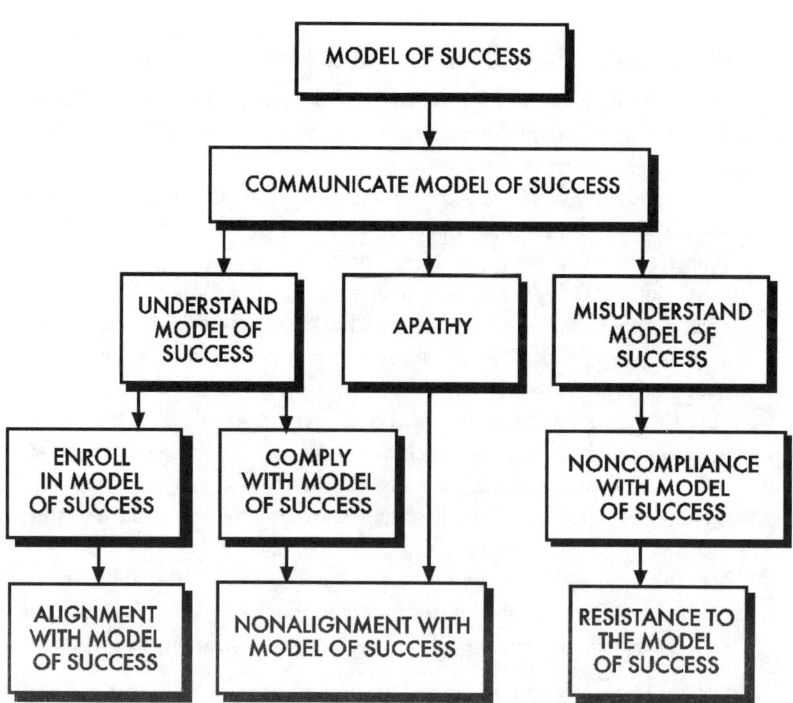

Figure 5.4 The Process of Pursuing Model of Success Alignment

The center path in the process of pursuing Model of Success alignment results is not a *resistance* to the Model of Success but a *nonalignment* with the Model of Success. These nonaligners could be suffering from apathy, which precludes an understanding of the Model of Success, or could be people who understand the Model of Success, comply with it because they don't want to lose their job, but aren't really aligned with it. Typically, the nonaligners have been exposed to program after program (Employee Involvement, Organizational Development, Quality Circles, Total Quality Management, etc.) and see the Model of Success as just another passing fad. Depending upon the level of MBF (Management By Fad), the nonaligners could represent somewhere between 20 to 50 percent of your employees. Over time these people have become numb to all of management's new programs, and therefore some significant time will be required in order to win them over. Persistent communication *will* awaken these nonaligners and bring them into alignment with the Model of Success.

THE CEOs SPEAK OUT ON ALIGNMENT

George Labovitz and Victor Rosansky, the authors of the book, *The Power of Alignment,* asked outstanding executives what the concept of alignment meant to them. Here is what they said:

Fred Smith, CEO of Federal Express, said "One of the first things we recognized is that most managers don't know what management is about. Alignment is the essence of management."

Dr. Dennis O'Leary of the Joint Commission on Accreditation of Healthcare Organizations said, "Alignment ensures that the organization is in balance—that all the pieces fit together. . . our accreditation process itself is consistently in search of organizational alignment. Alignment is what we do."

Lee Cox at AirTouch uses the analogy of a magnet to describe the impact of alignment. "If you drop a bunch of iron filings on a table from 10 feet, they'll be all over the place. Then as you start to put a magnet near them, you'll see the ones closest to the magnet start to move and twitch and start moving in the same direction. Getting into alignment is very difficult where there is none. Once you get there, staying in alignment isn't so difficult."

Labovitz and Rosansky go on to say that each of these CEOs aligned their organization by following the same deceptively simple tests:

- Carefully crafting and articulating the essence of their business and determining the Main Thing.
- Defining a few critical strategic goals and imperatives and deploying them throughout their organizations.
- Tying performance measures and metrics to those goals.
- Linking these measures to a system of rewards and recognition.
- Personally reviewing the performance of their people to ensure the goals are met.[21]

These insights and steps are the foundation of any Alignment Revolution.

Personal

Alignment doesn't occur to a *group* of people. Organizations do not get aligned, individual people do. This can be a difficult aspect of alignment in larger organizations, but it is critical nevertheless. The question for a Revolution leader is not "How can I get my organization aligned?" The question is "How can I get Bill or Sue or Bob aligned."

The important take-away from this point is the realization that actions, styles, and vehicles used to encourage alignment may need to vary with each person. What achieves alignment for one person may not work for another, and vice versa. So the action/style/vehicle must be customized for each person. It is also important to realize that the trust, credibility, and perception of the one requesting alignment is critical. For example, *Dr. Tompkins* can achieve alignment from some people who are impressed and motivated by individuals with higher degrees, but *Dr.* may be a turnoff for others who may desire alignment to be requested from *Bubba*. Usually alignment becomes a case by case project. But whatever time you as a leader put into this personal aspect of alignment is time well spent.

Practical

There must be a compelling, practical benefit to being aligned. People do not become aligned because it seems like the thing to do. There must be a real, viable, and practical set of reasons. Perhaps alignment will increase customer satisfaction which will increase sales which will increase profit sharing. Or, on a relational level, perhaps alignment will reduce friction between two people as they focus more on the Model of Success and its fulfillment than on their personal quirks. Whatever the benefit is, find it and communicate it. Make alignment make sense and appear practical; after all it does and is.

Progressive

Alignment is not something you can issue a memo on tomorrow and consider it done. Even if such immediate implementation did achieve alignment, it wouldn't last. Alignment simply does not last forever. It is like motor oil. It needs to be changed and upgraded from time to time. Alignment must be an evolutionary journey of growth in levels of commitment. Again, alignment, like most everything else in a Revolutionary context, is a process and must be nurtured over time.

Pledge-based

Alignment cannot be forced upon a person. Alignment requires a personal decision of enrollment, which is the acceptance of accountability for something that is going to occur. It is a movement from something *they* want to achieve to something *we* will achieve. I could easily see making alignment acceptance a semi-formal ceremony, where an individual publicly or privately enrolls their acceptance of and alignment with the Model of Success. Perhaps in this ceremony, the leader could recognize the individual's role in fulfilling the Model of Success. Think what that would do for the individual's morale and for peer respect. Of course, the level of alignment and the role the individual played in fulfilling the Model of Success would continuously grow; but such an enrollment would serve as a visible and emotional stimulus toward the alignment process. Whatever method you choose, make sure that the individual is consciously aware that they have accepted the Model of Success and have pledged to make it a reality.

Powerful

Alignment is to an organization what a magnifying glass is to the sun light. It provides a powerful focus and allows things to really heat up. Alignment brings a focused level of power that a nonaligned organization simply does not possess. An *aligned* organization will be a *focused* organization, and a focused organization is a *powerful* organization. It is powerful because the high level of commitment and loyalty result in the unified pull of all energies and powers toward Peak-to-Peak Performance.

Persistent

There are parts of alignment that require a lot of effort on the part of the leader. The largest demand is the demand for persistence. The process of the journey of alignment requires persistent, consistent repetition of the same thoughts, ideas, and concepts from the leader. Perhaps you need to schedule actions you can take to reinforce alignment in someone each week. Well after the speaker gets tired of repeating the same message, people will hear it for the first time and become aligned.

Model of Success Renewal

An organization's Model of Success should seldom change, but should routinely be subject to review. At least annually, the Steering Team should review the Model of Success and compare the company's progress, the changes in the environment and the marketplace, and any shifts in assumptions or paradigms, and thus either reaffirm or renew the Model of Success. The renewal of the Model of Success will typically involve a change in a word or a phrase. It is rare that the renewal will be major. On the other hand, if drastic shifts have occurred, there is no better way to send a signal to an organization than to make a significant change in the Model of Success. As the Steering Team reaffirms or renews the Model of Success, this should be communicated throughout the organization to maintain the focus on and alignment with the Model of Success.

Call to Action

How have you done with charting the vision of your organization? Are you currently trying to lead your Revolution with a one-sentence vision? If so, you are probably frustrated with the lack of understanding and alignment on the part of your employees. The solution? Develop a holistic Model of Success. The future of your company depends on it.

6

Leadership is a Verb

Revolution Principle #6:

A Revolution cannot be managed, it must be led.

Have you ever seen someone try to motivate a group of people to act by analyzing expense reports? Or has anyone ever tried to lead a group of people into Revolution by developing policies and procedures? No, and they never will. Management is not the stuff that creates a Revolution. It may help to carry it out and keep it on track, but it will never ignite it and will never keep the Revolutionary embers burning. To do that there must be leadership.

Let's face it, most Revolutions are personality cults. They are intensely centered on the leader, for good or for bad. That is because people are drawn to and motivated by a person who has the guts to move forward despite the consequence. They are inspired by visionaries and moved by idealism. They are fascinated by people who can see the big picture and who aren't set back by minor glitches. To have a strong Revolution, there must be strong leadership, for this is what keeps people moving.

In business, most companies have an abundance of management but a shortage of leadership. If that's so, how will they ever begin an Organizational Revolution? You can't manage your organization into Revolution, you must lead them there.

The science and practice of management is just a baby when compared to the history of leadership. Nevertheless, as organizational complexity has grown over the last fifty years, the focus of attention has been on management, not leadership; and many have battled over the differences. I believe it boils down to this: Just as a good basketball team must have both a good offense and defense, so too must a good organization have both good management and good leadership.

The problem, then, lies not in management versus leadership but rather in the out-of-balance situation most organizations find themselves in today. Most of them have an abundance of management and a shortage of leadership. To create balance, it is imperative that a management-to-leadership Revolution occur.

To begin the exploration of the Revolution from management to leadership, and to understand why this shift is necessary today, one only needs to reflect on how the words *management* and *leadership* are most often used. *Management* is most often used as a noun, and is defined as *the group of people who achieve orderly results by controlling schedules and budgets*. To the contrary, the word *leadership* is most often used as a verb, and refers to *the process of creating change to obtain results*. It is, then, by reflecting upon our present business climate that we may understand why this Revolution from management to leadership is needed today. In stable business times, when businesses are evolving to the future, it is appropriate for management to exert its controlling influence over an organization. To the contrary, in dynamic business times such as the present, it is absolutely critical that a Revolution toward leadership occur in order to bring about the required level of changes to adapt to the marketplace.

RETHINK THIS!

Although many managers aren't willing to face the necessity of a Revolution toward leadership, their actions betray their true understanding of this necessity. Think about this: What is the hottest topic in business circles today? What are people talking about? What are conferences being called? What is on the cover of all the business magazines?

Is the hottest topic controlling budgets? No, I think not. Is the hottest topic controlling schedules? No, that's not it. The hottest topic is *resomething*. What is resomething? Well, it's about creating change to obtain results.

Think about the following:

Realign	Reform	Reshape
Rebirth	Refresh	Retrench
Rebuild	Reimagine	Restructure
Recondition	Reinvent	Retransform
Recreate	Remake	Rethink
Redesign	Renew	Revamp
Rediscover	Renewal	Revival
Reengineer	Reposition	

In fact, a sure avenue to success in bookselling these days is to resomething. Why? Because management knows that in these dynamic times, we must create change to obtain results. They know we must redo management. Although they may have a difficult time facing reality, they know they must shift from management to leadership. Or is it a *re*shift from management to leadership . . . ?

Revolution Requires Strong Management and Strong Leadership

The most common management-bashing theme of the last ten years has been the short-term orientation of management. This has led many to the conclusion that we need to manage differently. To the contrary, management by its very nature has a short-term orientation. We don't need a new way to manage, what we need is a better balance between management and leadership. To understand the balance between management and leadership, it is useful to look at the following four combinations of weak and strong management and leadership:

Type 1. Weak management and weak leadership.
Type 2. Strong management and weak leadership.
Type 3. Weak management and strong leadership.
Type 4. Strong management and strong leadership.

A Type 1 organization, with weak management and weak leadership, is not long for this world. The organization will not know where they are (weak management) and will not know where they are going (weak leadership). There will be no focus on either the present or the future. In fact, there will be no focus at all, as people are simply going through the motions without any awareness of or concern for what is happening. These organizations are living *in* the past, *off* of their past. They will continue to exist only as long as their past will allow. Left to their own, these firms will die sad and lonely deaths. Other alternatives include a management and/or leadership Revolution, or an acquisition.

An effective management Revolution will result in a Type 2 organization, an effective leadership Revolution in a Type 3 organization, and an effective management and leadership Revolution in a Type 4 organization. Acquisitions have the full range of possibilities, from remaining a Type 1 organization and dying a sad and lonely death to being transformed into a Type 2, 3, or 4 organization. A Type 1 organization will either be transformed or it will die.

A Type 2 organization, with strong management and weak leadership, will have on hand an abundance of reports that document the organization's present performance. Unfortunately, there will be no focus or direction for the future. Risk will be minimized, control will be maximized, and decisions will be top-down and taken only after all alternatives have been analyzed and then a predictable path forward defined. Innovation will not occur, and changes in the marketplace will be viewed more as problems that need to be fixed rather than opportunities for growth and improvement. Type 2 organizations are the most common ones today.

In today's world of professional managers and MBAs, there are no large Type 3 organizations. The only Type 3 organizations found in business are small, entrepreneurial companies. These Type 3 organizations, which have strong leadership but weak management, have a focus on the long-term of their firm but little understanding of or focus on today's performance. A gambler mentality is prevalent, with little structure or assessment of risk. Decisions are made without a true understanding of the implications, and as growth occurs the organization spins out of control. Deadlines, promises, and budgets are not adhered to. Frustration and chaos loom. Type 3 organizations don't need a Revolution from management to leadership, but rather must achieve the proper management/leadership balance by adding professional management to their organization.

Type 4 organizations, which have both strong management and strong leadership, are the hallmark of success. If you are a Type 2 organization, you must become a Type 4 organization if you wish to be successful. This Revolution will create a balance between strong management and strong leadership that will result in the organization achieving Peak-to-Peak Performance.

The Succeed/Fail, Fail/Succeed cycle that I explained earlier may be viewed as a management/leadership cycle. Often when a new firm is created, it is created with an entrepreneurship that is strong on leadership but weak on management (Type 3). The founder realizes the firm's management shortcomings and brings in professional managers to run the company. The professional managers install budgets, policies, and procedures, and the company does very well. However, as time progresses, the bureaucracy that was once needed to create order becomes stifling. The company loses its edge and its profitability and upper management is fired. A new leader is brought in and Revolution takes place. New products are created that win in the marketplace and the company expands. Unfortunately, insufficient management controls are in place so mistakes are made. The leader is dismissed and professional managers are hired to regain control. Budgets, policies, and procedures are reinstalled, and now, with the new product line, success returns. The company does well. This recurring cycle exists because many organizations do not grasp the need to balance management and leadership.

The Challenge of Shifting From Management to Leadership

Professional managers have worked hard to become good managers. They have gone to school, held a variety of jobs, and read many books. They take great pride in being in charge, in being the person who makes decisions. The attitude often set forth is "The buck stops here." These managers enjoy the "burden" of management and have tied their ego to their being the decision maker, the problem solver, and the top manager. The suggestion that these managers transform from management to leadership is not well received, for these managers enjoy and understand management but are uncertain about leadership.

The greatest challenge, then, to the Revolution from management to leadership in a firm, is that the managers don't want to be moved out of their comfort zone. They are comfortable being managers. This is so sad, because in most firms where there is strong management and weak leadership (Type 2), there exist more rewards for leadership than for management. We have more managers than we need, but because of the management comfort zone, many managers will shortchange themselves and their organization by continuing to manage and failing to lead. It is in these situations that managers need to listen to Pogo when he said, "We have met the enemy, and he is us." The failure of these managers to shift to leadership restricts the growth and success of their organization. This is the greatest challenge in pursuing Revolution in leadership!

Shifting: How Leaders See Themselves

It was from the perspective of the managers and leaders that, at the beginning of this chapter, *management* was defined as a noun and *leadership* as a verb. Management is defined by who you *are*, whereas leadership is defined by what you *do*. A simple way to determine if a person is a manager or a leader is to ask what that person does for a living. If you were to ask the head of a human resources department this question, a *manager* would respond by saying "I am the Manager of Human Resources." If you asked this same question of the head of a human resources department who was a *leader*, the response you would get is "I work throughout the company to be sure we have the right people doing the right jobs with the right skills and training while being fairly compensated." You see, managers define their job by who they *are*, whereas leaders define their job by what they *do*.

Managers see themselves as a boss for whom people work. For this reason, managers think of themselves as being accountable. Conversely, leaders see themselves as working *for* their people, and therefore make their people accountable for their *own* actions. It is the manager's short-term, narrow focus that keeps their eye on the bottom line. To the contrary, leaders have a broader, long-term focus that keeps their eye on the horizon. Managers like the role of management and leaders like the role of leadership. Thus, for an organization to achieve the proper balance between management, leadership, and Revolution, individual managers must personally shift from management to leadership.

KEEPING HIS EYE ON THE HORIZON

What would you call a company that has a 75 percent market share in a fast growing market but wants to increase market share? The same company has a 58 percent gross profit margin with net earnings which make it the most profitable company of its size in the world. At the same time, the company doubles in size roughly every two years and is basing its future on beating AT&T, IBM, Matsushita, Motorola, Philips, Sega, and Sony. What would you call such a company?

One label is "hyperaggressiveness," another is "greedy," another is "competitively paranoid." It matters not what label is used, what you get is the very, very successful Intel. At its helm, the leader with his eye on the horizon is the "Mad Hungarian," Andy Grove. At a time when faced with greater competition than ever before (a product developed jointly by IBM, Motorola, and Apple Computer), how does this leader respond? By investing $1.1 billion in research and development and $2.4 billion in capital investment, while developing not only the product after next, but also the product after, the product after, the product after, the product after next, and pursuing a whole new market, consumer electronics.

How does Mr. Grove respond when asked about the rising competition? He says, "We needed a little threat, a good target. The juice is flowing." When asked if they would be doing what they were doing without the threat poised on the horizon, he responds, "Truthfully, no. We are making gutsier moves investment-wise, pricing-wise, every way, because we've got a competitive threat. The next result is we'll get to advance to the next level of competition."[1]

Now, that is leadership that keeps its eye on the horizon and sees all that it can see.

Shifting: How Leaders are Seen by Others

When asked to differentiate between managers and leaders, most people focus on one of three topics.

First, leaders demand accountability for performance. Whereas a manager may demand hard work, conformance to rules, and predictability, leaders are interested in results. Leaders are less interested in the *presentation* and more in the *innovation*, less in the *style* and more in the *creativity*, and less in *how* something was done and more in *what* was done. This manager/leader dichotomy flows directly from the manager's focus on *control* and the leader's focus on Revolution.

Second, managers believe in structure, in following a chain of command, and in a logical, orderly decision process. Leaders don't believe in structure, and in fact, often do not have organizational charts. Leaders do not follow a chain of command because they don't believe in a chain of command. Leaders feel no hesitation in talking to anyone and everyone in the organization. Although leaders desire a reasonable level of analysis, they understand that many opportunities are missed by the organization because it waited for just one more analysis prior to making a decision. The leader will often make a decision and boldly move forward in spite of the risk of failure. A manager will want one more analysis, one more task force, one more meeting, one more opinion . . . .

Third, a good manager is most often described by people as being very intelligent, a good decision maker, a good problem solver, a quick study, a person who asks difficult questions, a person with a good analytical mind, and so on. A good leader is most often defined as an inspirational person, a good listener, a person with a passion for the business they are in, a caring person, an enthusiastic person, a person of integrity, and so forth. Note how the good manager descriptions all refer to how the manager controls decisions, whereas the leader descriptions refer to how the leader relates to people.

Managers are clearly viewed by others as managers, and leaders are clearly viewed as leaders. Thus, for an organization to achieve the proper balance between management and leadership, individual managers must shift their relationship with people within the company from a relationship based on *control* to a relationship based on Revolution.

Shifting: What Leaders Do

When it comes to the actual tasks performed by a manager versus those of a leader, there is a very apparent difference. These differences are vital to you if you wish to be a leader. They define your role within the organization as opposed to the manager's role. Table 6.1 lists basic leadership functions and how they differ from management:

Table 6.1 Differentiating leadership and management functions

Role	Function
Leader	Define an organization's Model of Success.
Manager	Plan and budget.
Leader	Look at the long-term big picture, and define the organization's overall direction.
Manager	Define short-term specifics and allocating resources.
Leader	Obtain organizational alignment with the Model of Success.
Manager	Organize and staff.
Leader	Make sure people do the right things.
Manager	Make sure people do things right.
Leader	Define motivation.
Manager	Controlling people's performance.
Leader	Encourage results.
Manager	Monitor results.

Notice the differences between the leader's role and the manager's role:

- Management seeks *control,* leadership seeks *growth.*
- Management *administrates,* leadership *innovates.*
- Management relies on *systems and controls,* leadership relies on *people and trust.*
- Management asks *how and when*, leadership asks *what and why.*

Knowing the differences between management and leadership is your key to success in this area. Again, if you are to be a Revolutionary leader, you must know what that means practically. It does no good to espouse leadership rhetoric if you don't know how to respond to daily issues as a leader. You should read these simple differences each day. They will help you remember your role within the organization and remind you of how to gauge your leadership Revolution. You must come to the point where you naturally respond to the most mundane issues as a leader. This is the goal of Leadership Revolution!

Table 6.2 shows the differences between management and leadership:

Table 6.2 Differences Between Management and Leadership

Management	Leadership
Control	Change
Short-term	Long-term
Know where they are	Know where they are going
Who you are	What you do
Boss of people	Servant of people
Accountable for results (hold people accountable for conformance)	Hold people accountable for results
Narrow focus	Broad focus
Focus on bottom line	Focus on the horizon
Presentation, style, and *how* things are done	Innovation, creativity, *what* was done
Structure, chain of command	Orderly decision process: flexibility, openness, and progress
Described by how they control decisions	Described by how they relate to people
Dinosaur culture	Crocodile culture
Statistically consistent on change	Dynamically consistent on change
Planning and budgeting	Define Model of Success
Organizing and staffing	Obtain organizational alignment
People doing it right	People doing the right things
Controlling performance	Defining motivation
Administrates	Innovates
Relies on systems and controls	Relies on people and trust
Asks how and when	Asks what and why

Call to Action

Is your organization led or managed? Are you a leader or a manager? If you wish to pursue Revolution, you must Revolutionize your leadership style. Your organization's success will be determined by how you respond to this chapter. If you choose to continue to be a manager, you may maintain your position but you will eventually travel to a valley. But if you become a leader, you are choosing to bring your organization to new heights of success. Look to the horizon and lead your organization aggressively toward it.

Part III

Collaboration

Experts, consultants, union leaders, executives, professors, machine operators, and many others are agreeing with what is being said daily in newspapers, magazines, books, conferences, and seminars: "Successful organizations will be team-based organizations." Although since the beginning of the enthusiasm about teams there have been a lot of questions and concerns about "teaming," the concept is still essential. Based on what we have learned about teams over the years, I have switched from calling the process *teaming* to calling it *collaboration.* These may seem like synonyms at first glance, but they are intrinsically different. I will flesh that distinction out in Chapter 7.

Throughout my years of research and collaboration, I have also discovered that the concept is far broader than we all first believed. I have learned that collaboration includes two separate categories. First there is *intraorganizational collaboration.* This is what we have traditionally called teaming. It is the team process within the walls of an organization whose goal is to continuously improve business processes. The second category is *extraorganizational collaboration.* This is the joining of forces with those outside our organizations through the Revolutionary processes of customer satisfaction and partnerships. It is imperative to view each of these categories as collaboration because so many of their basic principles of success are related. It also helps to distill our thinking about them and group them under one heading, giving our thinking and learning greater focus.

As you read this section, the longest section in the book, I remind you that you are not trying to learn the latest fads, but are gathering the scientific data you need to begin a Collaboration Revolution. I have done all I can to make that information as accessible, interesting, and compelling as possible. The application of these principles is up to you.

7

The Power of Collaboration

Revolution Principle #7:

A Revolution cannot be carried out by individuals, it must be a collaborative effort.

The very nature of Revolution demands the intense collaboration of a group of people. There simply cannot be a one-person Revolution. Even if Revolution followers are forced into allegiance to the cause, they are the ones who actually carry out the Revolution. One individual who believes they can bring about Revolution on their own is usually viewed as a lunatic. But an individual who is able to gather a group of people around the cause instantly gains credibility, and usually a whole lot of media hype too.

However, not only can there not be a one-person Revolution, there also cannot be a whole group of individuals who do not collaborate. Groups of individuals who do not collaborate in their Revolution efforts usually end up in a counterrevolution, mutiny, or sedition. Interestingly, this is what happens to the majority of Revolutions—they splinter, thus losing their ability to ever accomplish significant Revolution.

Revolution is the science of synthesizing the energy of individuals into one collective force around a common set of goals. The synthesizing element of that definition is key to our understanding of Revolution. Where there is not synthesis, where individuals do not meld into the collective force, we have every reason to believe that the Revolution will fail or make the situation worse. There simply cannot be Revolution without collaboration, synthesis, and synergy.

The organization seeking to become a Revolutionary Organization should heed this warning well. Just as collaboration is key to Revolution in the non-business context, it is even more key within the business context. Your ticket to achieving success, Peak-to-Peak Performance, and Organizational Revolution is collaboration. Just as the individuals in a military Revolution must meld into the collective force, so the individuals in your organization must have the opportunity to do the same thing.

Possibly the greatest challenge in creating a successful organization is overcoming the existing paradigms of teams. Everyone is familiar with teams and has their own personal understanding of them, most of which today equals failure, frustration, and backfire. Unfortunately, rarely do two people have the same understanding because there are several different types of teams, several different levels of teams, several different phases of team evolution, and several different roles to be played on teams. This chapter will clarify these differences and lay the foundation for the next two chapters, in which the process of creating a Collaborative Organization is presented.

Teaming versus Collaboration

In Chapter 6, the question "What is good leadership?" was left unanswered, because it is in the context of understanding teams that the difficulty in answering the "good leadership" question may be further understood.

Any attempt to list the traits of a good leader results in frustration, as many of these traits can seem to be mutually exclusive. For example,

- A leader must be very intelligent, but also able to relate to people.
- A leader must be forceful, but also sensitive.
- A leader must be dynamic, but also patient.
- A leader must be an excellent speaker, but also an excellent listener.
- A leader must be decisive, but also reflective.

The simple fact is that no individual can combine all of these qualities. That's why we need teams. A team, as a totality, can possess all of these qualities. By combining all of these qualities, a team will be able not only to outperform any individual, but also the sum of the individuals on the team. This combining of parts to yield a whole that is greater than the sum of its parts (1+1=6) is called synergy, and is the power of collaboration.

I choose to use the term collaboration as opposed to teaming because teaming may or may not result in synergy; true collaboration always does. Successful companies do not form teams because they like teams, or because it is a fad. They form teams to reap the golden egg—synergy. It is the synergy factor that differentiates teaming from collaboration. The word collaboration implies the synergy factor in its very definition, whereas a team does not. I believe the failure of teaming in recent years is a result of companies pursuing teaming rather than synergy. Likewise, I believe the success of teams lies in pursuing the synergy factor and believing in the power of collaboration. Therefore I choose to call the entire collaboration process Business Process Continuous Improvement (BPCI). Collaboration is the means by which we improve our business processes, continuously.

What is a Team?

A team is a small number of people who use synergy to work together for a common end. Through this definition and an understanding of synergy, one can understand why leaders need followers as much as followers need leaders. In fact, the synergistic work of followers is what makes leaders, not the leaders who make the followers.

Leaders need to understand that committees, task forces, and groups are not teams. A whole company is not a team. The daily recognition of the value of teamwork (although very desirable) does not make a team. By definition, a team is a small number of people who use the power of synergy to work together for a common end. Therefore, to determine if a team exists, we must be able to answer the following three team-definition questions affirmatively:

1. Are there a small number of people involved?
2. Do the people use synergy to work together?
3. Do the people have a common end?

Now, given this understanding of teams, we can evaluate certain groups to see if they are teams. Is a choir a team? Yes, a choir consists of a small number of people. Yes, the members of the choir combine their voices via synergy (harmony). And yes, the choir has a common end of making beautiful music. So a choir is a team.

Does a church congregation singing a song on a Sunday morning qualify as a team? No, it is not a small number of people. What is a small number? It depends upon the circumstances; maybe 10, 20, or even 100. However, a church congregation of 600 is not a small number.

How about a baseball team? Yes, a baseball team consists of a small number of people. Yes, the members of the baseball team all want to win the game. A key question, however, is does a baseball team use synergy to work together? Well, some teams, yes, and some, no. On some baseball teams, each individual on defense only plays his position and there is no support, teaming together, or synergy. Similarly, on some baseball teams each individual on offense thinks only of himself and there is no synergism on hits and runs, squeeze plays, hitting away from the runners, sacrifice flies, advancing the runner, and so on. In these cases, baseball would not truly be a team sport. On other baseball teams, where on both offense and defense the players use synergy so as to play together, baseball is definitely a team sport.

How about a swim team? Is a swim team a team? Yes, a swim team consists of a small number of people who all want to win the swim meet. But, except for the relays, there is no use of synergy to work together and so, no, a swim team is not truly a team.

The Collaboration Process

Now that we understand the definition of teams, it is important to understand the process whereby an organization becomes a Collaborative Organization. As I said earlier, there is a major difference between organizations that "do teams" and organizations that believe in the power of collaboration and synergy. Doing teams is just another "flavor of the month" program. A wide variety of team programs have come and gone over the last 30 years. These programs (such as Participative Management, Job Enlargement, Job Enrichment, Organizational Development, Quality Circles, T Groups, Quality of Life, Employee Involvement, and so on.) have little to do with a company believing and engaging in collaboration. In fact, these programs drive organizations away from becoming Collaborative Organizations because of their lack of long-term success.

Although a successful organization may have "done teams" in their past, they now know that they will never break through to Peak-to-Peak Performance via a team *program*. The key to becoming a BPCI organization is the *process* of collaboration. The difference between team success and failure is the understanding that team *programs* don't work, but that a properly designed collaboration *process* can be made to work. The collaboration process presented in this book has been developed by Tompkins Associates over a 15-year period while working within hundreds of organizations. This process works, and will lead to success. The essence of the collaboration process I wish to define is not a program that you *do*, but rather a definition of *how* your company functions. For this reason, the process defined in this book should be taken as a whole. Adapt it to your situation, but don't skip portions of the process, or you too will become another failed team case study. In fact, as you might guess, I am often told of case studies of failed team programs and processes. One hundred percent of the time, these failures can be tracked to one or more omissions from the Revolution process defined in this book.

Different Types of Teams

As a starting point for the process of becoming a Collaborative Organization, it is important that you understand the five different types of teams that must exist in any Revolutionary Organization. These five team types are:

1. Steering Team
2. Leadership Team
3. Communication Team
4. Design Team
5. Work Team

Each of these teams is very different from the others, and with the possible exception of combining the Steering Team and Leadership Team in smaller organizations (less than 150 people), they all must be a portion of the process for an organization to become a Collaborative Organization. Each of the next five subsections of this chapter define one of these Collaborative Organization teams. These five subsections are summarized in Table 7.1.

Type	Objective	Number of Members	Frequency of Meetings	Other
Steering Team	To establish, communicate, and maintain focus on the Model of Success and to guide and support the Leadership Team.	5 to 10	Weekly until Model of Success and Leadership Team have been established. Then monthly.	Team should consist of top executive and key direct reports representing a broad organizational cross-section. Team leader should be top executive.
Leadership Team	To work toward Model of Success alignment; to define charter, orient, encourage, motivate, support, and accept accountability for teams; and to ensure performance.	8 to16	Twice weekly for first few weeks. Then weekly.	This team is the workhorse of the collaboration process. The people on this team will be required to spend several hours each week on the process.
Communication Team	To ensure that everyone in the organization has a clear understanding of the Model of Success, the status of teams, and the organization's status.	10 to20	Weekly, with monthly Communication Forums.	This team is a critical one in ensuring alignment and motivation. Information and understanding are power, and this team's job is to speed information and understanding throughout the organization.
Design Team	To design or redesign the company by using a blue-sky, clean-sheet, green-field process of innovation and creativity to bring about significant performance improvements.	Varies depending upon Design Team scope. Could be 3 or 4 or 10 to 20.	Varies depending upon Design Team scope. Could be 3 times daily to monthly.	This team is where the concurrent engineering and reengineering efforts within a company reside. An important element in breakthrough thinking.
Work Team	To bring the process of continuous improvement to life. To unleash the power of the people in the organization.	6 to 9	Weekly	Need to understand the differences between Cross-functional Work Teams and Functional Work Teams: Cross-functional Work Teams work across an organization for cultural transformation. Functional Work Teams work down an organization for performance improvement.

Table 7.1 The Types of Teams in a Business Process Continuous Improvement Organization.

Steering Team

In most organizations the Steering Team already exists and, for the most part, already functions like a team. The Steering Team should consist of the top executive and this executive's key staff, making the size of the team somewhere between 5 and 10 members. The Steering Team has the following two tasks:

Steering organization. The job of the Steering Team is to establish the Model of Success and to be the initial communicator of the Model of Success. Steering Team members should individually and collectively demonstrate a focus on the Model of Success. The Steering Team must consistently and persistently work toward the Model of Success alignment discussed in Chapter 6.

Steering Process. Through the definition, guidance, and motivation of the Leadership Team, the Steering Team should guide the overall collaboration process.

It is important that the Steering Team demonstrate their commitment to the process of becoming a BPCI organization by following the process. Therefore, even though the same group of people today may have the name Executive Committee, Management Committee, Board, or Policy Committee; have a regular meeting time; and have an ongoing *modus operandi*, this team should be called the Steering Team, should have a regularly scheduled meeting for just Steering Team business, and conform to the rules, procedures, and methods of the Revolution process.

Leadership Team

The Leadership Team provides the leadership for the Revolution to a Collaborative Organization. To do this, the Leadership Team must work toward Model of Success alignment; define, charter, orient, encourage, motivate, support, and accept accountability for teams; and ensure Peak-to-Peak Performance. The Leadership Team functions as the workhorse of the Revolution process. The Leadership Team should consist of 8 to 16 well-respected people, involved in all aspects of the company. If it is a union shop, it would be fine to include a couple of people from the union organization. The leader of the Leadership Team should be a well-organized, action-based person who has a broad-based perspective, a strong belief in the collaboration process, and strong communication skills. The Leadership Team should meet weekly and should proactively help each team overcome difficulties. The Leadership Team should follow this process:

1. Orientation
2. Define priorities
3. Charter teams
4. Provide team orientation
5. Encourage, motivate, and support teams
6. Ensure team progress
7. Monitor and report results
8. Grow process
9. Return to Step 3

PROCESS STUCK ON THE WRONG DEFINITION OF THE LEADERSHIP TEAM

A family-owned manufacturing company of about 500 people had an Executive Team of seven (to include three family members) who made most of the decisions about how the company functioned. The next level of the organization consisted of eight department heads, who in theory had a lot of autonomy in running their operation. A decision was made to combine the Steering Team into a single Leadership Team. A Leadership Team of 15 was created, a Model of Success developed, a Communication Team and four Work Teams chartered, and the process sat flat. There was no Leadership Team. What they had was a Leadership Group that consisted of the Executive Team (that really was a team) and eight other guys who did not feel comfortable dealing with the Executive Team.

After six months of frustration, the non-functioning 15-member Leadership Team was split into a seven-member Steering Team and an eight-member Leadership Team. Acting as a liaison between the Steering Team and the Leadership Team was a very thoughtful, clever- thinking, non-family member from the Steering Team. Guess what? The Steering Team started steering and after a while the Leadership Team started leading the process. Today, a successful, growing, profitable company has truly become a center of revolution. Oh, the glory of revolution, when things are done well.

Communication Team

Most organizations have two things in common:

1. Poor communications
2. Leadership who cannot understand why poor communications exist

Leadership is troubled, as they have worked hard establishing and then using a formal communications system. This formal communications system is top-down. Typically, bottom-up and horizontal communications don't work. Worse yet, many studies have shown that somewhere between 10 to 30 percent of all communications are lost as they travel through each level of an organization. That is to say, only 75 percent of what the president says, is understood by the vice president; that only 50 percent of what the president says, is understood by the director of operations; that only 25 percent of what the president says, is understood by the supervisor; and that the worker rarely understands at all what the president said.

Some leaders attempt to minimize this loss by communicating in writing. This helps, but not much. The thing that presidents don't realize is that their vocabulary, language, and assumptions differ from the workers' to such a degree that similar losses in written communication often occur.

The fact is, information and the understanding of information is power. Information and the understanding of information are to an organization's Revolution process what gasoline is to an automobile. This is even more critical during times of organizational transformation, because if the people don't have the information, the informal communications system will generate information that will most likely be detrimental to the process. Or going back to the analogy, when the automobile lacks gas, people in the throes of chaos put water in the gas tank.

It is clear that for an organization to achieve Revolution, a top-to-bottom, bottom-to-top, and side-to-side communications network must be established and used. It is the responsibility of the Communication Team to ensure that these communications take place.

The Communication Team's responsibility is to ensure that everyone in the organization has a clear understanding of the Model of Success, the status of teams, and the organization's status. The Communication

Team often consists of 10 to 20 members and meets on a regular weekly basis. Tools used by Communication Teams vary, but some that work well include:

Newsletters. Most organizations have some form of regularly produced newsletter. If one doesn't exist, the thought of developing a newsletter just for Revolution communications should be considered. Each newsletter should include the organization's Model of Success, updates on all teams, and recognition of all team activities.

Model of Success. The Communication Team should have the Model of Success attractively printed and framed. These framed Models of Success should be hung throughout the company and extra printed copies should be produced for individuals to hang in locations they deem appropriate. All team meeting rooms should have a framed Model of Success on the wall.

Bulletin Boards. The Communication Team should review all company bulletin boards. Appropriate Revolution information should be placed on the bulletin boards and maintained in a timely fashion.

Events. The Communication Team should evaluate special events for all employees. These special events should not be baseball games or picnics (although another team may wish to sponsor these types of events), but instead should be plant visits, video tapes, or guest speakers that will focus attention on the Model of Success, the Revolution process, and/or the organization's performance.

Word-of-Mouth. The members of the Communication Team should come from a broad cross-section of the organization. The members of the Communication Team should be posted and well known. Everyone in the organization should be encouraged to talk with the Communication Team members. While maintaining total amnesty of the sources of all communications, the Communication Team members should work to achieve the Communication Team objectives on a one-on-one basis.

Surveys. From time to time the Communication Team may wish to proactively seek inputs from the organization. These surveys should be done anonymously and should provide a forum for both structured tabular responses as well as for unstructured open responses.

Communication Forum. All organizations should have a regularly scheduled monthly Communication Forum. These forums are critically important to ensure organizational alignment, understanding, and celebration. A major shortfall in organizations today is the failure to celebrate our organizational successes, to provide feedback, to rekindle the "family" spirit, and to say "thank you." The Communication Forum is the opportunity for this all to occur and is the paramount regular event where an organization's transformation can be put on display. The agenda for the Communication Forum should consist of a review of the Model of Success and the Team Rules (to be presented in Chapter 8), and the team presentations. Each team presentation should be done by a team reporter who should spend three to four minutes reviewing the success, progress, issues, good things, and even weaknesses of their team. The people to attend the Communication Forum should be the Steering Team, the Leadership Team, the Communication Team, and one representative of each team. The Communication Forums should be fun, lively, and action-packed. After each presentation, people should be encouraged to ask questions, and these should be answered in a way that ensures full understanding.

To encourage Communication Forum interaction, the Communication Team may wish to create a Question Box. The purpose of this box is to obtain anonymous questions that will be asked at the Communication Forum. These questions should be asked of the appropriate party at the Communication Forum by a member of the Communication Team, while indicating that these questions came from the Question Box. Every effort should be made to make the Communication Forum a true celebration and a place to recognize and thank teams for their efforts.

Visual Management System. It is extremely important that the Communication Team work on organizational alignment, team information, team recognition, and performance visibility. A tool that can help in all these regards is a Visual Management System (VMS). A VMS is a large board that could quite easily be 20' x 8' and consume an entire wall. The four key elements of a VMS are:

- *Model of Success.* To maintain organization focus and alignment.
- *Team Listing.* To inform everyone what is being worked on.
- *Approved Projects.* To recognize team progress and success.
- *Visual Measurement System (VMS).* To act as a scoreboard to document and add visibility to the organizational performance and the organization's Evidence of Success.

A notebook version of the VMS can be provided to remote locations or to people who travel. Typically, this notebook version is updated monthly.

The Model of Success is typically displayed on the VMS in a permanent fashion. The team listings and approved projects should be fastened in such a way that they can be easily updated. The VMS should be updated at least weekly and perhaps even hourly. The Communication Team should accept responsibility for managing these updates. The questions to be answered when designing the VMS are:

- What organizational and team Evidence of Success should be regularly and frequently reported on, and what decisions or actions need to be taken?
- What information is required to measure the Evidence of Success, make the decisions, or take the actions?
- What data is needed to get the information?
- How do we obtain the data?
- How/who should convert data to information?
- How do we portray information, and how do we design the VMS?
- Where do we locate the VMS, and how many should we have?
- What will it cost to construct the boards?
- What should be the implementation plan?
- Do we have approval from the Leadership Team to proceed?
- Once a VMS has been implemented, how/who should train employees on it?
- How/who should audit VMS acceptance, refinement?
- How/who should upgrade and improve the VMS so that it can respond to everyone's needs?
- Who should educate new employees on VMS, and how?
- How can the Communication Team maintain the organization's interest in VMS?

The positive impacts of the visibility of, recognition of, and performance feedback on the VMS should not be underestimated. In many organizations where there has been little sharing of performance data, the implementation of a VMS will have major cultural and motivational impacts. Information is power, and the purpose of a VMS is to transmit information, so it isn't surprising that the VMS transmits power. This transmission of information and power will keep the Revolution going.

Design Team

While pursuing Revolution, the process of Peak-to-Peak Performance must be a focus, but so too must the process of design and redesign. The expression "If it ain't broken, break it" certainly is critical to the success of Revolution, but so too is the expression "If it's broken, fix it." Design Teams have to do with the process of design and redesign, and the expression "If it's broken, fix it."

Possibly the two most popular buzzwords of the early 1990s were *reengineering* and *concurrent engineering*. A true measure of the level of chaos created by a fad is the number of synonyms that are invented to say the same thing. Reengineering was also referred to as *work reengineering, work-systems redesign, rearchitecting, case management*, and *new industrial engineering*. Concurrent engineering was also referred to as *simultaneous engineering, design for manufacturability, mechatronics, winning manufacturing product development*, and *Taguchi methods*. The role of reengineering was *the design or redesign of organizational structures, systems, and procedures to improve performance*. Similarly, the role of concurrent engineering was *the design or redesign of products and manufacturing facilities to improve performance*. The role of a Design Team is the combination of the roles of reengineering and concurrent engineering: *to design or redesign organizational structures, systems, procedures, products, and facilities to improve performance*. Although all of these design or redesign efforts are different, it is absolutely critical that within a Revolutionary Organization these efforts not be segregated from the overall Revolution process, but be a fully integrated portion of creating Peak-to-Peak Performance.

The functions performed by Design Teams have not been executed well over the last 20 years. I believe that this is why the topics of reengineering and concurrent engineering were such fertile ground for buzzwords and their accompanying chaos. In a November-December 1993 *Harvard Business Review* article, the authors state:

> "In all too many companies, reengineering has been not only a great success but also a great failure. After months, even years, of careful redesign, these companies achieved dramatic improvements in individual processes only to watch overall results decline."[1]

And then in the bible of reengineering, *Reengineering the Corporation,* Hammer and Champy state:

> "Our unscientific estimate is that as many as 50 percent to 70 percent of the organizations that undertake a reengineering effort do not achieve the dramatic results they intended."[2]

And similarly with concurrent engineering, in a *Manufacturing Engineering* article Jean Owen states:

> "All this sounds great, but don't forget the land mines. The path to successful concurrent engineering is strewn with them, according to Dr. Daniel R. Tobin. Most of them are cultural, not technological. Seduced by promises of huge savings, many companies hired consultants, made massive investments in technology, tore down the walls between departments, developed multifunctional teams, bought the software and hardware to make it all happen, and found the return on investment pretty mediocre."[3]

And finally, from a *Business Week* article entitled "Flops":

> "If companies can improve their effectiveness at launching new products, they could double their bottom line. It's one of the few areas left with the greatest potential for improvement."[4]

To increase your company's design or redesign batting average is to be certain that design teams are chartered within the overall process of creating Revolution and Peak-to-Peak Performance, and to properly define the breadth and depth of the Design Teams within their charter.

Design Teams chartered with too narrow a breadth will not be successful, as they will only look at a portion of the total. At best, a suboptimization will take place. At worst, not only will improvement not occur, but overall performance will drop as the changes made to the portion of the total—although improving this portion—are detrimental to the broad picture. Design Teams should be chartered with a broad focus. This broad focus should relate to the creation of value in the ultimate company performance *as viewed by the customer.* Within the Design Team's charter, it should be clearly stated what performance improvements are expected to result from the Design Team. Once again, these performance improvements must be performance improvements from the perspective of the customer.

Design Team Charters that restrict the team will not allow them to penetrate to the core elements of the organization and to address the real opportunities so as to bring about Peak-to-Peak Performance. For this reason, Design Teams should be charted to allow an in-depth pursuit of the core issues impacting design. Design Teams should be chartered to:

- Leave the paradigms of the past behind.
- Develop recommendations independent of present practice.
- Establish a clean-sheet, blue-sky, green-field design for both today and tomorrow.
- Be innovative and creative.

As few restrictions as possible should be placed on Design Teams.

Table 7.2 presents several Design Team failures that resulted from charters that suffered from breadth and depth problems. The number of people involved in a Design Team can vary from 3 to 4 for the design of a process to 10 to 50 for the design of an automobile. Also, the frequency of meetings can vary from three times a day for the design of a product to monthly for the redesign of an entire organization. It is only through a well-developed and thoughtful charter that a Design Team can be successful. The failures of reengineering and concurrent engineering efforts have less to do with the process of reengineering and concurrent engineering and more to do with the chartering of these teams. Keys to chartering a Design Team include the following:

- The Design Team is a part of the Revolution process and creating Peak-to-Peak Performance and will conform to the Model of Success and the overall collaboration process.
- The Design Team will have intimate contact with the Leadership Team.
- The Design Team will work with the Communication Team to achieve awareness and understanding throughout the organization.
- The charter will include specific performance improvement expectations.
- The Design Team should have a broad focus that relates to the ultimate company performance as viewed by the customer.
- The Design Team should be chartered to allow an in-depth pursuit of the core issues.

- The Design Team's charter should not limit or restrict the Design Team's pursuit of performance improvement, but rather encourage and stimulate the Design Team to achieve Revolution and Peak-to-Peak Performance.
- Design Teams should be encouraged to look outside of their company's boundaries to pursue problems, challenges, and opportunities.
- Design Teams should be made aware of the fact that they will be involved with and responsible for the implementation of their designs.
- Design Teams should be encouraged to test new designs to whatever level possible, to refine the design, and minimize problems during implementation.

CHARTER STATEMENT	RESULTS OBTAINED/WHY
Improve company communications by redesigning receptionist position.	No results obtained. Charter too narrow.
Improve company communications but don't change phone systems, mail, or bulletin board.	No results obtained. Charter too restrictive, lack of depth of systems, opportunities to pursue.
Improve how company does business.	No results obtained. Charter too broad and too deep. No focus or real leadership direction.
Reduce inventories, but don't change inventory management systems or needs of the shop.	No results obtained. Charter too restrictive, lack of depth of inventory opportunities to pursue.

Table 7.2 Design Team Failures

AT&T SUCCESS WITH DESIGN TEAMS BRINGS MAJOR SUCCESS

Since the mid 1980s, AT&T had experienced lackluster performance from their Global Business Communications System business. This $4 billion business unit was not making progress, and by 1989 had hit a wall. Several Design Teams were created to redesign the business's core processes. The Design Teams found a system that did not work. There was no integration or accountability for how the business telephone systems sold by AT&T were eventually installed. In fact, the process from sale to installation required 16 hand-offs. Profits and customer service were unacceptable.

After a nine-month assessment the Design Teams recommended and received a green light to redesign the process with the goals of minimizing the time between sales and installation, minimizing hand-offs, and working as an integrated company to increase both customer service and profitability. After a full year of redesign including several trials, the team rolled out its new process in April 1991. The results have been amazing, with profits reaching record highs, customer willingness to repurchase climbing from 53 percent to 82 percent, adjustments for dissatisfied customers dropped from 4 percent to .6 percent, and an 88 percent customer service rating of Excellent.

Work Teams

Work teams are where the process of Revolution and creating Peak-to-Peak Performance resides. The purpose of Work Teams is to improve operations a little each day by unleashing the power of the people. The most shocking fact for leaders to note is that for Work Teams to produce many $100, $500, $1,000, $2,000, $5,000, $10,000, and $50,000 improvements, no new thoughts need to be generated. In organizations that have yet to become Revolutionary, there are literally thousands of ideas in the minds of workers that would significantly improve operations. In fact, it is not unusual for there to be over $100,000 in savings documented in the first few weeks after the collaboration process is initiated, savings that come forth simply because people are testing the sincerity of leadership to adopt the worker's ideas. Of course, leaders want to know why these ideas didn't come forth prior to pursuing the Revolution process. Listen to the answers:

> "I told this to my supervisor four years ago and he told me to go back to work. So, I went back to work."
>
> "I was told there was no money in the budget to do these types of things."
>
> "The only people in this organization who are allowed to have good ideas wear neckties and have an office up front. If one of the smart guys doesn't think of it first, it will never get done."
>
> "They don't listen to us. For years we have told them how to do it, but they will not or cannot listen."
>
> "I was told to go back to work. If they wanted my two cents they would ask."
>
> "The guys up front do not respect us. They think just because they went to college they are smarter than we are."
>
> "God gave me a good brain and a good pair of hands. At this company, they are only interested in my hands."
>
> "Six years ago John Smith told them how to improve his job and he got fired. You want me to speak up now?"
>
> "I told my supervisor how to do the job in half the time. He took my idea and he and his wife got a free dinner. He didn't even say thanks. That was the last time I'll ever tell management my ideas."
>
> "Why share your ideas? They don't listen to us. The guys set me straight 10 years ago. My job now? I get my 8 and hit the gate."

Work Teams differ from all other types of teams in that while only one Steering Team, Leadership Team, and Communication Team exist in a location, many Work Teams exist. Work Teams differ from Design Teams in that Work Teams focus on incremental improvement whereas Design Teams focus on innovation. Table 7.3 documents this Work Team versus Design Team dichotomy.

Table 7.3 Work Teams Versus Design Teams

PERSPECTIVE	WORK TEAM	DESIGN TEAM
Focus	Incremental Improvement	Innovation
Time Frame	Ongoing, long-term	Quick hit, short-term
Impact	Undramatic, ongoing	Dramatic, big splash
Pace	Small steps	Big steps
Improvements	Gradual and constant	Abrupt and volatile
Mode	Maintain and improvement	Scrap and start new
Timing	Continuous and incremental	Intermittent and non-incremental
Charter	How to improve	How to reinvent

There are two different types of Work Teams. The first are *Cross-functional Work Teams.* These are teams addressing a specific improvement opportunity (topic), with representatives across the company. Second, there are *Functional Work Teams.* These are teams addressing a specific geographical area (department), with representatives only from that area.

Cross-functional Work Teams have the largest impact on cultural Revolution, but Functional Work Teams have the largest impact on improved performance. For this reason, at the outset of the Revolution from individuals to teams, it is normal for three or four Cross-functional Teams to be chartered, and only after these teams have started to work as teams should the functional teams be created.

One point of clarification is needed. Several different companies have seen tremendous results flowing from Cross-functional Work Teams and thus they disagree that Cross-functional Teams have a primary focus of cultural Revolution. Typically what happens in these cases is that although the organization thought it was chartering a Cross-functional Work Team, what they really chartered was a Design Team. Certainly, Design Teams offer opportunities for tremendous results, and it is the lack of clarity between a Design Team charter and a Cross-functional Work Team charter that creates this confusion. Remember, Design Teams focus on innovation, Work Teams focus on incremental improvements.

Work Teams typically consist of between 6 and 9 members and meet on a weekly basis. The scope of the Work-Team charter should be consistent with the knowledge of the members on the team, and of sufficient focus to allow the team to achieve real performance improvements. When problems occur with the scope of the charter, consideration should be given to either a Strategy Team or linked Work Teams.

Strategy Teams, shown in Figure 7.1, become parents to several Work Teams for purposes of integrating the interrelated elements of a particular Peak-to-Peak Performance opportunity. Strategy Teams should meet weekly and should have at least one representative from each of its Strategy Team offspring Work Teams. The charter for each offspring Work Team should fully reflect the relevant aspects of the Strategy Team's opportunity, Evidence of Success, constraints, and expectations. Strategy Teams should not only support and integrate their offspring Work Teams but should also set the overall strategic direction for the opportunity being addressed.

Figure 7.1a Generic Illustration of Strategy Team

Figure 7.1b Actual Illustration of Strategy Team for a Consumer Appliance Company

Linked work teams, as shown in Figure 7.2, allow for the interrelationship of two or three Work Teams while the Leadership Team still provides the overall guidance and direction of the teams to be linked. If it is necessary for more than three Work Teams to be linked, the Strategy Team approach should be utilized, which will allow for more positive, efficient, and effective communication. The charter for each linked Work Team should indicate the linkage between teams and the relationships required to properly achieve the desired performance improvements. Linkage between Work Teams should be done either through team leaders, team liaisons, or both.

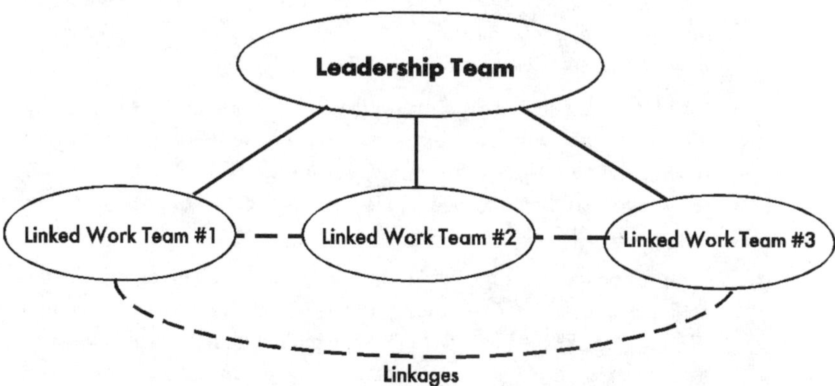

Figure 7.2a Generic Illustration of Linked Work Teams

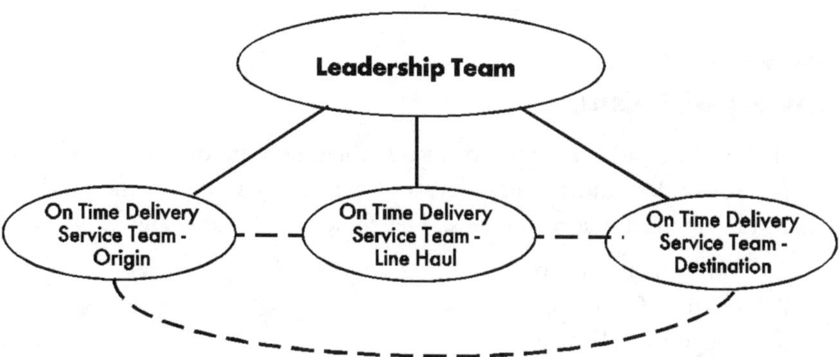

Figure 7.2b Actual Illustration of Linked Work Teams for a Trucking Company

CHRYSLER SCORES SUCCESS WITH NEON

The Japanese media has called the Chrysler Neon "the Japan killer." The United States press touted Neon as the first U.S. vehicle "with a real chance to challenge the Japanese dominance in the subcompact market." What makes this car so unique? Consider a few quotes from a June 1994 *Training* magazine article:

> Massive worker involvement has been Neon's hallmark. Production workers participated in the design of the vehicle and in decisions about the ergonomics of the production line. Early worker-involvement attempts at the Neon Belvidere plant date to at least 1987, when the plant was still building the Omni, but the pace really picked up in 1989 when worker teams were organized to suggest cost-cutting methods The full-involvement rollout came with Neon in 1992.
>
> Candor at the Belvidere plant is startling. Employees up to and including plant manager John Felice expound freely on Neon's flaws and what's being done about them. "The defects I'm talking about, the customer will never see," said Felice, "we find it, we eliminate it, we prevent it from happening again."
>
> The production workers were not eager at first to be involved with the design process. "There was not trust there," says union local president Rielly. "Our people honestly felt that no matter what they said, the engineers were going to do whatever they wanted. Once our people found out that what they said mattered and the engineers were going to accept it, it was 'Hey, if you've got something to say—say it.'"[5]

Levels of Teams

Just as there are different types of teams, there also are different levels of teams. Not understanding these levels of teams can bring on the total failure of the collaboration process. The six levels of teams are:

1. Traditional Group
2. Natural Group
3. Suggestion Team
4. Improvement Team
5. Semi-Autonomous Team
6. Self-Managing Team

Each of these levels has a progressive increase in autonomy, from Traditional Groups and Natural Groups that have no autonomy to Self-Managing Teams that have much autonomy. Each level is important to the Revolution process.

The first two levels of teams are not teams but rather groups. Groups differ from teams in that groups rely on the sum of the "individual bests" and not the synergy of the team. Groups do not collectively pursue performance improvement, but rather use the group to share information and opinions and to make *ad hoc* agreements to help one another. Groups do not have charters and have no predefined process, objectives, or evidence of success. The only commitment individuals have to a group is to attend the next meeting. After that meeting, a commitment may or not be made to attend the next meeting or to "send someone in their place." It is acceptable to send others in your place to a group meeting, as they can fill you in on the information and opinions presented and little will be missed. Since there is no synergy and no commitment, nothing is lost. To the contrary, it is never possible to send someone in your place to a team meeting. Team members must personally attend team meetings since it is through the team's complementary, common commitment that the team will obtain synergy and, therefore, significant process improvement.

Traditional Groups are people who come together from time to time to discuss topics. Sometimes the topics to be discussed are defined and sometimes they aren't. Rarely would there be an agenda followed or minutes taken. Traditional groups consist of individuals who will decide if they wish to participate in the group based upon how much they think the group will help them in accomplishing their objectives. Traditional Groups are useful to the point that individuals share information. Traditional Groups can be an asset to an organization or can be a total waste of time. There are no real processes, rules, or roles defined, so whether or not Traditional Groups will be worthwhile cannot be predicted or duplicated. Traditional Groups have meetings and every now and then something good happens; other than this, not much can be said about them. But then again, not much *needs* to be said, as we all have been part of many Traditional Groups.

Natural Groups are not teams but may at some point in the future become teams; although they still rely on the sum of the "individual best" they can be structured so that although they are not a team, they do respect the value of teamwork. Although Natural Groups do not have a charter, rules, agendas, and minutes, typically they do have the "natural" group leader, the supervisor. Natural Groups often meet on a regular schedule (like 10 minutes first thing each day, or 30 minutes at the beginning of the shift on Tuesday and Thursday, or whatever), and do have a topic of discussion predefined. Often the topic of discussion is quality and schedule attainment. Also, it would not be unusual for human resource issues, safety, product damage, and general business affairs to be discussed in a Natural Group.

It is also quite possible that from the Natural Group will come a requirement for creating a team. In these cases either the "natural" leader, the supervisor, would go to the Leadership Team and ask to be chartered, or perhaps the Natural Group would write its own charter and submit it to the Leadership Team for acceptance. The effort put into the formation of a Natural Group by the Leadership Team is either none or minimal. Not surprising, therefore, the results achieved are often none or minimal.

It is interesting, however, to watch how the Natural Groups fight to become and perform like a team, as an organization's culture is transformed from individuals to team. It is, in fact, this Natural Group evolution to teams that will often result in the formation of the majority of an organization's Functional Work Teams. The Leadership Team should encourage the existence of Natural Groups, provide a few hours of "Natural Group" leader training, monitor the Natural Group's progress and be ready to promote it to a team at the appropriate time.

A Suggestion Team is a real team with limited autonomy. The output from a Suggestion Team is a recommendation to pursue a specific path. Interestingly, although Suggestion Teams are most often called Suggestion Teams at the outset, they are not really teams yet, any more than a group of players is really a football team on the first day of practice. Nevertheless, a Suggestion Team will act like a team, be treated like a team, and will be expected to become a true team. A Suggestion Team will follow an accepted charter, team rules, roles, development patterns, and meeting guidelines. A Suggestion Team's charter will clearly limit the Suggestion Team to making recommendations.

This is not a trust thing, this is an evolutionary thing. One wouldn't expect a 2-year-old to get a job, or an 8-year-old to paint the house, or a 16-year-old to work full time, or a 22-year-old to be the president of a major company. A Suggestion Team at the outset is not even a team, so leadership would not be wise to allow this team to make major decisions. The Leadership Team is not restricting the Suggestion Team by making it a Suggestion Team at the outset any more than a parent is restricting a 2-year-old by not allowing the child to play in the street. At the same time, just as a parent should work to allow their children to grow, so too should a Leadership Team work to allow their Suggestion Teams to grow. Once a Suggestion Team has evolved by making several good suggestions and is truly functioning as a team, it should be promoted to an Improvement Team.

An Improvement Team is the logical next step for a Suggestion Team. At the appropriate time, the Leadership Team should officially upgrade the charters of Suggestion Teams to Improvement Teams. The autonomy of an Improvement Team involves the team having the authority and responsibility to solve certain types of problems themselves. An Improvement Team can implement changes given the constraints placed upon them in the area of capital expenditure, impacts on other areas, and whatever other constraints may be relevant. It is clear that the upgrade of the Improvement Team charter must be done well and without ambiguity, so that there are no surprises down the road. It must be made lucid to the Improvement Team that the charter is not meant as a ceiling on their activities but rather as a defining document, so that other teams are not caught off-guard by something being implemented that impacts them while they haven't been informed.

The fifth level of teams is a Semi-Autonomous Team—an adjusting point between an Improvement Team and a Self-Managing Team. In some cases, this level of team is skipped, and in other cases this is an important point of adjustment. When a Semi-Autonomous Team is created, it is clear who has the greatest level of adjustment: the supervisor. It is not clear who has the second greatest level of adjustment: the Semi-Autonomous Team, the Leadership Team, or the Steering Team. Care must be taken here to help the supervisor through this adjustment. (More information is presented on this topic in Chapter 9.) A Semi-Autonomous Team is responsible for planning, solving problems, implementing improvements, and participating in making decisions and setting goals. Once again, it is critical that the Leadership Team do a good job of upgrading the team's charter and clearly communicate these upgrades to the Semi-Autonomous Team.

The ultimate team in a Revolutionary environment is the Self-Managing Team, which, within certain guidelines, runs a portion of its business. Typically, only Functional Work Teams evolve to become Self-Managing Work Teams, and it almost always takes a team at least a year to reach this level. A Self-Managing Team is just what its name indicates; a team that manages its own affairs, hampered only by the constraints defined in their charter. In fact, other than having a contact person (maybe a leader, maybe not) participating in the Communication Forum and communicating its actions to the appropriate parties, a Self-Managing Team can decide on its own rules, roles, procedures, schedule, and so on. Some Self-Managing Teams may do everything but plan overtime; some may not want to be involved with hiring/firing, or want to do employee evaluations, and so forth. This team is truly self-managed.

Self-Managed, not Self-Directed!

A major, big time, don't-make-this-mistake warning is in order. Self-Managing Teams are your objective, a true sign of the Revolution from individuals to teams, a true indication of creating Peak-to-Peak Performance, and a key to the success of your organization. To the contrary, Self-Directing Teams are a huge mistake, a true sign that a company is lost, a true indication of failure, and a sure sign of a company's demise.

Why am I so hung up on the difference between Self-Managing and Self-Directing? Because Self-Managing Teams build a company up and Self-Directing Teams tear a company down. Think of the meaning of Self-Directing Teams: teams directing where the company is headed. There is no Model of Success, no Steering Team, and no Leadership Team. These teams decide their own direction and off they go.

Sound silly? Well it *is* silly; but behind a confused, misunderstood interpretation of empowerment, this is exactly what many companies have done, and they have created chaos. Although I will address the issue of empowerment later, let me be clear here that the use of the term *empowerment* with the use of the term *Self-Directing Work Teams* is dangerous—as in, *stay away*, *do not touch*, *run*! Get the picture? We do not want self-direction. We want leadership direction and self-management. This is the true indication of a BCPI organization, and I assure you that major success will abound. Self-Managing Teams are what successful organizations possess.

Call to Action

To conclude, let me remind you that if you wish to be successful, you must stop pursuing the teaming program and start believing in the power of collaboration. It is the synergy that issues from collaboration that is the gold at the end of the rainbow. Don't expect to throw together a few teams and reap the benefits of collaboration. Like everything else in a Revolution, collaboration is a process. Ask yourself these kinds of questions and then act upon them based upon what you have read in this chapter:

- What can we do to foster a collaborative culture?
- How can we overcome individualism?
- How can we communicate our belief in collaboration?
- How can we begin today the Revolution toward collaboration?
- How will we celebrate our success?

8

Team Anatomy

Revolution Principle #8:

Revolutionaries must be experts in the science of collaboration.

Far too many cavalier visionaries try to initiate Revolutions without understanding the physiological and psychological elements of group dynamics. Revolution may seem easy until the group begins to actually collaborate. If a Revolutionary force does not have a firm grasp on their expectations when they begin to work closely together, they can expect disaster. When under pressure and in such close proximity to one another, groups of people can do the most unexpected things. Those who want to succeed in their Revolution must make a science of expecting those unexpected turns.

Let me boil it down to this: Revolutionary ambitions require two things. First, the force must be expert on the issues they are trying to improve or the problems they are trying to solve. Second, the force must be expert in the science of collaboration and group-dynamics. Most of the time, Revolutionary forces are experts on the issues, but have not taken the time to learn how groups of people function and how to predict and overcome the common pitfalls of collaboration. This, once again, is asking for chaos and failure because unless a group understands the science of collaboration, they cannot collaborate successfully. The unexpected turns will take them down.

Business leaders must realize that there is also a science of collaboration in business. Many organizations have missed it, attempting to get people to collaborate without doing the scientific work of understanding what the process entails. Because I want your collaboration efforts to succeed, I want to give you the basic scientific underpinnings of the collaboration process. I believe that if you and your organization really understand what I present in this chapter, you are in a superior position. You will have gained the perspective that the majority of "teaming" programs have missed—the scientific perspective.

Team Conversion

I may be the only person alive who did not know intuitively that you never win a team over to the collaboration process. A consultant cannot single-handedly change an organization to a Collaborative Organization. I had to learn that we cannot convert masses, only individuals. Thus, the challenge of becoming a Collaborative Organization is not winning teams to the process but winning individuals to the process.

Think of each employee as having a mental collaboration switch which can be in either the Yes or No position. Yes means that the individual has been converted to collaboration, and No means that they have not. The conversion process usually occurs in five phases. Phase I begins with 100 percent of the people not being for collaboration. This is normal. Teams are unknown, new, and a change, so people tend to exhibit their natural tendencies against collaboration. Relatively quickly, however, several people will throw their switch. They may not truly believe in teams, but they are aware of the need for change, so they convert to a belief in collaboration. These are the easiest converts, but not necessarily the strongest.

As Phase II approaches, the majority of people do not support teams and a minority do. With leadership persistence the Phase II transformation takes place, and at the end of Phase II there are more people who have been converted to collaboration than not.

As we enter Phase III, team acceptance grows quickly. Phase III sees all but the last 5 percent not accepting teams. This is as good as it gets. You will never achieve 100 percent acceptance and should not be overly concerned with achieving it. The last 5 percent are hard to convert and you should continue without their support.

Phase V is an interesting phase. During this phase, even though the switches say Yes, there is a fall-off in results. This phase is actually a time to alter the charter and recycle to Phase I. Interestingly, Phase V is not well understood in the team development literature, even though we have experienced this phase with every team ever established. The team literature does an excellent job defining Phases I through IV. It is based upon these definitions and our personal experiences that the next five subsections define the five-phase conversion process.

Phase I—Forming

The first phase finds the team member asking the questions "Why am I here?" "What is expected?" "What is going to happen?" and "How do I fit in?" People feel a mix of anxiety and anticipation. The level of uncertainty is great, so many have decided not to speak but just to watch and listen. This watch-and-listen routine can result in the team going into a stall. The team leader needs to encourage and, if necessary, force participation. You cannot have a team where only the leader speaks. Things that will get people involved have to do with their pride in being chosen for the team and their attempts to understand their role. The few who accept teams at this phase are excited about them, and will immediately table several good ideas that have been known on the floor for years. It is critical that these ideas be fully pursued by the Leadership Team, and it is, in fact, these ideas that drive the process to Phase II.

Phase II—Storming

The second phase finds the team willing to vocalize their anxiety. The few that have accepted teams can't believe the other people don't understand and see the need for teams. The many who haven't accepted teams cannot believe that the few who have are so gullible. People are comfortable with their traditional role of taking orders and doing their jobs, and aren't at all sure they now want to "do management's job just because they can't!" Arguing, power struggles, frustration, anger, and politics grow. People ask "How can I get out of this?" and "Why do I have to waste my time on this?" "Where is all this going?" This is an opportunity for the team leader not to suppress the conflict but to manage it as an opportunity for growth, awareness, understanding, and acceptance of the team process. Although this "storming" may feel awkward, the fact is this is a very positive and important part of the Revolution. This is proved by the end of Phase II, when there are more people who accept teams than those who do not.

Phase III—Norming

Because of the conflict in Phase II, there is now an awareness and an understanding of the team purpose and the team charter. There are now more people who accept teams than not, so there begins to be a spirit of "we" instead of "me." This sense of trust, cooperation, and respect results in others accepting collaboration. Team members have various levels of trust at this phase. Some believe in collaboration, but have a hard time throwing out old paradigms. For this reason, in the Norming phase the ideas that are pursued are often not the best ideas team members have. They will be the trial balloon ideas. To ensure continued progress and movement from Phase III to Phase IV, the Leadership Team must pursue these ideas to their full extent.

Phase IV—Performing

Phase IV is when a team truly begins to function like a team. You can feel the excitement, the synergy. Ninety-five percent of all team members accept and are committed to teams. The team produces good work and does it well. There exists team confidence, loyalty, and pride in the results achieved. Team members still argue but this is now seen as an integral part of the evolutionary team process. Conflict and arguments are fine; they represent an opportunity for team members to grow and to investigate other perspectives. Questions asked by team members include: "What new issues should we address?" "How can we be more effective?" and "Are we continuously improving?"

Phase V—Maturation

Phase V is a phase that people who write books for a living do not understand. They believe in Forming/Storming/Norming/Performing and then living happily ever after. To the contrary, folks who have actually been through the entire team process have had the shock of their lives when they find themselves in the fifth phase of a four-phase process. Although the books all say Forming/Storming/Norming/Performing, believe me there is always Phase V—Maturation. Maybe the reason Phase V is omitted is that it is not a desirable phase. The maturity of the team that was evoked in Phases I, II, III, and IV results in the team getting tired, losing its edge, and falling into "groupthink." Groupthink is where team members all begin to think alike, there is no diversity, and no one wishes to dissent from their "wonderful teams." This leads to over confidence (false confidence) that results in faulty decisions and the accompanying falloff of performance. In addition, as a team matures the remaining problems to tackle become more difficult. This further adds to burnout and a tendency to fall back on the old way of "letting others do the thinking, I just want to do my job." At this point, one of four changes needs to be made by the Leadership Team:

1. If the team has completed its charter and performance is beyond the Leadership Team's expectations, disband the team, thank the team members, recognize their accomplishments, and move on to the next opportunity.
2. If the team has completed its charter and performance is not beyond the Leadership Team's expectations, alter the charter and put the team back to work. The charter alteration could be an upgrade in team level, an increase in scope, or an addition of another opportunity.
3. If the team has not completed its charter but Maturation is upon them, do an oil change. An oil change is a rotation of team members. This should not be done as a reward or punishment. People leaving a team should be selected randomly. Typically, with a seven-member team, two members would be rotated at an oil change.
4. If the team has not completed its charter but Maturation is upon them, do a team member upgrade. This involves sending one, two, or several team members to a conference, seminar, plant visit, and/or visit to customers or other locations of your organization. This outside look will often recharge a team for performance improvement.

Interestingly, no matter if the charter is altered, team members are oil changed, or team members are upgraded, when one of these things occurs, the team will return to Phase I. Now, it is very likely that the team will move through the phases much more quickly the second, third, and fourth (and so on) time, but never forget that you will return to Phase I, then II, then III, IV, and yes, you will then return to Phase V again. This is how creating BPCI performance should be. This is the process of team development and of Revolution.

Team Roles

I did not understand that the four phases of team development were actually the five phases of team development until after I had gone through the four phases several times. There has also been an evolution in understanding of the roles of teams that has occurred over the last ten years. It is now clear that for a team to successfully evolve and perform, there are six team roles that must be filled. These roles are:

1. Team Sponsor
2. Team Liaison
3. Team Leader
4. Team Reporter
5. Team Recorder
6. Team Member

Team Sponsor

A team sponsor is the person who defines the need for a team. This person sells the opportunity of the team to the Leadership Team and sometimes writes the first draft of the charter. The team sponsor may move on to become the team leader, liaison, member, or may not be further involved after the team is chartered. The team sponsor will often gather some initial statistics and define the potential for improvements. Sponsors can be company presidents, new employees, and even people outside of the company.

At a company picnic a few years ago, a production foreman's sixteen-year-old daughter asked why the company was so obviously divided between office workers, production workers, and management. The production foreman asked her daughter what she meant and the daughter pointed to several things at the picnic (where people sat, who ate first, how people interacted, and so on) that indicated where everyone fit into the pecking order. In this case, the sixteen year-old daughter became the team sponsor of a company culture team that was very instrumental in the company's Peak-to-Peak Performance success.

Sponsors come from different educational levels, backgrounds, and experiences. The Leadership Team should encourage team sponsors to come forward. The Leadership Team should create easy, non-threatening avenues for potential sponsors to share their thoughts. Of course, the easiest method of learning from team sponsors is to listen—go to the floor, be among the people, and listen. About half of all successful team sponsors are people you would not necessarily think of as obvious team sponsors. This tells us the need for teams is as well understood at the top of the company as it is at the bottom. All people associated with an organization should be encouraged to put forth their ideas and be a team sponsor.

Team Liaison

A clear indication whether an organization is pursuing self-managing teams or self-directed teams is the existence of a team liaison. Organizations pursuing self-management will have team liaisons; organizations pursuing self-direction will not have team liaisons. A team liaison provides direction for a team as it pursues its charter. A team liaison is a person from the Leadership Team assigned to the team to ensure the team is following the Revolution process and that progress against the charter is being made. There is a different reporting arrangement when a Strategy Team exists because in this circumstance there will be a team liaison from the Strategy Team to the Leadership Team and several different team liaisons from the Strategy Team to each of the offspring Work Teams. The team liaison, however, is not a member of the team, and thus should only be involved in support of the team leader. The liaison assures that the team focuses on their charter and responds to questions from the team. The team liaison has the authority and the responsibility to speak for the Leadership Team (Strategy Team). Each question asked of the team liaison by the team can receive one of four responses:

1. I do not understand the question, please clarify by helping me understand . . .
2. Yes. The team may go forward.
3. No. This should not be pursued and the reasons why are . . .
4. I don't feel comfortable responding to that, but I will take it to the Leadership Team (Strategy Team), get their response, and be back to you in a week.

Of course, the team liaison needs to be fully accountable to the Leadership Team (Strategy Team) for all responses provided to the team. The team liaison acts as the communication conduit between the Leadership Team (Strategy Team) and the team. The team liaison should report to the Leadership Team (Strategy Team) at each Leadership Team (Strategy Team) meeting and accept responsibility for working with the team leader to achieve team success. Especially early on, the team liaison should meet with the team leader after each meeting and help the team leader help the team make progress. The specific responsibilities of the team liaison are:

- Support the team leader.
- Ensure that the team meets on a regular schedule.
- Address any team member attendance problem.
- Ensure that a recorder is assigned at the beginning of each meeting to take legible/understandable minutes, and that minutes are submitted for typing/copying in a timely manner.
- Ensure the team adheres to the team rules.
- Focus the team on the Model of Success.
- Create a climate of trust and openness.
- Evolve the team, grow the team, assess team progress, and change oil.
- Manage team conflict by proactively inquiring into other's viewpoints.
- Identify team training opportunities.
- Attend team meetings.
- Once a team achieves self-managing status and regular weekly meetings are not held, check with the team leader on a weekly basis to ensure team evolution on performance and continuous improvement.
- Participate in team meetings on an as-needed basis. Be aware of the fact that the team liaison is not the team leader, not a team member, but an observer, facilitator, and resource. Be an active listener by listening well, fostering an environment for listening well, and being a cheerleader as appropriate.
- Report to the Leadership Team on the team's successes, problems, evolution, and status.

- Provide the team with input on how to best structure their recommendations to ensure Leadership Team understanding. Help the team develop quality recommendations. Communicate recommendations from the team to the Leadership Team and communicate back approval, rejection, and/or feedback.
- Follow up on all Leadership Team approved projects and provide regular status updates to the Leadership Team.
- Emphasize the Model of Success and ensure team alignment with the Model of Success.

Team Leader

The team leader role is critical. The team leader must be action-oriented, sensitive to others, and a good communicator. Good team leaders instinctively know that the reason for the team's existence is to improve performance through the synergistic interactions among team members.

Unlike group leaders whose task is to optimize the contributions of the group members, the Team Leader's task is to obtain real team performance which exceeds the sum of the contribution of the team members. Team leaders ensure quality communications and participation, run meetings, provide focus on the Model of Success and the team charter, build commitment, grow team members, manage team boundaries, and accept responsibility for team growth and progress. In addition, a team leader is also a team member, and so the team leader does real work, participates in decisions, and has opinions just like all other team members. It is the team leader being a team member, however, that can cause difficulties.

The team leader must understand when it is best for them to be involved and when it is best to let another team member step forward. Some team leaders want to do too much themselves and some too little. It is critical that the team leader carry their own weight but that they do so while projecting the attitude that they do not have all the answers and that their input is just one of many. The team leader should not be making team decisions and should clearly project the attitude that the team will not be successful without the synergistic interplay of the entire team. This team leader role is a narrow path and one that must be walked carefully, but differently, with each team. No two team leaders will ever have identical teams, so no two team leaders should ever act the same.

An aid that has been useful in helping team leaders understand their role is the comparison between Supervisory Leadership, Group Leadership, and Team Leadership. Table 8.1 presents these roles. Since team leaders have more experience practicing Supervisory Leadership and Group Leadership than Team Leadership, it is normal for team leaders to err on the side of too much involvement, control, guidance, and direction. The team leader must focus their energy on this delicate balance, and the team liason should help refine it.

APROACH TO	SUPERVISORY LEADERSHIP	GROUP LEADERSHIP	TEAM LEADERSHIP
Change	React to change	Encourage change	Work with team to create change
People	Direct people	Involve people	Help people grow and obtain synergy
Diversity	Minimize diversity	Allow diversity	Build upon diversity as team asset
Decisions	Explain decisions	Get input for decisions	Facilitate and support team decisions
Development	Train people	Develop people	Develop people and team
Coordination	Manage one-on-one	Coordinate group effort	Build trust and team identity
Conflict	Minimize conflict	Ignore conflict	Use conflict as opportunity to learn

Table 8.1 Role Comparison Between Supervisory Leadership, Group Leadership, and Team Leadership

Team leaders are selected by the Leadership Team (Strategy Team) and should have a "no-fault" option of declining the team leader role. The team leader should not pick the team members; this, too, should be done by the Leadership Team. There is no such thing as co-team leaders. Each team can have only one team leader. The requirements to be considered by the Leadership Team when selecting a team leader include:

- Must believe people are the company's greatest asset
- Must believe that the growth of people is natural
- Must believe that team growth is never ending
- Must realize that the team leader is a facilitator, coach, and counselor
- Must believe that Business Process Continuous Improvement is a process, not a program
- Must believe mistakes are OK and a part of learning
- Must be open, honest, and worthy of trust
- Must accept change and realize change is natural
- Must promote teamwork
- Must be open to new ideas

The specific responsibilities of the team leader are:

- *Listen to Team Members.* The team leader must set the example by actively listening to team members. The team leader must involve the entire team in the discussion. They must draw quiet team members into the discussion and be certain only one person speaks at a time so that no one is interrupted and no one talks all the time.
- *Create a climate of trust and openness.* There must exist both a climate of trust and openness within the team and between the team leader and the team members. It is only by developing this trust that team members will be open and feel safe enough to say what they really think.
- *Eliminate fear.* Fear is a natural emotion as the continuous improvement process asks team members to change their roles within the company. This takes time, and the team leader, by creating a climate of trust and openness, must work to help team members overcome their fear. Team leaders must be patient for this to evolve over time.
- *Value diversity.* By encouraging active participation by all team members, the team leader encourages team members to present their views. It is very important that different views are encouraged, dissected, and understood. Different views should be openly and straightforwardly addressed. Team diversity is the heartbeat of team synergism.

- *Focus on Model of Success, Team Charter, and Team Results.* A key role of the team leader is to be sure the team is making progress on their charter while maintaining focus on the Model of Success. The team leader should plan several thresholds for team results and help the team make progress toward these thresholds. Time is of the essence and team leaders must be accountable for effective time utilization and for real performance improvement.
- *Share information*: A supervisory leadership role has always been to hoard information and to only share information on a "need to know basis." This does not produce success. The only way team members will actively participate in teams is if they feel they understand what is happening. If they feel information is being withheld from them or if information is not honest, there is little chance of the team members supporting the process of Revolution and creating Peak-to-Peak Performance.
- *Lead effective meetings.* It is the responsibility of the team leader to keep the team energized, structured, functioning in accordance with the team rules, disciplined in their problem solving methodology, performing assignments between team meetings, and clearly moving forward.
- *Break down barriers.* It is the team leader's job to identify and destroy any and all barriers to team success. These barriers may be cultural, political, or just a few individuals who do not support the team process. There will be some supervisors who do not want their people to attend meetings. There will be some managers who will talk against the process. The team leader, with the support of the team liaison, must take action to break down these and other barriers.
- *Support team growth.* The team leader must help both the individual team members and the team to grow. The team leader must help the team learn from mistakes, go outside the team for information as necessary, and encourage learning through understanding other team members and both individual and team self-assessment.
- *Encourage creativity, risk-taking, and creating Peak-to-Peak Performance.* The team leader, with the help of the team liaison, must help the team leaders to think creatively and outside of their present situation. The problem solving and decision making skills of the team should be enhanced, as should the team's ability to reach a conclusion. The team leader must encourage team mem-

bers to support the decisions of the team and to actively support the implementation of these decisions.

AN OVEREXTENDED SUPERVISOR BECOMES A SUPER TEAM LEADER

Bob had a bad case of ulcers, and was not doing so well, from either an effectiveness or a physical perspective. Bob's department had quality, schedule, and budget problems. The vice president of manufacturing had two chats with Bob about early retirement. Bob did not want to leave but knew he was not pulling his weight. Then the company became collaborative and Bob became an extremely effective team leader. Within eight months, Bob provided the leadership for his department to become a self-managed team with amazing quality, schedule, and budget turnarounds. In eight months, the company's poorest supervisor became the company's best team leader. Looking back, it became clear that no supervisor could have been effective prior to the installation of the collaborative process. There simply was no way one person could deal with the materials, scheduling, engineering, machine utilization, training, setup, and other day-to-day challenges. There were 18 to 24 hours of work to be done in each 8-hour day. Look what happens when you create a realistic environment in which a person can perform. Maybe even more amazing, last month's checkup indicated Bob's ulcers no longer existed. Amazing, the power of a Collaborative Organization!

Team Reporter

The role of the team reporter seems outwardly as merely the spokesperson for the team at the monthly Communication Forum. This certainly is an aspect of the team reporter's task, but this is not the entire task. The team reporter role should be a month-to-month assignment. Next month's team reporter should be selected at the first team meeting after each month's Communication Forum. In this way, although the assignment is to make a presentation at the Communication Forum, the team reporter acts as team progress champion for the next month. You see, the reporter does not want to have to stand up in front of the Communication Forum and say, "My team met four times since the last Communication Forum and we are actively looking into three projects, but we have no results to report."

The team reporter wants to be able to report on how well the team is performing. Thus, the hidden portion of the reporter's role is to act as a motivator for closure, progress, and action. When reporters stand up at the Communications Forum they will have several significant things to say to demonstrate their team's progress and the real Peak-to-Peak Performance improvements coming from their team.

Team Recorder

Team recorders are assigned at the beginning of each meeting and should be rotated among all team members except for the team leader. The apparent role of the team recorder is to take the minutes of team meetings. These minutes should be a record of the meeting (date, time, location, attendees, topics discussed, decisions made, assignments, and call for next meeting) and should provide an understanding of what happened at the team meetings to both team members and non-team members. Team members should use these minutes as a thread of consistency from team meeting to team meeting.

A second important role of the team recorder is to function as an equalizer and a hook of involvement for all team members. Within the team meetings, there are no titles, no bosses, no pecking order. All team members are equal. The equal assignment of recorders around the room is an illustration of this equalization. It is very helpful for a worker to see the president of the company be assigned the task of team recorder just as they were in earlier weeks. The recorder task also provides for the involvement of all team members. Being responsible for writing the team minutes requires the recorder to pay attention and to truly listen to all team members. This practice will facilitate the team's overall ability to listen to one another. An important mistake to avoid is having the team recorder responsible for producing the minutes. It works much better if after a team meeting the recorder gives the team minutes to the team leader. This allows the team leader to help the recorder not only with production and distribution but also with spelling, grammar, and accuracy that may cause some embarrassment to the team members. To some, the recorder's role is not going to seem important and these people are going to want to assign a permanent recorder who always does minutes. This is a mistake and will slow down the evolution of the team and the growth of team identity. Trust me, use a revolving recorder.

Table 8.2 Members of an Ideal Team

Type	Typical Features	Positive Qualities	Allowable Weaknesses
Company Worker	Conservative, dutiful, predictable	Organizing ability, practical, common sense, hard-working, self-disciplined.	Lack of flexibility, unresponsiveness to unproved ideas.
Chairman	Calm, self-confident, controlled	A capacity for treating and welcoming all potential contributors on their merits and without predjudice. A strong sense of objectives.	No more than ordinary in terms of intellect or creative ability.
Shaper	Highly strung, outgoing, dynamic	Drive and a readiness to challenge inertia, ineffectiveness, complacency or self-deception.	Prone to provocation, irritation, and impatience.
Plant	Individualistic, serious-minded, unorthodox	Genius, imagination, intellect, knowledge.	Up in the clouds, inclined to disregard practical details or protocol.
Resource Investigator	Extroverted, enthusiastic, curious, communicative	A capacity for contacting people and exploring anything new. An ability to respond to challenge.	Liable to lose interest once the initial fascination has passed.
Monitor/Evaluator	Sober, unemotional, prudent	Judgment, discretion, hard-headedness.	Lacks inspiration or the ability to motivate others.
Team Worker	Socially oriented, rather mild, sensitive	An ability to respond to people and situations and to promote team spirit.	Indecisiveness at moments of crisis.
Completer/Finisher	Painstaking, orderly, conscientious anxious	A capacity for follow-through. Perfectionism.	A tendency to worry about small things. A reluctance to "let go."

Team Members

Similar to the "What is good leadership?" question I previously discussed is the "What are the characteristics of the members of an ideal team?" question. Neither can be answered. Although there has been extensive research on this topic, there are no magic formulas to ensure team success.

In the most in-depth analysis of what makes up the ideal team, Dr. R. Meredith Belbin spent over nine years of research in the composition of teams. The result of this work indicates that an ideal team consists of the people described in Table 8.2. The challenge in trying to configure such a team is that in the real world, there are only a certain group of people who have the technical understanding and involvement with the scope of the team to be positive contributors. Therefore, we must learn from Dr. Belbin's work that what we want on a team is diversity. This diversity of team membership should include diversity in talent, personality, age, background, experience, education, sex, race, and all other member features. An interesting result from Dr. Belbin's work about the diversity that is required to have a successful team is the corollary that what results in the poorest team is a "pure team." That is, a team that consists of all the same type of people will not be a successful team. The reason this is so interesting is that many organizations, in an effort to ensure successful teams, go through an extensive testing process to ensure all team members meet the organization team profile. This effort to ensure successful teams, in fact, does just the opposite; it ensures team failure. In fact, if during the selection of team members someone says, "Don't place Bob on a team; he is just a troublemaker." I will decide that I want Bob on the team. You want troublemakers, you want diversity. Select team members to maximize diversity and you will select successful teams.

Team members should be nominated to serve on teams and should be required to attend a team orientation session, but should be given a "no-fault" opportunity to decline to serve on the team. At the orientation, the potential team member should be given an overview of the team process, participate in a review of the team charter, and be told that the definition of a team member is a person who has agreed to be committed to the team, to work with the team, and to work toward team success. If, after the team orientation, the person decides not to be a team member, this is fine. The Leadership Team should replace the people not wishing to serve and should hold a second team orientation. Allowing people to have a "no-fault" opportunity to decline to serve on a team will cause most people to want to serve on a team. Having a few decline to serve on teams early in the process of implementing teams is good since it allows everyone to see that no one is forced into "doing teams."

Team members should understand that their role has the following requirements:

- To be aligned with the Model of Success and to understand the impact of the Model of Success on them
- To support and have ownership of the team charter and to accept responsibility for the level of team empowerment specified in the charter
- To honestly advocate from their own perspective while actively listening to the positions of others and to be flexible in weighing the positions of others in making decisions
- To respect diversity and to learn from others
- To trust the team leader and other team members
- To participate in meetings by communicating openly and honestly
- To be focused on creating Peak-to-Peak Performance for both the task at hand and the team
- To support the team leader
- To use their talents and energy to work for the team's success
- To do assignments on time and to the best of their ability
- To exercise self-restraint in an effort to allow other team members to contribute and to grow
- To sacrifice for the benefit of the team
- To support all decisions made by the team
- To be accountable for the implementation of all team recommendations
- To accept full ownership of team-recommended improvements

Team Progression

There are two team progression philosophies. The first is what I call the train, train, train approach to becoming a team-based organization. This philosophy advocates having everyone in the company attend a large amount of team training. This training may require each person to attend 40 hours, 100 hours, 150 hours, or as much as 200 hours of communication, team management, problem solving, or listening training. Needless to say, this training is very expensive and can easily take six months or longer to complete. All the while, the company continues to operate "business as usual." Even though this training often has excellent content, it is rarely well received by the workers. They are not interested in learning things that at the time seem to be irrelevant. Further, only a small amount of this learning sticks. There is no place to apply the things learned as there are no teams until the training is complete.

The progress reports from the *train, train, train* philosophy don't describe improvements in operations, but rather the number of hours of training provided. Eventually, the training ends and some team efforts are pursued. Unfortunately, since the emphasis was on training and not on the process of becoming a Collaborative Organization, rarely are these teams successful. Typically, management concludes the effort and moves on to a new program. They feel satisfied because their team is now ready to face the challenges of tomorrow because the people in the organization are now much better trained to work as teams to do their jobs, blah, blah, blah! This is not a team-based process. This is training for training's sake and has nothing to do with success.

The second team progression philosophy is called the process-based approach to becoming a Collaborative Organization. This approach advocates doing teams by creating a team. Then create another team. Will mistakes be made? Sure. That's great! Mistakes are opportunities to learn and should be embraced as opportunities to learn. Will training be required? Sure. How to do it? How about Just-In-Time training? You develop the training in advance but then you present the training when a team indicates it needs the training, Just-In-Time. Team leaders and team liaisons should look for opportunities to train. The philosophy of Just-In-Time training says that when a team uncovers a need for training then the team should receive training, which should then be (Just-In-Time) applied by putting the new knowledge into practice (Recovering). This Uncover, Discover, Recover process of Just-In-Time training allows both individual and team member growth, as well as for team collective growth and for the performance improvements that result from putting the new knowledge into practice.

The team progression that should be followed to pursue a process-based approach to becoming a Collaborative Organization is:

- Team charter by Leadership Team
- Team orientation
- Team reviews charter
- Team accepts/refines charter
- Team creates team ownership of charter
- Team pursues process as defined on team charter
- Leadership Team reviews progress of existing teams and takes appropriate action. When time is right, Leadership Team re-cycles to Step 1.

Characteristics of Successful Teams

Successful teams are not necessarily teams where morale is high and people are happy. Morale and happiness are individual characteristics and not team characteristics. What is important in defining a successful team is not the individuals on the team, but the team as a whole. The ten characteristics that define a successful team are:

1. *The team has a collective and expanding understanding of the Model of Success and the team charter.* The team members have struggled and from time to time continue to struggle with the meaning of the Model of Success and the content of the team charter. This struggling is good, since it builds team commitment. The team members share a common vision of where the team is headed and realize that their success can only be achieved through the entire team working together as one.
2. *Team commitment and confidence are growing.* There is an ongoing increase of trust, respect, and support. Individual commitment and confidence flows from the pride in the growth of the team's commitment and confidence. There evolves a sense of team excellence, and mediocrity will not be accepted. Conflict is viewed as an opportunity to learn; there is no win/lose attitude but rather an attitude of mutual discovery and support of the team's growth in understanding.

3. *There exists a feeling of interdependency.* As individuals acquire new skills and talents, these are viewed not as individual assets but as team assets. Each team member feels they are important to the team and that they can and will influence the team. The team will listen equally to all team members and is stronger as a whole than they are as individuals. All team members have a sense of belonging.
4. *The team feels good about their opportunity to make presentations at the Communication Forum and, as a team, takes pride in the credit and recognition the team receives from these presentations.* The team works hard to document performance improvement results and to present these at the Communication Forum.
5. *The team is action/progress-oriented and is achieving significant Peak-to-Peak Performance improvement results.* The team pulls together to each do their part to achieve team results. The team members are prepared for team meetings and responsive to the needs of other team members.
6. *There exists clear, honest, open, and effective communications.* Team members openly express themselves and feel free to ask questions with the confidence that other team members will respond with candid answers. There are no hidden agendas, no politics, and everything is above board. Team members not only answer the questions asked but in the spirit of the questions asked too. Team members avoid the practice of providing narrow responses that require other team members to play "twenty questions" to obtain a real understanding. The team has a common language that allows all team members to gain the same understanding of what team members are saying. Team members share common access to all information relevant to the team. Team members are anxious to share information as information is viewed as key to each team member's contribution to the team.
7. *All team members value and appreciate team diversity.*
8. *The team members have a shared perspective of how their team functions.* There is a shared understanding of the collaboration process, the team roles, and how the team will achieve success.
9. *The team members believe in and conduct self-assessments to improve their performance and their ability to accomplish more.* The team members believe that the team should continuously improve. It is in this spirit that the team members ask of themselves, "How

well are we functioning as a team?" "What barriers are preventing us from being more successful?" and "What can we do to achieve more?"

10. *Team members have a common and shared view of how the team is progressing.* Team members have shared Evidence of Success and have the same view on Evidence of Success status. They feel comfortable with the team's progress but anxious for greater results. They are optimistic about continued success and how this success will be measured.

Call to Action

As you read this chapter, did you find yourself saying, "I never realized that collaboration could be so scientific. When we tried teams, we just got a group of people together and tried to solve a problem." If you are frustrated and disappointed in the result of your collaboration efforts, it is probably because your organization didn't approach it scientifically. If you really want to be a Revolutionary Organization, you must become a Collaborative Organization. I challenge you to begin the collaboration process again or perhaps for the first time. Understanding team anatomy can make the difference between failure and success. I want you to succeed.

9

Demystifying the "E" Word

Revolution Principle #9:

A Revolution must push its power down to its lower ranks.

A sure way to tell whether or not a Revolution is serious about the changes it is seeking, or if it is merely a self-serving exploit of its leader(s), is by observing where the decision making process takes place. Are all decisions made by one or a few individuals at the top, who then trickle their directives downward to those below? Or are the lower ranked people given power to make decisions themselves, and is their knowledge tapped in a significant way? A Revolution that harbors all of the power among a few top-level people, simply trickling decisions downward, cannot be serious about Revolution. But, unfortunately, this is the common approach.

Think about it: If a leader or a group of leaders sincerely wants to change and improve a condition in society, the best way to do it is by allowing those closest to the situation, and thus who know the most about it, to play an integral role. These "grassroots" individuals must be tapped in a significant way in order to fully understand the problem and its solution. Further, to reap the full benefit of their knowledge, these individuals must be given the power to make decisions and carry them out. Otherwise, the success of the Revolution is determined by the knowledge of the leader, who may or may not have a full understanding of the problem.

In a Revolutionary context the power issue distinguishes the genuine from the false. True Revolutionaries have no ego stake in power. They are far too concerned about improvement to bother with protecting their power. On the other hand, false Revolutionaries, who often have a low self-esteem, a shattered identity, immense insecurity about their own abilities, and thus an inflated ego to cover it all up, believe power is the objective of the Revolution, not change. This is dangerous! This is how dictatorships begin and where oppressive forms of government have their root. If there are real changes that result from such a Revolution, they will be changes that further embellish the egotist leader's power.

The kind of Revolution that the world must take seriously is the kind that genuinely involves the lower-ranked people in the formulation. When Revolution leaders push their power down to the people, giving them the approved authority to make decisions and carry them out, then we know we have a serious Revolution on our hands. Why? Because then we know that the Revolution is tapping the reservoir that contains the answers to the problems at hand, not simply amassing power for itself.

I believe the answers to the business challenges we currently face are contained in the same place—in the minds of the lower ranks. A leader who is leading an Organizational Revolution must tap the knowledge and abilities of front-line employees at all levels. Not only must they tap them, but they must push power and authority down to those employees, allowing them to play a more central role in the Revolutionary pursuit. This process of pushing power down to lower level employees has traditionally been called *empowerment*. Although there is a great amount of confusion surrounding the topic of empowerment, I believe it is central to your success, for all the reasons I have described earlier and more. In this chapter I want to dispel the myths of empowerment in the business arena and define for you exactly what it is and how you may benefit from it.

The Great Misunderstanding

Probably one of the hottest terms of the 1990s was the word *empowerment.* As a buzzword, empowerment came to the forefront almost overnight. It was thought to have magical powers and then, just as quickly as it came upon us, got a bad reputation and was dismissed as a mistake. In one Gallup survey probing the empowerment subject, 66 percent of the respondents said that employees had been encouraged to get involved with decision making, but only 14 percent felt that employees were authorized to make the kind of decisions management was talking about. In another survey, 96 percent of the companies indicated they believed in teamwork and empowerment, but only 24 percent of the companies had a commitment to providing a process for this to occur. Interestingly, although smaller firms have reported greater success with empowerment, the 24 percent of all companies committed to the process are not uniform across all sizes of companies. Only 13 percent of the companies in the 0 to 99 employee range, 25 percent of the companies in the 100 to 499 employee range, and 36 percent of the companies having over 500 employees have a commitment to providing a process for empowerment to take place. Another interesting split in the understanding of empowerment stemmed from the level of the person in the company. Fifty percent of all executives believed their company understood how to empower, but only 9 percent of the managers and supervisors felt their company understood empowerment. Why this lack of clarity? Why this misunderstanding? Why all the empowerment mistakes? It has to do with understanding. It has to do with the definition of terms and everyone using the terms in a consistent manner.

"E" Word War Stories

What happened to the empowerment train after such a grand send-off from the train station? The concept of pushing decision-making authority down to the appropriate level in an organization seems so logical. How could empowerment get hit so bad that some are afraid to even use the term (thus the concept of the "E" word). Here are some common "E" word war stories:

- Empowerment was based upon sharing power. So what happened is the new "power people" started wielding authority with the same disregard for teamwork as the old people, and chaos prevailed.
- Empowerment was based upon being accountable for our own performance, so good "performance people" made decisions that, although contrary to the good of the whole, allowed them to look good.
- They told us that empowerment is natural for mature adults. They told us empowerment would occur almost magically. "Zap and it would be done."
- Empowerment allowed workers to make their own decisions and so all the middle managers were no longer needed. They said that empowerment is the key to delayering and downsizing an organization. Lower cost, happier people, and better performance. "It doesn't get any better than this."

What is Empowerment, Really?

The kind of "E" word misunderstandings described above all lead to problems. In fact, these "E" word misunderstandings of empowerment are so prevalent that before I define empowerment, it is important to say what empowerment is not:

- Empowerment is not abandonment.
- Empowerment is not letting people do their own things.
- Empowerment is not letting people or teams define their own direction.
- Empowerment is not a style of management or leadership.
- Empowerment is not a concept or philosophy.
- Empowerment is not the expansion of authority for employees to make more decisions.

So, what it empowerment? First, it is critical to understand that empowerment is a process. Empowerment is not something that has been done, empowerment is something that is being done. Leaders do not grant, give, install, or bestow empowerment. Empowerment is something leaders cultivate, grow, and harvest. Empowerment is not giving power or redistributing power, but the building, developing, and increasing of power through a synergistic process of cooperation, sharing, and working together. Individuals cannot grow power through synergy, only teams can do this. Synergy, by definition, is what teams do, and so empowerment cannot be an individual thing but must be a team thing. Based on these factors, I have developed a definition of empowerment:

> Empowerment is the leadership process of building, developing, and increasing the power of an organization to perform optimally through the synergistic evolution of teams.

Please read this definition a few times. Try to really understand it, and please be sure that when you use the word empowerment, the people to whom you are communicating understand this definition. A key characteristic of a Revolutionary Organization is the universal understanding of this definition of empowerment. Revolutionary Organizations understand the following:

- Empowerment is a leadership process.
- Empowerment is building, developing, and increasing the power of an organization to perform.
- Empowerment is the synergistic evolution of teams.

Leadership's Empowerment Role

In the Revolutionary Organization, leadership has the responsibility for empowering and teams have the responsibility of performance. Leaders cannot succeed without teams and teams cannot succeed without leadership. This is why Part II of this book deals with leadership and Part III with teams. This is as it must be. Revolutionary Organizations must have strong leaders who accept accountability for empowering teams and strong teams who accept accountability for performance. The following ten factors define the role of leadership in the process of empowerment:

1. *Leadership must define organizational direction and ensure alignment.* The Steering Team must define an organization's Model of Success and obtain the organization's alignment with the Model of Success.
2. *Leadership must define the collaboration process.* The Steering Team must define the team process just as the rules of play must be defined for a baseball game. The Steering Team must define the topics in regards to:
   - Types of teams
   - Levels of teams
   - Team development
   - Team roles

   The Steering Team must also address the mechanism for teams to succeed.
3. *Leadership must define the flows of information within an organization.* The information flows in a Revolutionary Organization will be different than the information flows in a traditional organization. In a traditional organization, there exists a hierarchical information flow from the work level up through a Management Information System (MIS) to a Financial Information System (FIS) and an Executive Information System (EIS). Unfortunately, the MIS/FIS/EIS have nothing to do with leadership, little to do with the management of performance, and even less to do with team performance. For this reason, the information systems in a Revolutionary Organization must be significantly altered from the information systems that existed in the traditional organization. The MIS/FIS/EIS systems must be replaced with the following:
   - Leadership Information System (LIS):

     Customer Satisfaction, Financial Results, and Market Position Information
   - Performance Information System (PIS):

     Operational Scoreboard, Business Trends, and Customer Service

- Team Information Systems (TIS):

  Peak-to-Peak Performance, Operational Improvements, and Results versus Goals

With this reconfigured flow of information, the Steering Team, Leadership Team, and Communications Team will utilize the LIS, PIS, and TIS to do their jobs. Design teams will focus on the PIS and Work Teams will utilize both the PIS and the TIS. Revolution Leaders know that information is power. The process of empowerment demands that leadership provide the information that allows teams to accept accountability for their team performance. Revolutionary Organizations will thrive on the availability and abundance of truly relevant information.

4. *Leadership must define the thrust of teams.* It is the task of the Leadership Team to define teams. This thrust must define why a team exists, what issues are to be considered, and what the Evidences of Success are for the team. The team thrust should define the subject of a team's endeavors and serve as the guiding light for the team's evolution.
5. *Leadership must define the time frame for performance improvement.* The Leadership Team must set specific, time-based goals for the team. These goals act as a guide to a team by defining the time frame in which results are expected. The Leadership Team must exhibit care that the goals established relate to measurable enhancements to the Evidence of Success and not the specific improvements that will result in the improved performance.
6. *Leadership must define team participants.* The Leadership Team must define the team leader, team liaison, and team members. It is the responsibility of the team liaison to bring the team leader on board with the team and to support the team leader bringing the team members on the team. The Leadership Team must also define how much time should be spent by the team leader and members on the team activities.
7. *Leadership must define constraints.* The Leadership Team must define the scope of teams, things that the team cannot change, and the authority within which the team must function. Specific budgetary issues should be addressed so no questions exist as to what a team can and cannot do.

8. *Leadership must define the evolution of team authority.* Earlier I presented how the process from a Suggestion Team to an Improvement Team to a Semi-Autonomous Team to a Self-Managed Team evolves. The Leadership Team must define an overall plan for the evolution of the empowerment process for a team. This plan should be specific in that it should define specific tasks but be flexible in time frame. The time frame should then be defined by the Leadership Team as a team evolves. Table 9.1 presents an example of how a Leadership Team may define the evolution of team authority.

GUERRILLA AND RENEGADE TEAMS: LOST IN SPACE

Unbelievable! In an article entitled "Guerrilla Teams: Friend or Foe," a Guerrilla or Renegade Team is defined as a team that springs up in the middle of a traditional organization where senior management does not support a team process. The article explains that although the team will likely be "quashed" and even if they enjoy some initial success, they will most often be "too worn down by the struggle to continue," that there are some friendly tips on how to keep Guerrilla Teams "alive and well." Give me a break!

This type of analysis is so shallow and lacking in understanding of leadership, teams, and empowerment that it is almost funny. The thing that makes it not so funny is that the article appeared in the magazine *Training,* which is an excellent magazine for materials on leadership, teams, and empowerment.[1] Let me not just pick on this one article. I have a whole file of articles and, yes, even a whole shelf of books, that do not really have a clue about the topics on which they speak. The point here is not to throw stones, but rather to send a word of caution about what you read and what you believe. Please help others understand the truth about leadership, teams, and empowerment. We do not need our companies making detours via Guerrilla or Renegade Teams or whatever is next, and getting lost in space.

Type Team	Authority	Time Frame (Effective Date)
Group	None	1998
Natural Work Group	Provides input on housekeeping, safety, damage, materials, and quality.	Early 1999
Suggestion Team	As above, plus makes performance improvement suggestions to Leadership Team on productivity and quality improvements.	Mid 1999
Improvement Team	As above, plus implements inventory accuracy, attendance, quality, and production reporting challenges.	Mid to late 1999
Semi-Autonomous Team	As above, plus schedules changeovers, overtime, holidays and vacations, budgeting, capacity and planning, and interfaces with purchasing and sales.	Late 1999 to early 2000
Self-Managed Team	As above, plus customer interface, partnership evolution, team management, team member selection and appraisal, and product design.	Some time in 2000

Table 9.1 The Empowerment Evolution for the Assembly Team

9. *Leadership must define the team support structure.* The Leadership Team must be sure that the team has available the necessary resources required to perform their task. These resources may include access to information, people, computers, clerical support, and so on. These resources should be described as specifically as possible and should not only be communicated to the team but also to the people impacted by this allocation of resources.

10. *Leadership must define the deliverables expected from the teams.* The Leadership Team must set forth the specific deliverables expected from the team for the team to ensure their interconnectedness with the rest of the organization/process. These deliverables should include minutes, presentations, reports, and recommendations.

A review of these ten factors indicates that the first three factors are tasks that must be done by the Steering Team. These tasks (define direction and assure alignment, team process, and information flows) are all foundational tasks upon which the evolving Revolutionary Organization will be built. The last seven factors are all Leadership Team tasks that are a part of the ongoing Team Chartering process. A key aspect of a Revolutionary Organization is this chartering process. It is this chartering process that allows the Leadership Team to pursue the empowerment of teams.

LEADERSHIP MUST UTILIZE BRAINPOWER

Intellectual capital is the most valuable asset of your company. Your company's competitive edge in the marketplace is the sum of everything everybody in your company knows. A key here is realizing that what is meant by "everybody" is *everybody*. Not just the research people, the engineers, or the "knowledge workers," but everybody. The Revolution Leader understands that everybody is every employee and thus accepts the responsibility of empowerment of the entire organization. It is in fact the empowerment of an organization's brainpower that results in the greatest use of its intellectual capital. It does little good in an organization to have wise people sitting around being wise. It is by empowering the wise people that the Revolution Leader, through the synergy of teams, can maximize his return on investment in intellectual capital.

Chartering Teams

The seven steps of the process of chartering teams are:

Step 1: Leadership team defines thrust for new team

Step 2: Sponsor drafts charter

Step 3: Leadership Team reviews charter

Step 4: Leadership Team approves charter

Step 5: Team reviews charter

Step 6: Team accepts charter

Step 7: Team charter evolution

Step 1 involves the Leadership Team deciding what Work Teams should be created. At the outset of the process of creating a Business Process Continuous Improvement (BPCI) organization, the early teams should be cross-functional teams, since it is cross-functional teams that provide the greatest opportunity for the organization's cultural Revolution. Surprisingly, the Leadership Team process of selecting the first priorities is not straightforward. This, in fact, is more a reflection of the Leadership Team being a new team and going through the Norming/Storming stages than the Leadership Team's difference of opinion. Nevertheless, if this hurdle is not overcome, the evolution of the organization can get bogged down in defining these early teams. After the first teams have been chartered and become operational, additional cross-functional and functional Work Teams should be created by the Leadership Team in accordance to the potential for performance improvement.

Step 2 of the chartering process involves the selection by the Leadership Team of the person best qualified to write the team charter and this person preparing a draft of the charter. The person who prepares the first draft of the charter may or may not be a member of the Leadership Team. The person who prepares the charter is referred to as the Team Sponsor. Often, if the Team Sponsor is a member of the Leadership Team, this sponsor will also become the Team Liaison. If the Team Sponsor is not a member of the Leadership Team, then a different Team Liaison will have to be selected. The form that should be used by the Team Sponsor to draft the team charter is the charter form that will be used throughout the chartering process. A blank team charter form is given in Figure 9.1.

Charter for the ____________________ Team __________________
Team Sponsor: ____________________
Date: ____________________

Leadership Team Preliminary____________________
Leadership Team Final ________________________

___________Team Review____________________
___________Team Acceptance_______________

1. OPPORTUNITY: (What is the reason this team exists?)

2. PROCESS: (What are the steps to be followed and what are the questions to be answered by this team?)

3. EVIDENCE OF SUCCESS: (What results are expected in what time frames for this team to be successful?)

4. RESOURCES: (Who are team members, team leaders, and team liaison; who will support the team if needed; how much time should be spent both in meetings and outside of meetings; and what additional resources are available to the team?)

5. CONSTRAINTS: (What authority does the team have, what is the overall time frame for the evolution of the empowerment process, what things cannot be changed, what items are outside the scope of the team, and what budget does the team have?)

6. EXPECTATIONS: (What are the outputs from the team, when are they expected to be complete, and to whom should they be given?)

Figure 9.1 Team Charter Form

Step 3 of the process of chartering teams is the review by the Leadership Team of the preliminary charter. Typically, the Team Sponsor would present the preliminary charter. The Team Liaison records team comments and revises the charter accordingly for Step 4, the Leadership Team approval of the team charter. The Team Liaison then meets with the Team Leader to discuss the charter and, if the Team Leader has not been a Team Leader previously, to help the Leader understand not only the charter, but also the role of the Team Leader. The Team Leader receives a Team Leader orientation and given the Team Leader's acceptance of their role, the Team Liaison then works with the Team Leader to have a Team Orientation. All Team Members are invited to the Team Orientation. At this meeting, the Team Leader, Team Liaison, and Team Members are all oriented into the BPCI process and review the Team Charter (Step 5). At this point, the Team Leader and Team Liaison work together to help the Team Members understand the Team Charter. After Step 5, individuals are given an opportunity to decline the opportunity to serve on the team. If people decline to serve, the Team Liaison goes back to the Leadership Team to obtain approval for potential new members. The Team Liaison and/or Team Leader repeats Step 5 for any new members. Once the Team Membership is solidified, then the team meets again (Step 6) to accept their charter. The Team Liaison has the following three choices in dealing with changes to the Team charter that are made by the team:

1. For items considered to be refinements and not major changes in the Charter—accept the refinements as they are defined.
2. For items considered to be major that change the thrust of the Charter—either reject the changes as they are defined or place the changes on hold, discuss them with the Leadership Team, and return to the next meeting with a clearer direction.
3. For items when the Team Liaison is uncertain—place the item on hold, discuss them with the Leadership Team, and return to the next team meeting with a clearer direction.

Once the team accepts its charter (Step 6), then the Team Charter may be published and distributed. Now the team is off and running. The team understands not only their level of authority, but also the empowerment path forward as the Team Charter evolves (Step 7).

BOUNDARYLESS, SPEED, AND STRETCH

In a recent annual report letter, Jack Welch, CEO of General Electric, defines the following three operating principles that are the key to General Electric "building a work force with an absolutely infinite capacity to improve everything":

Boundaryless—"Piercing the walls of 100-year-old fiefdoms and empires called finance, engineering, manufacturing, marketing, and gathering teams from all those functions in one room, with one shared coffee pot, one shared vision, and one consuming passion—to design the world's best jet engine, or ultrasound machine, or refrigeration."

Speed—"Speed means that new products are coming out with drumbeat rapidity." Speed also means focusing GE efforts on "the speed of our order-to-remittance cycle (from time of order to when we get paid) as well as allowing us to shift the center of gravity of the company rapidly toward the high-growth areas of the world."

Stretch—"Stretch is a concept that would have produced smirks, if not laughter, in the GE of three or four years ago, because it essentially means using dreams to set business targets—with no real idea of how to get there."

Mr. Welch states that he is looking for "leaders at every level who can energize, excite, and coach rather than enervate, depress, and control. In some cases, this means parting company with some impressive people who won't block for others or play as a part of a team."[2] What an endorsement for the use of boundaryless and speed-based teams that respond to stretch charters to coax an organization into being better and better. There's no doubt that Jack Welch is a Revolutionary Leader.

Call to Action

Where has your organization confused the concept of Empowerment? What "E"word war stories can be heard inside your walls? The 10 Leadership empowerment roles I outlined in this chapter are your path forward to making empowerment successful. Read that list again and begin to take action in each area. Empowerment is a lot more work than you may have thought, but you will enjoy great success if you do it right.

10

What Do You Know?

Revolution Principle #10:

Revolutionaries must be masters of the art of learning.

Revolution is predicated upon the awareness of a problem and the proposal of a solution. Then, for a Revolution to continue its success, it must continue to identify problems and offer further solutions. This entire problem/solution discovery process is the result of *learning*. Before a Revolution can ever get off the ground, learning must take place. And for the Revolution to continue, the learning must continue, and continue, and continue . . . .

As I have thought this issue through over the years, I have come to believe that a Revolution cannot go beyond what it knows. A Revolution cannot address problems it doesn't know exist, and cannot offer solutions it has not discovered. There is no better Revolution that illustrates this point than the *Computer Revolution*, which we have witnessed before our very eyes over the last twenty years. We have watched as the way the entire world communicates, manages business, gives business presentations, designs products, produces cartoons, does research, and on and on, has drastically changed. This is nothing less than a Revolution.

The interesting thing to me is that the Revolution has been successful primarily because of learning. What started with computers that filled entire rooms and did relatively little, has "learned" its way into desk top and lap top versions suitable for any need. Then think of the software. What started as clumsy, user-unfriendly, and extremely limited packages has "learned" its way into software that even kids can use and that fits just about any application with custom precision. It has been amazing! But I have to remind myself that these products and these technologies did not just land on us, they were learned. And the learning is still occurring, the Revolution is still happening. This is the power of learning and it has unbelievable Revolutionary implications.

Let me apply this to business. The Computer Revolution has taken place primarily within the business sector. What I mean is that those who made the greatest strides in developing, implementing, and profiting from the technology have been companies. Even more, the number of companies who have made the greatest strides have been relatively few. Those companies took the task of learning very seriously, have changed the entire world with what they have learned, and are now enjoying the success. This really excites me, because the same potential lies within many other products, technologies, and services. There are countless other Revolutions waiting to begin. If we would answer the call to become learners who then start a Revolution based on what we have learned, and then continue the Revolution through further learning, the possibilities would be endless. In this chapter I want to explore the fascinating topic of learning. I hope to inspire you to become a Learning Organization because I believe it is key to your becoming a Revolutionary Organization.

The Training Fallacy

There are two fundamental approaches to learning: The *process-based* or *results-driven process* and the *training-based* or *activity-centered process*. In understanding which method is correct, you must get beneath the surface-level, common-sense rhetoric in the philosophies and see the traps. Consider the following common sense statements:

> "Continuous improvement requires a commitment to learning. How, after all, can an organization improve without first learning something new?"[1]
>
> —David A. Garvin
> *Harvard Business Review*

> "Quality takes a long time to learn and I wish we had accepted that earlier. It would have saved us a lot of anxiety and frustration. . . . People spend what seem like huge amounts of time reading about quality or going to training courses, only to realize they don't know much and their company hasn't really started quality management. . . . One of the surprises is the length of time it takes to actually begin, in our case it took two years."[2]
>
> —Patricia A. Galagan
> *Nations Business*

Pure common sense you say? Well, then it also follows that:

- To become a team-based organization, a company must practice continuous improvement.
- Continuous improvement requires continuous learning.
- Continuous learning requires training.

Therefore, according to this logic, the approach to become a Collaborative Organization is training, and so what we must do is pursue a training-based process. This common-sense approach leads to the following:

- The retention of a consulting firm to conduct training.
- A classroom training program that makes every school teacher smile.
- Huge expenditures on training that result in little true performance improvement.
- Success stories like these:
    - "318 people have completed all 90 hours of the XXX program."
    - "250 people have completed the 60-hour XX program."

- 79 people have completed the 40-hour X program."
- Positive morale.
- Good feedback on training.
- No performance improvements.
- No results.

This is not common sense; this is nonsense that doesn't work. Although there are many, many consultants out there providing a train, train, train program that may feel good, they do not produce results. Let me be clear: The training-based or activity-based or activity-centered process to become a team-based organization is wrong, will not work, and cannot be made to work. The problem lies in a total misunderstanding of the learning process. The kind of learning your organization needs has little to do with training as practiced by organizations today.

Think about learning. Most of us see a mental picture of sitting in a classroom. A teacher is at the front of the room actively involved in the process of teaching. You passively listen. The teacher is responsible for the learning process. This "formal education" picture is clear in our minds because most of us have spent many years participating in this kind of learning process. Thus it is not surprising when asked to think about learning that we pull out our old mental image and once again think about the classroom.

Unfortunately, this thinking about learning is wrong; it is obsolete, and it is the culprit in leading many organizations astray from their pursuit of becoming a collaborative organization. Why does classroom training most often fail to fulfill the learning needs of the organization? Here are the top ten reasons:

1. *Training is not done Just-In-Time.* The proper philosophy of learning is Uncover - Discover - Recover. Uncover the need for knowledge. Discover new knowledge. And Recover by placing new knowledge into action. Classroom training typically only addresses the Discover element. By not being Just-In-Time, the leading responses to classroom training are:
    - "They talked about a lot of things I will never need to know" (failure to Uncover the need for new knowledge).
    - "Not sure that what I learned has application to what I do" (failure to Recover by putting knowledge to work).

2. *Training is not a part of the process of creating Peak-to-Peak Performance.* Training is seen as this month's program and not a part of an overall process. Teachers teach their program but do not tie their program into the organization's Model of Success or to what is happening in the organization today.
3. *Training is inflexible.* There is an assumption that one size fits all when in fact it is clear that the needs vary from "extra-small" to "extra-extra-large." Generic training is provided independent of need. In fact, what is key is not what is learned, but what programs have been attended.
4. *Training is sabotaged.* Managers and supervisors do not support training. They see training as a waste of time, and so they undercut its effectiveness and often will make fun and openly criticize the training.
5. *Training burnout occurs very quickly.* Especially for people in operations, the thought of sitting in a classroom for four or more hours in a day is unbearable. Regardless of the effectiveness of the teacher, many people turn off well before the teacher does.
6. *Training is not built into the schedule.* When people return from training all of their work awaits them. They resent the training as it takes time away from their "real job."
7. *Training accountability does not exist.* There is no or little training follow-up and little or no measurement of the effectiveness of training. Students logically conclude, "If there is no follow-up, how important can this training be?"
8. *Training is of individuals, not of teams.* Training is given to individuals, but not to the people around the individual, and so there exists little empathy to be involved with what was learned. Even worse, sometimes there exists resentment toward the people who did not go to the training from the ones who did.
9. *Training is not viewed as an organization priority.* Although all the right words were said, when decisions have to be made on attending or not attending training, often the decision is taken to not attend the training. Urgent problems take precedence over training, and thus a lack of training continuity exists.

10. *Training objectives are not focused.* Poorly focused training objectives result in too much trying to be done in too short a time frame. This time compression leads to a lecture-only format which is counterproductive to real learning.

The formal education mental picture has little to do with organizational learning, successful teams, Peak-to-Peak Performance, and leading an Organizational Revolution. This formal education mental picture must be replaced by a process-based or results-driven process of learning that will support the Revolution from individuals to teams. This process-based approach to organizational learning may be called "learning-by-doing," "action learning," or "team-based learning." The purpose of this chapter is to show how to lead a successful Learning Revolution and how to become a genuine Learning Organization.

What is a Learning Organization?

We have all heard about the solution to the 1990s—the Learning Organization. But what is a Learning Organization? In the popular book *The Fifth Discipline: The Art and Practice of the Learning Organization*, by Peter Senge, he tells us the answer, but then goes off on an intellectually stimulating treatise on learning and never gets back to the process of creating a Learning Organization. Let me delay for a moment in telling you what Senge says, and instead, see if I can get you to think through this with me.

First, can organizations learn? Well, what does it mean to learn? What is learning? According to the dictionary, learning is "the acquiring of knowledge or skill."[3] D. H. Kim adds insight to this definition by pointing out that knowledge is "knowing why," which implies the ability to understand concepts, and that skill is "knowing how," which implies the physical ability to produce. For example, a carpenter who is good at woodworking (skill) without the conceptual understanding of building a table (knowledge) has really not learned to be a carpenter. Or, to the contrary, a carpenter who has the knowledge to conceptually design tables, but does not have the skills to produce the tables, has not really learned how to be a carpenter.[4] It is from this perspective that D. A. Kolb defines learning as "the process whereby knowledge is created through the transformation of experience" and Kim defines learning as "increasing one's capacity to take effective action."[5]

Now, in answer to our first question, "Can organizations learn?" the answer is no, not really. Only individuals can learn. So, this leads to our second question, "If only individuals can learn and not organizations, what is organizational learning?" The scholars have had no shortage of ideas here. Garvin has compiled the following definition from over ten years of discussion:

- "Organizational learning means the process of improving actions through better knowledge and understanding."
- "An entity learns if, through its processing of information, the range of its potential behaviors is changed."
- "Organizations are seen as learning by encoding inferences from history into routines that guide behavior."
- "Organizational learning is a process of detecting and correcting error."
- "Organizational learning occurs through shared insights, knowledge, and mental models."[6]

The dilemma then is, how can there be organizational learning if only individuals can learn. Argyris and Schon pose this issue as follows:

> "There is something paradoxical here. Organizations are not merely collections of individuals, yet there are no organizations without such collections. Similarly, organizational learning is not merely individual learning, yet organizations learn only through the experience and action of individuals. What, then, are we to make of organizational learning? What is an organization that it may learn?"[7]

This leads to the third and target question: "What is the definition of a learning organization?" Garvin's answer to this question is:

> "A learning organization is an organization skilled at creating, acquiring, and transferring knowledge, and modifying its behavior to reflect new knowledge and insights."[8]

Wick's answer to this question is:

> "A learning organization is an organization that continually improves by rapidly creating and refining the capabilities needed for future success."[9]

Senge's answer to this question is:

> "A learning organization is an organization where people continually expand their capacities to create the results they truly desire, where new and expansive patterns of thinking are nurtured, where collective aspiration is set free, and where people are continually learning how to learn together."[10]

Then, to be certain the meaning is clear, Senge really tells us what we need to know:

> "Team learning is vital because teams, not individuals, are the fundamental learning unit in modern organizations. This is where the rubber meets the road; unless teams can learn, the organization cannot learn."[11]

Thus, a Learning Organization is a Collaborative Organization where teams are pursuing Peak-to-Peak Performance. Amazing as it may seem, when one does a thorough review of the five "component technologies" of the Senge learning organization (Systems Thinking, Personnel Mastery, Mental Models, Building Shared Vision, and Team Learning), what is understood is that this book presents a process that fully defines how to do these five things. Similarly, if one does a thorough review of Garvin's five building blocks (Systematic Problem Solving, Experimentation, Learning From Past Experience, Learning From Others, and Transferring Knowledge), once again we see that this book defines how to do these five things. So, in a way this book is the "How-To" guide to becoming a Learning Organization. In fact, given a robust definition of a Learning Organization, a Revolutionary Organization is a Learning Organization.

At the same time, caution must be exercised since there are holes in the Learning Organization literature that have resulted from the failure to actually pursue Revolution. For example, although Senge understands the issue of alignment, he does not understand empowerment. He states:

> "Alignment is the necessary condition before empowering the individual will empower the whole team. Empowering the individual when there is a relatively low level of alignment worsens the chaos and makes managing the team even more difficult."[12]

We know that alignment is the necessary condition before empowering a team, but that a team will never be empowered if first the individuals are empowered. Similarly, although Kim defines learning as "increasing one's capacity to take effective action," he also says:

> "All organizations learn, whether they consciously choose to or not, it is a fundamental requirement for their sustained existence. Some firms deliberately advance organizational learning, developing capabilities that are consistent with their objectives; others make no focused effort and, therefore, acquire habits that are counterproductive. Nevertheless, all organizations learn."[13]

This is not true. All organizations are not increasing their capacity to take effective action, no more than all organizations are improving teamwork or performance by creating teams. Creating a shift from individuals to teams, becoming a team-based organization, becoming a Learning Organization, becoming a Revolutionary Organization, is not something that will just happen. If leadership does not properly pursue a methodical process, these things will not happen.

AT CITICORP LEARNING AND INNOVATION GO HAND-IN-HAND

Citicorp has long been thought of as a bank of innovation. The Citicorp record on certificates of deposit, automated teller machines, bank credit cards, foreign banking, electronic funds transfer, and so on, is one of aggressive pioneering. The stimulation for this innovation was an emphasis on learning. Some of the stories told about Citicorp include:

- Leadership authorizes many experiments. Almost any good idea is supported.
- Leadership believes "Having a lot of activity going on and learning from it" is the best way to improve the bank.
- Bright, unconventional nonbankers are brought in and encouraged to experiment. When they succeed, they are promoted; when they fail, they are assigned to a routine job for a while, allowed to recover and recharge, and then assigned to another experiment.
- Mistakes are viewed as opportunities for learning.

Is it any wonder that Citicorp continues to learn and, therefore, be successful?

Becoming a Learning Organization

If you wish to become a Learning Organization, you must embrace the following learning issues:

- In the introduction to this chapter, the concept of Just-In-Time learning and the philosophy of learning Uncover-Discover-Recover was presented. It is this philosophy of learning that explains the critical nature of organizational alignment with the Model of Success. It is only when an organization uncovers the gap between the present organizational position and the vision that the organization has a true understanding of why they must become a Revolutionary Organization.
- A Revolution Leader will be intimately involved with learning. I stated earlier in the book that "the first task of a Revolution Leader is to shape the organization's culture." A key element of a Peak-to-Peak Performance culture is learning, and so leaders must shape their organization's culture to encourage learning. I also stressed the importance of the leader personally learning, providing leadership to the learning process and the team-based process. A Revolution Leader is one who has a total awareness of learning.
- There is an old saying that "success breeds success." This is a nice saying but unfortunately it isn't true. More often than not, success breeds contentment which eventually breeds failure. In fact, it is more true to say that failure breeds success.

  If this seems funny to you, consider the following:

  - Babe Ruth not only had 714 career home runs, he also had 1,330 career strike outs.
  - R. H. Macy failed in retailing seven times before he became a success with his store in New York.
  - Pete Rose holds not only the record for the most hits in baseball: 4,192, but also the most outs: 9,518.

Abe Lincoln and Thomas Edison both had many more failures than successes. But we call both these people successful. The point, however, is not to try to fail but rather to not be afraid of failing, and if you do fail, to learn from it. In fact, in a Revolution culture where risk taking is encouraged, a failure is seen as a learning opportunity. When no one is failing, when no one is making mistakes, there is no risk-taking, there is no growth, and there is no learning. In a Revolution, there will be lots of failures, lots of mistakes, lots of learning, and yes, lots of success.

- Directly related to the saying "failure breeds success" is the topic of active learning. Active learning says the best way to learn is by doing, by being involved, by participating. Allow me to adopt an old Chinese proverb by thinking from a team perspective:

  > "We hear and we forget, we see and we remember, we do and we understand." My translation? "Go, Go, Go!" The more you try, the more you learn.

- Revolutionary Organizations learn by making mistakes and by being involved, but they can also learn by observing and understanding the experiences of others. By watching others' successes and failures and adopting what was learned to one's own situation, there is an opportunity to learn. This may be done by visiting plants, reading trade publications, attending industry meetings, conferences, and seminars, retaining consultants, and participating in benchmarking studies. The experts in this type of learning have been the Japanese, who prior to each trip, are given training on "How to look, How to listen, and How to ask." During each trip, large amounts of information, audio tapes, video tapes, and pictures are taken and after each trip detailed debriefing and trip reports are prepared. We never want to miss an opportunity to learn and if we are aware of what is happening around us, we can learn from the success and failure of others.
- An important type of learning that is very difficult for some to accept is *unlearning*. Unlearning is the process of discarding old knowledge and skills and adopting new knowledge and skills. A term that has become popular as a result of the excellent video *The Business of Paradigms* by Joel Barker is the term *paradigm*. A paradigm is a model, a framework, a way of thinking, or a scheme for understanding reality. Unlearning is a process that may be likened to a paradigm shift, where old ways of thinking are thrown off and new ways are adopted. I believe many misunderstand the process of paradigm shifting and unlearning in that they only think about the acceptance of new ways of thinking and they forget the equally important aspect of leaving behind old ways of thinking. Revolution Leaders fully understand all aspects of unlearning and paradigm shifting.

- A distinguishing characteristic between a Revolutionary Leader and a Traditional Manager is their outlook on learning. A Revolutionary Leader seeks out every opportunity to learn whereas a Traditional Manager waits to be taught. The Revolutionary Leader understands that learning is a part of every day whereas the Traditional Manager believes learning occurs in a classroom. The Revolutionary Leader believes they are personally accountable for their own learning, whereas the Traditional Manager doesn't really think about accountability for learning, but certainly doesn't think it is their job. The Revolutionary Leader sees each day as a part of their lifelong learning process, whereas the Traditional Manager sees their learning as primarily being complete. The Revolutionary Leader is concerned with the entire organization's learning as they believe learning is required for continued business success, whereas the Traditional Manager is not concerned with organizational learning and does not see any linkage between business success and learning. In fact, a good measure of a Revolutionary Leader may be obtained by simply asking the person about learning within their organization. Within minutes, you will know if you are speaking to a Revolutionary Leader or a Traditional Manager.

MOTOROLA: THE LEARNING ORGANIZATION

Motorola spent the 1980s focusing on quality, and as a result of their six sigma defect–reduction programs, and excellent basic and statistical process control training, won the Malcolm Baldrige National Quality Award and, even more importantly, the finest reputation for quality in Corporate America. But its leaders have understood that as the competition catches up, quality will have gone from a goal to a strategic advantage to a given. Motorola believes the next set of weapons to win the competitive war will be responsiveness, adaptability, and creativity, and to arm these weapons, what will be required is a focus on teams and lifelong learning. The goal is a workforce that is disciplined yet free-thinking, with a depth of understanding while having independent-mindedness. Two keys to Motorola's focus on learning is how they link learning to business strategies and what they call "embedded learning." This ensures that Motorola people are not just learning for the sake of learning, but that learning is done so as to achieve Peak-to-Peak Performance. The learning being tied to business strategies results in uncovering

(continued)

the need for knowledge and the embedded learning through both team-based and apprenticeship's results in the Discovery and Recovery phases of the education process. It is clear Motorola is a Learning Organization and, in fact, probably the prototypical Revolutionary Organization.

Call to Action

Let me put the question to you bluntly: If you aren't taking every opportunity to learn, what makes you think your organization will survive into the next century? I believe that only those organizations that become Learning Organizations will be prepared to meet tomorrow's demands. You can be sure of this: Every Revolutionary Organization is learning how to excel tomorrow, and some of those organizations are your competitors. Rather than allowing your competitors to do all the learning about your markets, why don't you become a Learning Organization and lead the way to tomorrow's success?

11

Applied Science

Revolutionary Principle #11:
Revolutionaries excel at applying the science of collaboration.

Revolutionaries understand that there is a science of collaboration, but they also understand that to achieve the benefits from the science, the science must be applied. Collaboration succeeds only when there is positive, customized application of the collaboration process. Conversely, where Revolutions fail to apply the science they will remain stagnant, or worse, fail altogether.

In many ways, the application of the science of collaboration is a specialty unto itself. For example, if a military revolution understands the scientific process of getting people to work together to create synergy, they must also understand how to properly conduct a strategy meeting so as to best facilitate the synergy. This is applying the science of collaboration and it is vital. Without sound application, a Revolution will sit on the idea table with little or no execution. However, if a

Revolution has successful execution as its goal, then application must become a high-level priority.

The application principle is crucial to everything I have said thus far concerning collaboration in business. My goal for you is implementation of the collaboration process. I believe that in order for this to happen, you must have a solid path forward for application. This chapter gives you that application.

Another Meeting?

Although none of us like meetings or need more of them, we must be aware of the fact that for the Revolution from individuals to collaboration to occur, there must be team meetings. In fact, people learn to operate as a team in team meetings. Therefore, a key to Revolution is learning how to have successful team meetings. Here are the basic guidelines:

- *Make good first impressions.* The first impressions received by the team members will have a big impact on how they support the team and the process, particularly early in the Revolution process. These first impressions will include how they are invited to the team orientation, the team orientation itself, the first meeting after the orientation, and so on. Every effort should be made to help team members become comfortable with the process at the outset and to break down barriers. Team Liaisons and Team Leaders must work extra hard early in the process to minimize team member surprises, hassles, and awkwardness.
- *Adhere to team meeting etiquette.* All team members must understand and adhere to the following:
  1. Team members may not send "someone in their place" to team meetings, but must personally attend all meetings.
  2. Team members must all be punctual and team meetings should start and stop on schedule.
  3. No telephone calls or interruptions should be allowed during team meetings. Beepers will be turned off.
  4. Within the team, there are no bosses, supervisors, or rank. All team members are equal.

5. Team members will not seek to win an argument. Team members should balance advocacy and inquiry and should speak candidly, openly, and clearly, and listen actively.

- *Assign team roles.* As presented earlier, the roles within a team are Team Sponsor, Team Liaison, Team Leader, Team Reporter, Team Recorder, and Team Member. It is important that all these roles are filled and that everyone clearly understands who is filling them. Many teams have had unsuccessful team meetings because they failed to identify or fulfill one of the team roles.
- *Follow team rules.* There are six team rules that we have found to be necessary to support successful team meetings. These rules facilitate trust, openness, and participation. These rules should be hung on the wall in the team meeting rooms and should be reviewed at the outset of each team meeting. The team rules are:

  1. Total honesty
  2. Total amnesty
  3. Listen to others
  4. Stay focused
  5. Manage time
  6. Be prepared

  The Team Leader should be certain the Team Members have the following understanding of these rules:

  1. *Total Honesty*. Team Members are encouraged to say what they think. No politics, no playing games, and no adversarial relationships are allowed. Everyone is encouraged to express their views and to contribute their beliefs to the team.
  2. *Total Amnesty.* There will be no repercussions for things said at team meetings. Individual views and beliefs will not be quoted in the team minutes. This rule is not meant to create a veil of secrecy but rather to encourage total honesty without fear of negative reactions.
  3. *Listen to Others*. Team Members are encouraged to listen actively to others. Team Members must be aggressive in trying to understand what others are saying. To do this well, Team Members must listen both for facts and feelings, make eye contact, minimize listening distractions, and paraphrase back to the speaker what the listener heard to ensure purity of communication.

4. *Stay Focused.* Team meetings should stay on the agenda topics. All comments should contribute to the discussion at hand. Side talk should be minimized.
5. *Manage Time.* Team meetings should run as scheduled. The majority of the time, team meetings should be 60 minutes or less. Once a team gets used to dealing with a 60-minute time frame meeting, efficiency and effectiveness will improve.
6. *Be Prepared.* At the end of each team meeting assignments will be made. Team Members are responsible for completing these assignments on schedule. Not completing assignments in a timely manner is not accepted. Team Leaders and Team Liaisons, as appropriate, should support Team Members in completing assignments on schedule.

- *Be oriented toward action.* Team meetings must bear fruit. The Team Leader and Team Liaison should plot the team's progression and should share with the Team Members the timing and path forward in accordance with the team charter. A sense of urgency and direction to the team meetings should always exist. For team meetings to be successful, the majority of the Team Members must believe the team meetings are worthwhile and action-oriented.
- *Follow a team meeting agenda and keep team meeting minutes.* All team meetings must follow a written agenda and should result in an orderly progression of thought on the "agendized" topics. A typical team agenda should include the following:

  1. Assign recorder
  2. Review meeting rules
  3. Review Model of Success
  4. Review last meeting
  5. Pursue objectives
  6. Review assignments

  The first four items should take 2 to 5 minutes. The last item should take 2 to 5 minutes. Thus, the majority of the meeting time should be spent pursuing the meeting objectives. After the meeting, the Team Recorder should give the Team Leader the meeting minutes. These minutes should record decisions, actions items, and assignments. The Team Leader should review the minutes, have them prepared, and distributed.

- *Keep the meetings focused.* Team meeting focus must flow from the team charter. The Team Leader should frequently refer to the Model of Success and the team charter to provide the context and purpose of all team deliberations. The Team Leader should help the Team Members stay on target and progressively lead the team to achieving results.
- *Work hard at communication.* Team communications should be natural and spontaneous. All barriers to effective communications must be eliminated. The Team Leader should work to achieve an overall balance in team participation. The entire team should work together to assure that all that is said is both heard and understood.
- *Create a thinking environment.* A normal day does not include much time for most people to think. The day-to-day harried, rushed pressures of the moment prevent many of us from having the opportunity to sit back and think. Successful team meetings should not only be a time to think but also a time where our thinking is stimulated by the thoughts of others. Team meetings are where the synergy of collaboration occurs. The Team Leader must create an environment where ideas flow and Team Members are stimulated to think outside of the box.
- *Assess team meetings.* If a team is not having successful team meetings, it is important for the Team Leader and/or Team Liaison to take action to improve performance. A good method of highlighting the difficulties of a team is the utilization of a Team Assessor. A Team Assessor is a Team Member who is assigned the role of assessor. The assessor should be a meeting observer and should use one of the following two formats to help the team improve team meeting performance:
    1. *Freelance.* The Team Assessor should take notes during the meeting and then spend a couple of minutes just prior to the meeting's conclusion giving the team feedback. Both positive and negative aspects of the meeting should be discussed by the Team Assessor and the team.
    2. *A-B-C-D.* All team meeting deliberations may be defined as:

       A = Administrative: Routine housekeeping team issues.

       B = Building the Business: Working towards the Model of Success, the team charter, and team success.

C = Crisis: Urgent, fire fighting, hot activities that demand immediate attention.

D = Dispensable: Things that do not contribute to the topic at hand or to the team moving forward.

In this case, the Team Assessor would keep track of the time spent on each of the A-B-C-D categories in the meeting. At the end of the meeting, the Team Assessor would report on what percent of the meeting time was spent on A, B, C, and D discussions. It would not be surprising to see a new team report its activities as:

A = 30%

B = 10%

C = 30%

D = 30%

Similarly, it would not be unusual to see a performing team receive an assessor's report that says:

A = 5%

B = 90%

C = 5%

D = 0%

- *Report team meeting assessments.* At the end of the meeting, the Team Assessor reports areas of strength, areas of weakness, and a total score to the team. On a monthly basis, problem areas and team progress should be discussed.

Organizing for Success

Figure 11.1 illustrates the traditional hierarchical pyramid organization structure that has resulted in silos of organizational awareness. Information only flows down vertical silos and the majority of the people in the organization do not have a clue what is going on. The hierarchical pyramid organization is now widely seen as ineffective and must be augmented by the flatter, more integrated, responsive, customer-driven, collaboration-based organization structure given in Figure 11.2. This latter structure is the Revolutionary structure.

Interestingly, many have discussed the collaborative structure using the labels *open networked organization*, *relational organization*, *cluster organization*, *human networking*, and so on. In many of these discussions, there seems to be no awareness of the need for the coexistence and overlapping of the two organizational structures. Figure 11.2 could only be the organizational structure for a company that had every line and staff function covered by a self-managing work team. This is neither practical nor desirable. Therefore what needs to exist is both a hierarchical pyramid organization structure to represent certain organizational relationships, and at the same time, a collaborative organizational structure to represent other organizational relationships. It is only by understanding both of these structures and their overlap that an organization will have the true understanding of the role of individuals and teams in an organization.

Revolution leaders rely on individuals to be accountable for certain tasks and teams for other tasks. Everyone within a Revolutionary Organization knows which teams are accountable for which tasks and which individuals are accountable for which tasks.

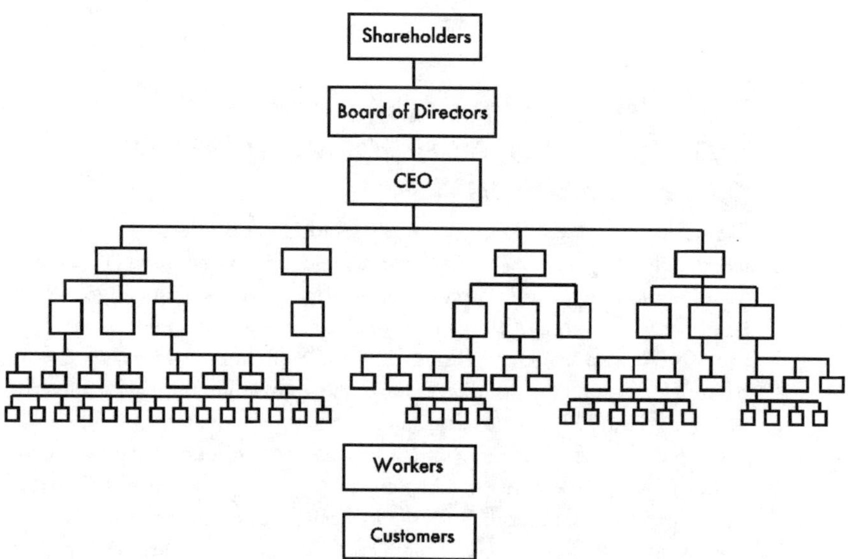

Figure 11.1 The Traditional Hierarchical Pyramid Organization Structure

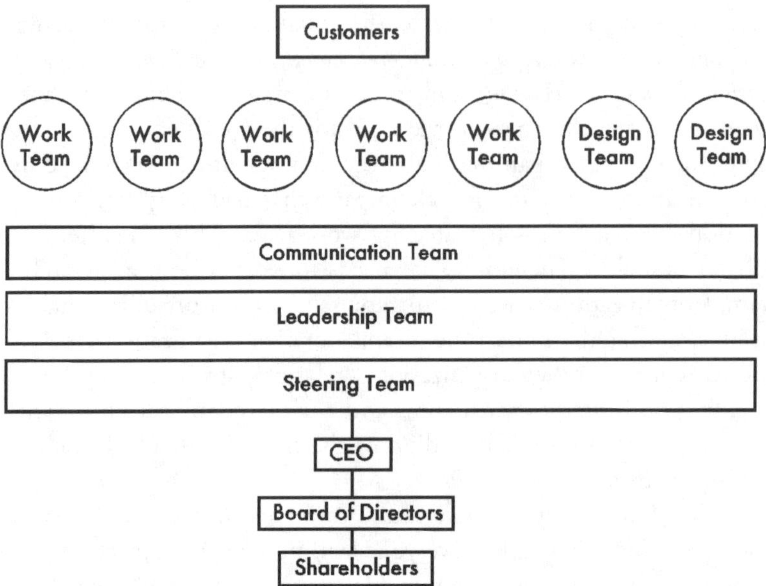

Figure 11.2 Collaboration-Based Organization Structure

CAUTION: CREATING TEAMS DOES NOT AUTOMATICALLY ALTER JOB DESCRIPTIONS OR RESPONSIBILITIES

A Steering Team was created in early October. A Leadership Team and Communication Team in mid-October. By mid-November, three cross-functional work teams were norming to performing and two functional work teams were chartered. All was fine. By mid-December, the company and the process were approaching chaos. How could this happen? Easy. A single person had a misunderstanding of the authority of teams and, in an attempt to move forward, upset the many middle managers who then fought back.

Let me be more specific. Richard Span was a natural leader on the C Track assembly line. He was told in mid-November that he was to be the C Track Assembly Line Team Leader. Bob Hendry from data processing was to be the Team Liaison. Richard is an excellent communicator, well respected in the shop and a good thinker with an orientation toward action. Richard believed in the team concept and, in fact, had read a few empowerment books.

(continued)

Bob was very quiet, very intelligent, new to the company, and uncertain of the collaboration process. The C Track Assembly Line Team charter was weak. The charter did not define the level of the team, the constraints, nor the time involvement expectations of the Team Members. The Leadership Team had addressed all these issues for the initial cross-functional Work Teams, but for some reason did not think functional Work Teams needed this guidance since "everyone knows what we want to achieve." Well, Richard and his team started work. In the first three weeks, Richard and his team did the following:

- Changed the layout in two sub-assembly areas without interaction with Industrial Engineering (who is responsible for the layout).
- Purchased two new fans and mounted them over the line to improve air circulation. The fans were bought directly, without the support of purchasing, and the fans were connected without input from maintenance. Purchasing and maintenance are responsible for these functions.
- Changed from a size eight screw to a size nine screw for motor mounting without approval from engineering (who controls product design and documentation).
- Changed the inspection process on sub-assemblies without approval from the people responsible in quality.

Well, guess what? Industrial Engineering, Purchasing, Maintenance, Engineering, and Quality all went nuts. What was going on here? Who is in charge? If the teams can do anything they want, then what is my job? And so on. . . . World War III. What went wrong? Well, for starters, a weak charter, then a weak Team Liaison, then an over-anxious Team Leader, and finally no outside facilitator to run interference. In short, a mess. How was it fixed? A strong charter was written, the team leader and team liaison were provided support from an outside facilitator, and an apology was issued to Industrial Engineering, Purchasing, Maintenance, Engineering, and Quality. How did it work out? Richard did fine as did the team, Industrial Engineering, Purchasing, Engineering, and Quality. The Maintenance guy never agreed to this team stuff and as this book goes to press, is still a question mark. Bob Hendry, the Data Processing guy, left the company and was replaced by Sue Carnevale from Quality as Team Liaison. Sue is doing well and has helped the team stay focused. Was this a major mistake? Yes. Did it hurt the company? No. Was it good for the company? Yes, they learned from this mistake and have not to this date again approved a weak charter nor allowed a team to automatically alter the responsibilities of others just because the team exists.

Beware: Speed Bumps Ahead

Many organizations today are not enjoying the success of teams. I believe a large part of the failure is due to the cavalier attitude with which many organizations approach teams. Just as it would be a mistake for you to do surgery without an experienced surgeon, it is a mistake for you to pursue teams without an experienced team expert. Thus, the following list of team mistakes will be helpful in allowing you to understand the challenge of making teams successful, but it is not possible to create a comprehensive list. In fact, your organization, your people, and your teams will think of new and unique ways for teams to fail. Only through the eyes of an experienced team facilitator can you avoid team failure. Nevertheless, the following list of the ten most dangerous team mistakes should be studied as a key to achieving collaboration success:

1. *The collaboration process is not customized.* Although this book advocates a specific process for Organizational Revolution, the simple truth is that the process explained here has never been followed. The process presented here is an excellent baseline, but each organization has a unique culture, a unique history, a unique group of leaders, managers, and people, and a unique collaborative background that must be taken into consideration when designing and refining a specific organization's collaborative process. Rarely will we find an organization that is beginning the collaborative process. For better or worse, the process has been evolving for years. This evolution may have involved Employee Involvement, Participative Management, Quality Circles, Job Enrichment, Organizational Development, and so on. It is critical that the past be understood and considered when implementing the collaborative process in the pursuit of Revolution. The past may result in a change in the Model of Success terminology and/or format. The past may result in the combination of the Steering Team and the Leadership Team. The past may result in how the Communication Team evolves. The past may mandate the adoption of existing teams or the prioritization of early teams, and on and on. It is critical for an organization to customize their collaboration process while maintaining the essence of the process to create the required Revolution from individuals to teams.

2. *The Steering Team is not actively steering.* The Steering Team must actively and visibly demonstrate a focus on alignment with the Model of Success. The Steering Team must actively, visibly, and consistently exhibit a support of the Leadership Team and clearly communicate to the entire organization that the collaboration process is not a fad or "another program." The Steering Team must take care to avoid the leadership disease "Attention Span Deficit Disorder." Because of past bouts with this disease, an organization requires ongoing assurance that it will become team-based and that there is no turning back. A test of a Steering Team is when a member of the Steering Team changes. When a key person or even *the* key person leaves an organization, the Steering Team should stay the course and demonstrate their commitment not only to the Revolution but also to bringing the new key person up-to-speed on how the organization functions.

THE ROCKET SHIP IS LEAVING THE LAUNCH PAD

The president of the more than 500-person company knew he had to place a stake in the ground. His company had pursued many fads and had done the hat, lapel pin and banner things. He needed to let the entire organization know that this was different, that this was not a program, but that this was how the company was going to function. He called a meeting for the last five minutes of first shift and the first five minutes of the second shift. This type of meeting was unprecedented. In fact, there was no place to hold such a large meeting. The president set up a microphone on the shipping dock and all the people stood outside in the truck wells (fortunately, it was a nice day). The President introduced the entire company to the Model of Success, the collaboration process, the membership of the Steering Team, and the Leadership Team, and then made the statement:

> "We have done many programs here. I want you to know that this is different. This is not a program, but the beginning of a process that will define how we do business forever. Folks, we will become Revolutionary, and here today, we are making a first step, a new beginning. The rocket ship is leaving the launch pad and there is no turning back. This is how we will run our business. This is how we will all be successful. I appreciate and expect your active involvement and look forward to working with you as we begin anew. Thank you."

The impact was amazing. The results six months later were even more amazing. The rocket ship truly did leave the launch pad and not only was there no turning back, there was not even any looking back.

3. *Middle management/supervisor's roles are not changed.* Middle managers and supervisors are threatened by teams. Middle managers and supervisors feel that teams will undercut their authority, power, and control. The self-esteem of the middle manager and supervisor is tied to their job as it has been. They believe they have earned their position and are now losing it. Their career path seems broken. From these perspectives, it is not hard to understand why middle managers and supervisors are often against teams. At the same time, middle managers and supervisors have had a lousy job and their satisfaction is among the lowest in industry. Middle managers and supervisors typically have all the responsibility for performance, but little authority to achieve performance. It is time for us to realize that in general, the middle manager/supervisor job is broken. When asked to describe their job, middle managers and supervisors use words like firefighter, policeman, power broker, paper pusher, stock chaser, baby-sitter, disciplinarian, problem fixer, and priority settler. When asked which of these roles they enjoy, the majority of middle managers and supervisors say none of the above.

   This is a major problem because the people who fill these positions are promoted because of their above-average performance and tremendous potential. So what we do is take our best workers and promote them into a job that is broken. How intelligent is this? In fact, one of the important results of becoming a collaboration-based organization is the recapture of all the talent that is today wasted on middle management and supervisory positions. In a Revolutionary Organization, there will be fewer middle managers and no supervisors. This does not mean people will be fired. To the contrary, these people are some of the best people in our companies and they will be moved into much more satisfying, relevant, value-added work where their talents may be more fully utilized. Some of these people will fulfill the role of coordinator, where they will support the Revolutionary process. Instead of old words like firefighter and power broker to describe the old middle manager/supervisor role, the new coordinator job will be described as coach, planner, trainer, motivator, people developer, and sounding board. These coordinators will really feel good about themselves and their contributions, and they will never want to go back to their old positions. The challenge, however, is in making the middle manager/supervisor to coordinator transformation in sync with the evolution of the teams.

Depending upon the team and the middle manager/supervisor, this synchronous transformation may be easy or difficult. For example, if a middle manager/supervisor has evolved with a Natural Group and has a positive relationship with the group and a clear understanding of the required role transformation, it is possible this person could still retain the role as middle manager/supervisor, be a Suggestion Team member, an Improvement Team member; then become a coordinator and work as a member of a Semi-Autonomous Team; and ultimately a Self-Managing Team. The middle manager/supervisor transitions with the team and becomes the coordinator while serving as a member of the team. The team defines the roles and the transformation would be straightforward.

By contrast, there will be some traditional groups where the middle manager/supervisor is not able to transition to a Natural Group. Here, when the Suggestion Team is formed, the middle manager/supervisor should not serve on the team, as this would prevent the team from evolving. The Team Liaison and Team Leader should work with the middle manager/supervisor to help them evolve their interaction with the team. As the team transitions to an Improvement Team, the team needs to work through the Team Liaison and Team Leader to transition the middle manager/supervisor's role. Depending upon the team and the middle manager/supervisor, this may involve the middle manager/supervisor joining the team.

Each circumstance needs to be assessed and synchronized by the Leadership Team with the input of the Team Liaisons and Team Leaders. Eventually, the transformations will all be complete and all Self-Managed Teams will have coordinators. Managing this team and role transformation is the responsibility of the Leadership Team. This responsibility requires that at every point in time each middle manager/supervisor/coordinator and each corresponding team have a clear definition and understanding of roles. Roles that need to be assigned include the following:

- Scheduling: Work prioritization, assignments, and reporting
- Quality: Address quality problems, coordinate quality improvements, and reporting
- Administration: Attendance, overtime, vacation, work schedules, and payroll reporting
- Human Resources: Performance reviews, hiring, and training
- Maintenance: Housekeeping, maintenance problem solving, and coordination
- Safety: Address safety problems, coordinate safety improvements, and reporting
- Materials: Coordination with purchasing, receiving, warehousing, and material handling

4. *The team charter is poorly executed.* Some common charter mishaps include the following:
   - *Team Charters are not effective.* An ineffective Team Charter is a charter that does not focus or motivate a team.
   - *Team Charter is not tied to the Model of Success.* Team Members do not understand how fulfilling the charter will help the company.
   - *Team Charter is not understood by the team.* The Team Members simply do not know what the charter says.
   - *Team Charter is so broad that it does not provide any focus to the team deliberations.* The charter can be interpreted many different ways so there is a lack of team direction.
   - *Team Charter Evidence of Success are not measurable, understood, or relevant.* Evidence of Success in the Team Charter do not relate to the Evidence of Success in the Model of Success.
   - *Team Charter has not clarified the role of the team.* Is the team a Design Team or a Work Team? Is the team a Suggestion Team, an Improvement Team, A Semi-Autonomous Team, or a Self-Managing Team?

- *Team Charter does not identify a topic for team deliberations but rather an attempt is made to use a team to rubber stamp a solution already identified by leadership.* The team will see through this charter and will be unwilling to be used in this manner.

5. *Teams are improperly staffed.* A key to the success of a team is the staffing of the team with the correct people. Useful guidelines to consider when staffing a team include the following:
   - People should not be placed on teams as a reward or a favor. Teams should not be staffed with people because of their loyalty to company leadership.
   - People should only be placed on a team where they have personal knowledge about the topic the team is pursuing. Team Members should have a stake in the output of the team.
   - People should not (in fact, cannot) be forced to be a part of a team. If a person does not want to be on a team after the team orientation, they should be allowed, without negative repercussions, to not serve on the team.
   - People with diverse perspectives, talents, age, and personalities should be placed on a team. It is the diversity of Team Members that results in the synergistic evolution of the team.
6. *Team Leader and/or Team Liaison not doing job.* Team recommendations should be handled in a timely fashion and, for the most part, should be accepted. Team Leaders and Team Liaisons should support a team to help them get results. Not getting these results will result in the following:
   - A loss of team energy and enthusiasm
   - A sense of helplessness
   - A lack of direction
   - A loss of focus to discussions
   - Ineffective meetings
   - Cynicism and mistrust
   - The failure of the team

7. *Teams not allowed to work.* The three things that will prevent a team from being successful are:
   - Members of early teams are subjected to peer pressure and the Leadership Team does not properly handle this pressure.
   - Teams are prevented from obtaining the information they need to address their task.
   - Adequate time is not allocated for Team Members to participate in the teams.
8. *Leadership Team is not working.* The Leadership Team does not provide for the proper management of the team evolution (Suggestion Team, Improvement Team, Semi-Autonomous Team, and Self-Managing Team) or development (Forming, Storming, Norming, Performing, and Maturation). Or, to the contrary, the Leadership Team attempts to micro-manage the teams and does not allow the teams to evolve. The micro-management challenge for the Leadership Team is typically a result of the Leadership Team and/or the Steering Team lacking patience. Although the whole purpose of the Revolution process is creating Peak-to-Peak Performance, care must be exhibited early in the process not to place too much early emphasis on results at the expense of the evolution of the team. The teams will be expecting the leadership to take charge and "make something happen." The Leadership Team must sit tight and allow the cultural transformation and team evolution to take its natural course.

PATIENCE IS A VIRTUE: BUT IT ISN'T EASY

The Leadership Team charters a team with a focus on company-wide cost reduction. The first thing the team tackles—the paper towels in the bathrooms. After four weeks of team meetings, a recommendation comes forth to replace the paper towels with cloth towels. No investment required, and an annual savings projected at almost $150. That is correct, not $150,000, but $150. The Leadership Team went bananas; they just went nuts. Finally, cooler heads prevailed and they decided to do nothing and to just be patient. The second project the team tackled—the cups used for coffee in the company. After six weeks of deliberations (think eight people, one hour a week, for six weeks) the recommendation was to stay with the present cups. The Leadership Team wanted to fire someone, anyone.

(continued)

They were crazy with anger. The outside facilitator kept them under control and they decided to do nothing and be patient. The third project had to do with tool life and saved the company about $55,000 per year. The fourth project involved the reduction of set-up time in the press department–annual savings of around $490,000. The moral of the story? You sometimes have to live through the paper towels and the coffee cups before a team believes in themselves: patience, patience, patience!

9. *Communication Team is not working.* It is the responsibility of the Communication Team to assure everyone in the organization has a clear understanding of the Model of Success, the status of teams, and the organization status. When the Communication Team does not work, it means that people within the organization are lost, uninformed, or both. This is totally unacceptable and results in Team Members not being able to contribute effectively at their team meetings. This causes ineffective team meetings which will then result in an ineffective collaboration process. The Communication Team must be effective and thus must apply several of their available tools to assure organizational awareness and understanding.
10. *Legal aspects of teams are poorly handled.* Although this continues to be an evolving issue, the bottom line is that teams should not be used as a mechanism to deal with "grievances, labor disputes, wages, rates of pay, hours of employment, or conditions of work." As long as teams are restricted from these topics, there should not be any difficulties in either a union or a non-union shop proceeding with teams.

Path Forward for Success

In this chapter I have explained how to have successful team meetings, how to organize for success, and how not to fail. Thus, the methodology for achieving team-based success has been presented. What remains to be done here is to define the steps to be followed to actually lead the Revolution from individuals to teams. These steps are presented in Table 11.1.

Table 11.1 The Steps to Shift an Organization From Individuals to Teams

Step	Who	What
1	Steering Team	Revolution Orientation
2	Steering Team	Define Model of Success
3	Steering Team	Charter Leadership Team
4	Steering Team	Refine Model of Success
5	Leadership Team	Revolution Orientation
6	Leadership Team	Charter Communication Team
7	Leadership Team	Define Priorities for Cross-functional Work Team
8	Leadership Team	Charter Cross-functional Work Teams
9	Cross-functional Work Teams	Revolution Orientation
10	Cross-functional Work Teams	Pursue Charter
11	Communication Team	Revolution Orientation
12	Communication Team	Pursue Charter
13	Steering Team	Support Leadership Team and Overall Process
14	Leadership Team	Liaise, Support, and Evolve Teams
15	Leadership Team	Charter New Teams
16	New Teams	Revolution Orientation
17	New Teams	Pursue Charter
18	All	Go to Step 12

Steps 1, 5, 9, 11, and 16, shown in Table 11.1, are all the same—Revolution Orientation. This orientation is a review of the first four chapters of this book. In addition to these orientations, if there is a union in the organization, it would be a good idea to conduct this exact same orientation for the local union leadership between Steps 5 and 6. Steps 1, 2, 3, and 4 in Table 11.1 are preparation steps for the Steering Team, as Steps 5, 6, 7, and 8 are for the Leadership Team.

Typically, the first Work Teams created should be Cross-functional Work Teams (Steps 8, 9, and 10), as Cross-functional Work Teams allow for the greatest exposure and cultural transformation. Once these early Cross-functional Work Teams have moved into a Norming phase, then new teams should be created (Steps 15, 16, and 17). This then begins the continuous process of Steps 12-13-14-15-16-17 and back to 12, and so forth. This process will never end but will cycle through the creation and completion of Cross-functional Work Teams and Design Teams and the creation of and evolution to Self-Managing Functional Work Teams. This will lead an organization to Peak-to-Peak Performance and will be the ongoing process of the Revolution.

Step 14 in Table 11.1 involves the Leadership Team, through the Team Liaison, supporting the team development through the phases of Forming, Storming, Norming, Performing, and Maturation.

Call to Action

The aspects of applying collaboration are every bit as important as the philosophy. How you run a team meeting, how you structure a collaborative organization, how to avoid team failures, and how to actually make the Revolution from individuals to collaboration are the things most organizations fail to do well. However, Revolutionary Organizations excel at the application of collaboration, leaving everyone else far behind. My advice? Study this chapter and master it. Make sure every team in your organization excels at application. Don't get bogged down in merely talking about Revolution; rather make collaboration work for your Revolution, for your success, and for your next performance peak.

12

Customer Service Isn't Enough

Revolution Principle #12:
A Revolution must satisfy those it serves.

Have you ever thought of who the customer is in a Revolution? Is it the leader? No, unless the leader is a dictator. Is it the government? No, unless the government is totalitarian. If it's not the leader and not the government, then it must be those whose lives benefit from the result—the general population.

This is central in understanding the theory of Revolution. If Revolution is genuinely seeking to improve the lives of the general population through the activities of a representative number from that population, then it is the population who must be served. They are the audience. They are the shareholders. Whenever a dictator becomes the leader, or the government becomes the leader, we have a big problem on our hands (just think of communism). Genuine Revolution is always by the people for the people.

I draw this distinction to point out another crucial principle of Revolution. For Revolution to be successful and remain successful, the audience must not only be served, but be satisfied as well. If the changes a leader promises are not delivered or are delivered poorly, the audience will become dissatisfied and will seek a counterrevolution. They will never remain impressed by a leader's noble attempts if the changes never occur. For example, since in the former Soviet Union, the collapse of communism, the end of the cold war, and the new openness to foreign trade, the groundwork has been laid for real economic and political Revolution. But so far, it's not working. There have been a lot of promises, a lot of attempts, and a lot of alliances formed, but is the average Russian satisfied? All the statistics indicate that they are not. They are not personally reaping the benefit of this new era, and therefore their Revolution has not been successful, at least not yet. Will communism return? Will another dictator rise up? Will the people bow their heads once again in oppression? If it puts bread on their tables and a roof over their heads, amenities many Russians do not currently enjoy, you bet they will.

A Revolution must always seek to satisfy the people, to improve their lives. Revolution leaders must constantly poll the people to be sure they are being satisfied, and find ways to increase satisfaction. This care for the people will build allegiance and commitment like no speech or general hype ever could.

Who is the customer in your Organizational Revolution? Is it a wholesaler, distributor, retailer, the end-user, or all of them? And the real question is, are they personally satisfied with the way you serve them? Do you improve their lives in a tangible way, and offer them a quality of product or service they cannot find elsewhere? Customer satisfaction is the beginning of level two in the collaboration process. It is the first step toward Extraorganizational Collaboration. I believe that Extraorganizational Collaboration in general and customer satisfaction in particular are at the heart of your success in the next decade and century. In this chapter I present what I feel is the most current and most scientific approach to customer satisfaction.

I have been overwhelmed by the seminars, books, articles, video tapes, audio tapes, software packages, and newsletters that have been crossing my desk on the topic of customer service. From one perspective, this is good news, since it appears that we are beginning to understand that the whole reason to be in business is to satisfy the customer. It really is that simple.

If you don't have satisfied customers, you will not be in business over the long-term. From another perspective, however, this is bad news because virtually all of the customer service materials available today are basic sales tips that have more to do with business etiquette than satisfying customers. For example, consider the following topics that are presented as keys to achieving customer satisfaction:

- *Smile:* A secret to customer service is smiling. If you smile a lot, even when on the telephone, the customer will feel good about doing business with your company.
- *Like Yourself:* If you like yourself, the customer will like you and be more inclined to do business with your company. You are a special person; be happy with who you are.
- *Appearance:* You are how you look. You gain confidence by looking your best. If you dress well and are confident, customers will be more likely to do business with your company.
- *Listening:* Listen to your customers and especially to their complaints. Complaints are good for the company as they let you know where you can improve.
- *Empathy:* Always put yourself in the customers' shoes. When empathizing with their perspective, customers will be less dissatisfied when they have complaints.
- *Complaints:* The beginning of a satisfied customer is a complaint. By listening and empathizing, we can turn complaints into opportunities for customer service.
- *Empowerment:* Give customer service people the authority to handle all customer complaints. It is through empowerment that customer service gains its ability to respond.
- *Promises:* Be sure not to promise more than you can deliver. It is always best to under-promise and over-deliver.
- *Speech:* Customer satisfaction will result from how loudly you speak, how fast you speak, how clearly you speak, and how to use the right words and phrases.
- *Positive Attitude:* When you have a positive attitude, your customers will too. This will result in happy customers, which will make your business happy.

and on, and on, and on. . . .

One piece that recently crossed my desk described the job of customer service as:

- *An acrobat*: The ability to balance customer wants and company needs.
- *A mind reader*: Reading between the lines of what a customer says, so you know just how to respond.
- *A juggler*: Keeping the conflicting facts and reality all in the air at once.
- *A lion tamer*: Knowing how not to put your head in the lion's mouth with the wrong words or tone of voice.
- *The ringmaster*: Keeping the customer's anger in one ring, your own anger in another, and the actual problem in a third.
- *A magician*: Keeping everyone happy as you deal with a huge variety of customers—and problems—simultaneously.

What are we doing here? Have we decided that, independent of the quality of the product we produce, or independent of the selling price of the product, or independent of the quality of the value-added support we provide, the key is to smile, like ourselves, look good, listen well, empathize, solve complaints, empower people, under-promise, speak clearly, and have a positive attitude, and customer satisfaction will follow? Baloney! Have we decided that all we need to do is practice our circus acts and the audience will clap? Come on. This is all fluff! This fluff is not all bad and, in fact, we should probably do some of these things (I am not against smiling, for example), but the problem lies in the myth that this fluff has something to do with customer satisfaction. It is in fact a focus on this fluff instead of a true emphasis on customer satisfcation that has resulted in our currently sorry state of customer service satisfaction.

Well, what do you think? Is customer service a priority? How is your customer satisfaction? Do you want my stories or will your own suffice? Here are examples of customer dissatisfaction I experienced in the last week:

- A rental truck was not available even though I had reservations for it, to help my daughter move.
- A motel reservation was lost and for $149 a night I slept on a pull-down bed.

- Airplane food? The flight attendant tells me she would not eat it either.
- A bank teller ordering concert tickets on the telephone happily ignored the line of bank customers.
- A mail order shipment arrived with the wrong color shirt.
- I arrived home with my fast food—one sandwich short.
- A rude check-out person told me, in a monotone voice and with no eye contact, "Have a nice day."

Where does it stop? Some people say we are moving toward a service economy; to me it seems more like a non-service economy. Customer service is not a smile. Customer service is not a department. Customer service is a way of doing business and it is a prerequisite to Extraorganizational Collaboration, Peak-to-Peak Performance, and an Organizational Revolution.

How to Measure Customer Satisfaction

At the core of the challenge concerning customer service is the definition of customer service. Customer service is defined as everything done to enhance customer satisfaction. The challenge with this definition is a misunderstanding of the definition of customer satisfaction.

Customer satisfaction, although a possibly elusive concept (as opposed to traditional customer service), can be measured. Here is the basic formula:

Customer Satisfaction = Perception of Customer Service Received − Expectation of Customer Service

This customer satisfaction formula presupposes two critical points, which every organization seeking to Revolutionize customer satisfaction must understand:

1. Customer satisfaction is based on our customers' perceptions and expectations, not on our self-centered view of what the customer may want.
2. The level of customer satisfaction will change as the customers' expectations change.

Revolution toward customer satisfaction must begin here—in an organization's basic beliefs about customer service. Customer satisfaction requires us to divest ourselves of our self-interest, and instead become consumed with the needs, expectations, and perceptions of those to whom we provide products and services. This requires organizations to know and be able to identify the special needs of each level of its customers. They must understand the Customer Tier.

The Customer Tier

No company has only one kind of customer. A customer base is made up of people, and no two people are alike. Each has their own set of expectations, and each requires different services and value-addeds to be satisfied. Identifying the many different nuances of a company's customer base is a vital key to today's and tomorrow's success. Nuance identification can be as broad and as thorough as a company chooses. But the fundamental principle that drives all nuance identification activities is that every customer is different and demands different levels of service to be satisfied.

Because customers change while they are our customers, companies cannot maintain customer satisfaction with the same set of services and value-addeds that satisfied customers yesterday. As customers continue their patronage, they will expect more and will require more to be satisfied. In his book, *Managing Quality: The Strategic and Competitive Edge*, David Garvin identifies the elements of quality as they relate to customer progression. I have presented those elements in Table 12.1.

Table 12.1 Elements of Quality

ELEMENT	DEFINITION	AUTOMOBILE ILLUSTRATION
Performance	The operating characteristics of the product	Acceleration
Secondary Features	Characteristics that supplement the product's basic features	Air conditioning
Reliability	The anticipated failure rate of the product	Length of time to failure of the starter

(continued)

ELEMENT	DEFINITION	AUTOMOBILE ILLUSTRATION
Conformance	The lack of defects in the product when delivered	Fitting of trunk, hood, and doors
Durability	The useful life of the product	Number of years before car deteriorates to the point where it should no longer be repaired
Serviceability	The ability to obtain satisfactory repair	Availability of engine parts and ease of installation
Aesthetics	The customer's feeling about the appearance of the product	How the customer views styling
Perceived Quality	The customer's overall feeling about the product	Subjective judgment of the customer as to which is the best automobile

Customer satisfaction adheres to the first principle of revolution: *Revolution is a process, and in a true revolutionary scenerio, a continuous process*. Customer satisfaction cannot be a policy to implement; that is only customer service, and is insufficient for today's business climate. Customer satisfaction is a process to be continually pursued. Rather than being implemented, customer satisfaction is nurtured.

The customer satisfaction process begins by understanding the basic Customer Tier. This enables companies to pursue customer satisfaction in a highly focused and specialized manner. The tier is made up of three levels of customers with three corresponding levels of satisfaction.

Level One: *Visitors*. Visitors are new customers who occasionally purchase our products and services, but have no lasting commitment to us. They often have low expectations and therefore, to them, customer satisfaction has to do with the fundamental aspects of the product. Level one customers define satisfaction in terms of product features and cost.

Level Two: *Associates*. Associates are customers who regularly, but not exclusively, purchase our products and services. Because our associates' experiences have grown since they were visitors, so too have their expectations. As they become associates, they begin to take features and cost for granted, and turn their attention to quality. This is a real challenge because quality is defined differently by different customers.

Level Three: *Partners*. Partners are customers who have moved you to the primary position on their list in your product category. Over time they have come to the place where they always choose you first; they prefer you. But once again, because their experiences continue to grow, so do their requirements for satisfaction. They still expect features, cost, and quality; but now their quest for satisfaction turns to other value-added support, such as special handling, special delivery, extra services, training, and so forth. So, what we need to understand is that customer satisfaction depends upon the level of the customer's experience. Therefore, customer service is not something you define for the marketplace, but something that each customer will define for you. I will flesh out these partnerships fully in the next chapter.

The crucial take-away from this Customer Tier is the realization that our customers evolve through these levels while they are our customers. To maintain satisfaction, slowly converting visitors into partners, companies must know their customers well enough to evolve with them, and then be willing and able to make the evolution. This is the Revolutionary process that will win continuous customer satisfaction.

To illustrate how the Customer Service Formula and the Customer Tier work together, consider a situation in which a company produces an excellent product at a competitive cost with high quality, but little extra value added. Let's say the customer's perception of customer service was 100 points. Then, for a level one customer whose expectation of customer service was only 40, their customer satisfaction is very high, at 60 (100 – 40 = 60). However, the level two customer who expects an excellent product, competitive cost, and high quality, had a customer service expectation of 90, so their customer satisfaction is low, at only 10 (100 – 90=10). Still worse, a level three customer, who expects an excellent product, competitive cost, high-quality, and considerable value-added support, had a customer service expectation of 110, so their customer satisfaction is –10 (100 – 110 = –10). To put this in other terms, the level three customer had a customer *dis*satisfaction of 10.

This example illustrates a real problem that occurs for many companies. The problem occurs as customers' expectations increase—from level one, to level two, then to level three—without a corresponding increase in the customers' perception of customer service received. This causes customer service inflation, and is when we hear statements like "I am delivering the best customer service I have ever delivered, but the level of customer satisfaction is at an all time low." Companies fail when customers' perception of product/price/quality/service does not keep pace with their customers' expectations of their offerings. Since the failing company was self-centered in their view of their offerings, they did not notice that although their offerings had been improved, the customers' expectations had increased well beyond this level of improvement, and thus customer satisfaction was low. This low customer satisfaction positions a company for failure. If they had recognized the Customer Tier, and evolved with its customers as they traveled along it, they would have had higher levels of satisfaction and a greater hope of success tomorrow.

SCANDINAVIAN AIRLINE SYSTEM: CUSTOMER SATISFACTION BASED ON THE CUSTOMER'S PERCEPTIONS

When Jan Carlzon took over Scandinavian Airline System (SAS), the company had an $8 million loss on top of a $20 million loss the year before. The next year SAS made $72 million, and has continued to be successful ever since. What was the key? According to Carlzon, the key was and continues to be customer satisfaction. Instead of continuing a trend of defining customer service by marketing, Carlzon delegated customer service to the front-line SAS employees, the people who had direct contact with the customers. Carlzon explains, "Last year each of our 10 million customers came in contact with approximately five SAS employees, and this contact lasted an average of 15 seconds each time. Thus, in the minds of our customers SAS is created 50 million times a year, 15 seconds at a time. These 50 million 'moments of truth' are the moments that ultimately determine whether SAS will succeed or fail as a company. They are the moments when we must prove to our customers that SAS is their best alternative."

It is the customer's perception of these moments of truth that will result in the customer satisfaction perception of SAS. It is not that SAS defines customer service, but the customer and the basis for the customer's perception of customer service is not a corporate slogan, program, or outreach, but rather these 50 million "moments of truth." SAS has great customer satisfaction because they truly understand that the customer defines customer satisfaction.

Another way to view the formula for customer satisfaction is by growing the customer expectation for service, but growing the customer's perception of customer service at even a faster rate. Table 12.2 illustrates this scenario. As may be seen for a Level I Customer, a perception of customer service received of 100 results in a delighted customer. For the same perception of customer service received of 100 for a Level III, we have a lost customer. At the same time, increasing the perception of customer service received for any level of customer allows for the progression from lost customer–dissastified customer–satisfied customer–appreciative customer–delighted customer–Invincible Customer Service.

Table 12.2 Growing Customer Satisfaction

Customer Level	Perception of Customer Service Received	Expectation of Customer Service	Customer Satisfaction	Description of Customer Satisfaction
I	0	40	(40)	Lost
I	20	40	(20)	Dissatisfied
I	60	40	20	Satisfied
I	80	40	40	Appreciative
I	100	40	60	Delighted
I	130	40	80	Invincible
II	50	90	(40)	Lost
II	70	90	(20)	Dissatisfied
II	110	90	20	Satisfied
II	130	90	40	Appreciative
II	150	90	60	Delighted
II	170	90	80	Invincible
III	100	140	(40)	Lost
III	130	140	(20)	Dissatisfied
III	160	140	20	Satisfied
III	180	140	40	Appreciative
III	200	140	60	Delighted
III	220	140	80	Invincible

Laying a Customer Satisfaction Foundation

The foundation for customer satisfaction must be laid by leadership. Leadership must adopt a customer satisfaction culture and define the organization's Model of Success and motivation to include the customer point of view. Leadership must be certain that everyone in the organization understands the answers to the following three key questions:

1. Who is the customer?
2. What does the customer want?
3. How do we increase customer satisfaction?

In many companies, there is disagreement over who is the customer. If you are a brewery who sells through a distributor organization, who is your customer: the distributor, the retailer, or the person who drinks the beer? If you are a pharmaceutical firm that sells controlled drugs, who is your customer: the wholesaler, the doctor, the pharmacist, or the person in need of your product? If you produce baby food, who is your customer: the wholesaler, the retailer, the parents, or the baby? In each of these situations, the answer is yes. All of the people mentioned are customers, and they are the ones who define customer service.

At the same time, the question "who is the customer?" is answered by many as the "king" or the "boss." The attitude here is that "the customer is always right." This "customer-driven" attitude is dangerous. Your customer is not always right, is not the king, and certainly is not the boss. There have been many "customer-driven" organizations that believed the customer was always right as the organization went bankrupt pleasing the customer.

A better way to think about the customer is that the customer is your mother (or the memory of your mother). With this attitude, service does not stem from a platform of weakness or submissiveness, but from a platform of honor, respect, and love. Despite the fact that your mother isn't always right, you always are interested in her best interests because without your mother (customer), you would not exist.

The second question, "what does the customer want?" can be answered in several ways. First, as I said in the introduction to this chapter, the customer does not want fluff. Second, the customer wants more features, lower prices, higher quality, and more value-added support. Third, and most accurately, the answer to this question should be "don't ask me, ask the customer." In fact, only when we really understand that it is the customer who answers the question "What does the customer want?" can we tackle the third question, "How do we increase customer satisfaction?"

The answer to the third question is straightforward for an organization in pursuit of Revolution:

1. Leaders define culture, direction, and motivation for increased customer satisfaction.
2. A collaboration process of creating Peak-to-Peak Performance is installed.
3. Organizations listen to customers and then via the collaboration/BCPI process improve the organization's performance to increase customer satisfaction.

The Science of Listening

The greatest challenge to listening is found in the iceberg of listening. The iceberg of listening indicates that only 8 percent of all opportunities to improve customer service are known by upper management, 16 percent by middle management, 32 percent by supervisors, 64 percent by your staff, but 100 percent by your customers. To whom are you going to listen? First and foremost listen to the customer, then respond to and take action based on the customer's input.

How should you listen to your customers? The most popular but the least useful method of listening to your customer is through their complaints. Complaints tell you about problems that should be addressed and about things causing dissatisfaction, but complaints do not tell you anything about improving customer satisfaction.

In addition to complaints not being a source of ideas for creating Peak-to-Peak Performance, they only represent a very small percentage of dissatisfied customers. Most dissatisfied customers will complain to their friends and take their business elsewhere, but they will rarely be outraged enough to go through the process of submitting a complaint.

Customer interviews also tend not to result in an accurate understanding of customer satisfaction. The problem with interviews lies with people being unwilling to truly speak their minds, to commit the time for sharing their thoughts, and wanting to avoid controversy. Therefore, the best approach to listening to the customer is with a customer survey. However, the benefit one receives from a customer survey has a lot to do with the design of the survey. The surveys used by many motels and restaurants are excellent examples of ineffective designs. The only people who complete these cards are customers that either are very satisfied or very unsatisfied. These two groups do not represent the majority of customers and will rarely provide information relevant to creating Peak-to-Peak Performance. The only real benefit from these surveys is in identifying major problems, but that's all. To the contrary, a properly designed survey provides for a clear understanding of the customer's satisfaction with all aspects of your relationship. Some key considerations in the design of a customer survey include the following:

- Keep it simple, straightforward, and short. Your customer's time is valuable. Don't expect them to spend a lot of time on the survey.
- Make most questions multiple choice. This makes it easier for the customer to complete and for you to compile and analyze.
- Always have some open-ended questions. Many great ideas have been obtained from customers.

There are three approaches to disseminating the customer survey. The first approach is the easiest but results in the poorest response rate; it is including the customer survey with the customer order. The second approach is to mail the survey so that it will be received by the customer a few days after the order. This approach results in an improved response rate but requires additional coordination. The best approach from both a customer satisfaction and a response rate perspective is to call the customer a few days after they receive the order and ask them:

1. Were there any problems with the order?
2. Who would be the best person to receive the customer survey?
3. Would this person be willing to complete a customer survey?

Then, send the survey and refer to the telephone conversation. This third approach is recommended and will result in the best feedback from the customer on their satisfaction. Based on the feedback from these customer surveys, teams should be created to address these opportunities. The collaborative response to these opportunities will lead to the improvement of customer satisfaction.

"MAYBERRY BUYS BIGGEST BANK IN TEXAS"

Teamwork drives the Peak-to-Peak Performance process at NationsBank. "I can't think of anything we do that doesn't involve cross-functional teams," says Brinkley. "Teamwork is a value in our company. It is definitely part of our structure." One example is the Acquisitions Team. For every NationsBank acquisition, a team of managers navigates the perils of each acquisition, folding the new operation into the overall corporation. Throughout the team-based process, serving the customer remains the focus of the bank. "The General Bank is concentrating on several primary business objectives," explains Brinkley. "One, we want to increase the retention of our current customers. Two, we want to continue to attract new customers from bank and nonbank competition. Three, we want to broaden and deepen all of our customer relationships." Jim Trigg, Change Management Executive, adds, "The first question we ask ourselves is, 'How do we satisfy customers?' "

To answer this question, NationsBank must find out what their customers want. According to Amy Brinkley, direct input from customers through customer surveys plays a big role. In addition, NationsBank concentrates on what Brinkley calls the "behavior of the customer." The bank examines the type and volume of customer transactions. Follow up research is then done for customers who remained with the bank as well as those who left. Based on this type of information from its customers, NationsBank develops fairly accurate predictive models, helping the bank choose which products or services to introduce or modify. NationsBank uses this type of database modeling to tailor products and services to fit specific customer segments. In the Washington, D.C. area, for example, the bank experimented with special video/telephone banking for customers whose hectic lifestyles don't fit into bankers' hours. In another area, modeling helps the bank consider the location and customized services of their automated teller machines (ATMs), such as allowing customers to print out interim bank statements.

Right now, the Model Banking Program only directly involves the NationsBank General Bank area, which operates full-service banking centers, commercial banks, and business offices. The process of creating Peak-to-Peak Performance, however, touches the bank's Institutional Group and Financial Services area as well. In fact, as Brinkley states, Model Banking "has implications for customers no matter where they are." The team-based process represented by the Model Banking Program allows NationsBank to concentrate on the customer and maintain its leadership role in the banking industry.

The Revolution Toward Invincible Customer Service

What do customers really buy? Customers of Tompkins Associates, Inc. do not buy consulting services; they buy confidence in the solutions implemented. Customers of IBM do not buy hardware or software; they buy solutions to business problems. A TGIFriday's restaurant does not sell food; they sell a good time, a celebration, an opportunity to unwind. At Rubbermaid, it has been discovered that, yes, customers buy quality products, low prices, and product innovation. But these are not the things that allow Rubbermaid to provide invincible customer satisfaction. According to the Vice President of Management Information Systems and Invincible Customer Service (a real title), what retail chains buy from Rubbermaid is quality, prices, innovation, and, most importantly, information about the satisfaction of the ultimate customer—the consumer. It is this information that differentiates Rubbermaid from the competition. What do your customers really buy? Do all your customers buy the same thing? As a starting point to invincible customer satisfaction, understand what your customer buys.

Invincible customer service recognizes that knowledge is service. Information like in the Rubbermaid case, innovative ideas, suggestions that help a customer achieve success, business experience, and technical expertise are all a part of value-added support that leads to invincible customer service.

Interestingly, customer satisfaction is not a surrogate for customer retention. While it may seem logical that increased customer satisfaction will result in increased customer retention, this is not true. Between 65 percent and 85 percent of customers who change suppliers say they were satisfied or very satisfied with their former supplier. In the automobile industry, although satisfaction scores range from 85 percent to 95 percent, repurchase rates average only 40 percent. Companies that provide invincible customer satisfaction know that customer loyalty today is not tied to customer satisfaction as much as it is to the following:

- Consistently delivering invincible service.
- Consistently improving the customer service provided.
- The cumulative impact of many, many successful interactions.
- Ease of working together.

- Loyal relationships between people in the organizations.
- No-hassle problem resolution.

Customer loyalty will be a frequent topic of discussion among firms that wish to provide invincible customer service.

STATE FARM'S INVINCIBLE LOYALTY-BASED SYSTEM

Consider the following statistics:

- State Farm insures more than 20 percent of the nation's households.
- State Farm has the lowest sales and distribution costs among insurance companies of its type.
- State Farm agents' incomes are generally higher than agents working for other insurance companies.
- State Farm has one of the fastest growth rates of any multiple-line insurer.
- State Farm agents remain with the company at a much higher rate than the rest of the industry.
- State Farm agents have a 50 percent higher productivity than industry norms.
- State Farm customer loyalty is reflected in the highest customer retention rates in the industry, in excess of 90 percent.
- How does State Farm achieve such phenomenal results? They say it all has to do with their Loyalty-Based System. They have actually built a system that cultivates loyalty. What is this Loyalty-Based System? Here are a few of its elements:
  1. State Farm agents work from neighborhood offices which allow them to build long-lasting relationships with their customers and to provide personal service.
  2. State Farm agents are rooted in the community and become a part of their customer's family, proudly offering discounts for honor roll performance, and sternly warning young drivers about the responsibilities of driving.
  3. State Farm pricing policies are a magnet for retaining good customers by offering discounts for accident-free customers.

(continued)

4. State Farm agent commissions are designed to encourage long-term relationships. Commission rates are the same for both new and renewal business.
5. State Farm provides a full life-cycle product line giving the agents an advantage in economically servicing multiple-line customers.
6. State Farm agent retention is a result of both a lengthy recruiting and selection process before appointment and because State Farm agents are independent contractors who exclusively sell and service State Farm products.
7. State Farm business systems measure customer retention and defections and are distributed throughout the organization.

The results of the invincible Loyalty-Based System at State Farm is invincible customer service, where State Farm has not only built a super business, but where agents benefit, and most importantly, where customers obtain an outstanding value.

A tool that was used as a sales tool for years has now become an invincible customer service tool. This tool, *customer training*, has undergone significant changes as it has progressed from sales tool to invincible customer satisfaction tool. The traditional sales-tool training consisted of seminars, books, and videos that focused on how to use a supplier's product and why the product was the best product to use. Today, in companies providing invincible customer service, customer training is focused on helping the customer be successful. In many cases, the supplier will not only recommend how to use the product, but will also give guidelines and suggestions on how to reduce costs, increase safety, improve quality, and improve performance. A much more holistic approach is taken to customer education, often with the specific product being sold included only as a secondary consideration.

SMITHKLINE BEECHAM OFFERS BOTH INVINCIBLE CUSTOMER SERVICE AND INVINCIBLE NON-CUSTOMER SERVICE

The animal-health division of Smithkline Beecham has run many educational programs over the years on how to use a specific product to prevent or cure a specific disease. Several beef-packing plants reported problems with meat quality because some cattle vaccines had been incorrectly administered. John Landon, the Smithkline Beecham Marketing Manager for the company's cow/calf products, said "Because we manufactured some of those products, we felt a challenge to train the customer in the proper use of the product so the image of beef wasn't damaged. The producers' livelihood depends on that image and ultimately ours depends on it too."

Therefore, Smithkline Beecham developed an education program that not only helped beef producers administer vaccines properly but also included the value of good facilities, how to ensure animals don't become bruised, how to process cattle with as little stress to the animal as possible, and other practices for working cattle to produce the best end product. The education program was offered throughout the United States and was sponsored by 40 states. The education was flexible in that it consisted of wall charts, videos, slide shows, brochures, and other written materials. The materials could be used in a self-taught mode, a presentation, or a demonstration, where Smithkline sales representatives delivered the seminar while working with live animals. Due to the success of the initial education program, Smithkline has added a second program for producers who raise calves and a third that presents the advantages of communications among various groups in the industry.

The only possibly questionable portion of this educational outreach was Smithkline's decision to not only include customers, but to also include producers who do not use Smithkline products. Smithkline Beecham explains this approach as follows: "Rather than selling a product, we're more interested in selling a solution to a problem over the long term. We aren't interested in a one-time sale." That this approach works is evidenced by what Mike Smith, Director of Animal Health and Education for the Colorado Cattle Feeders Association, states: "Personally, I find that these programs clearly testify to the Smithkline commitment to the beef-cattle industry. It is a bold step to offer this to non-customers, but I think it sets up a win-win situation for the entire industry."

So, although product features, price, quality, and value-added support are important factors, for the most part, with today's sophisticated customer, they are a given. To move beyond good customer service and achieve invincible customer service, we must focus on these factors:

- Understanding what the customer really buys.
- Providing knowledge to our customers.
- Customer loyalty.
- True customer training.

Call to Action

Where has your focus been—on serving your customers or satisfying them? If you really want to be a Revolutionary Organization, you must go beyond customer service. This chapter has provided you with the tools to begin your Customer Satisfaction Revolution. Let me encourage you to apply what you've read by giving you a three-fold path forward:

1. Identify your Customer Tier.
2. Make sure everyone in your organization can answer these three questions:
   A. Who is our customer?
   B. What does our customer want?
   C. How can we increase customer satisfaction?
3. Evaluate and improve the way you listen to your customers.

These three action points will thrust you into the realm of customer satisfaction. But remember, don't just talk about satisfying your customer; actually satisfy them.

13

I Choose You

Revolution Principle #13:

A Revolution must be willing to join forces with other like-minded Revolutions.

The only thing more powerful than a well-executed Revolution is two well-executed Revolutions, both working toward similar goals. It always humors me to hear of some small group who is convinced they can overthrow an entire government. Even if their ambitions are noble—that is, if the government is corrupt and harming the people and they wish to stop the abuse—they are foolish to believe they can start the Revolution themselves.

However, my ears perk up when I hear that a number of different groups are banding together to accomplish similar goals. Instantly, there is greater manpower, greater intelligence, more financial resources, more weaponry, and more diversity. The more groups that band together the greater the reality of accomplishing their Revolutionary ambitions.

The strength that suitable allies foster can rarely be equaled by individual sects, states, or nations. Wise Revolutionaries will always search for like-minded Revolutionaries with whom they can join forces.

The willingness of a Revolutionary force to follow this principle says a lot. A leader who wishes to be a silo of power, who does not wish to share the efforts and the victories with anyone else, and who ultimately believes that their's is the only worthy group, will find this principle repulsive. However, if the leader wants to accomplish the Revolutionary goals of improvement, wants as many people to benefit as possible, and wants there to be total satisfaction among the general population, then this principle will be a foregone conclusion.

The same principles are applied to business. When it comes to Extraorganizational Collaboration, Revolutionary Organizations must not only maintain customer satisfaction, but must be willing to work with other Revolutionary Organizations. If the goal is to satisfy the end-user, not to create silos of power, then partnerships are critical. Think of it: If the links of your supply chain were synthesized, causing one continuous flow of product to the end-user, extending to them as much value as possible, what would that do to your business? There would be greater demand for the product, greater responsiveness to the customer, causing repeat sales, which would benefit each member of the supply chain. I believe that this Supply Chain Synthesis (SCS) will be the *modus operandi* for business in the next century. I am advising business leaders the world over to investigate its opportunities and implement the process now. In this chapter I want to begin to explore partnerships, and I hope you will begin to see your need for them as you pursue Organizational Revolution.

It has been reported that a major corporation provided the following instructions to its purchasing managers:

1. Offer exaggerated growth projections.
2. Establish very early long-term contract rules but do not negotiate in detail.
3. Resist all suggestions that some costs are controllable and others are not.
4. Focus all activity on reducing the immediate price dramatically
5. Destabilize the supplier with repeated meetings and 'urgent' demands for information.

6. Set deadlines for suppliers to meet but increase anxiety by deferring decisions.
7. Tie up the short-term price, but keep nibbling at the "eleventh hour."

These seven guidelines were referred to as "The Purchasing Vise" with which to squeeze their suppliers. Is it surprising that this same company has had a problem with supplier loyalty? Is it surprising that this company has both an internal and external challenge with trust? At the same time, many companies are leveraging and negotiating their way to success on their supplier's backs. The whole Just-In-Time concept has often been twisted and used as a hammer to force suppliers into a "survival of the fittest" contest. Consider these traditional characteristics used by purchasing departments:

- The best way to cut costs is to maximize competition.
- Suppliers are interchangeable.
- Multiple sourcing allows us to maximize our supplier leverage.
- Only share the information required to address the contract on the table and be sure to hold confidential information on product designs and production schedules.
- Maintain relationships at arm's length.
- Pursue short-term contracts to keep the suppliers on their toes and to maximize your flexibility.
- Evaluate all contracts on cost and play suppliers off of each other.

Interestingly, many of these practices have been pursued while pursuing strategic alliances. Is it surprising to you that several studies have reported the failure of strategic alliances? For example, just in the automotive industry, failed alliances include: General Motors and Daewoo Corporation, General Motors and Isuzu Motors, Chrysler and Mitsubishi Motors, Chrysler and Maserati, Fiat and Nissan, to name a few. It is time for a restart, a shift, a new relationship: A Partnership Revolution.

There has been some movement in the partnership direction, but it is not clear if organizations truly understand the magnitude of the challenge. We need partnerships, but as Tom Peters said, "The fact that the rhetoric of partnerships outstrips the reality is really no surprise; not so long ago we didn't even have rhetoric."[1] The Revolution toward partnerships, just like the Revolution from manager to leader, and the Revolution from individual to team, is a fundamental Revolution that must take place for you to be successful into the next century.

Trust Me

For the Revolution from customer/supplier to partners to take place, we must begin with a true understanding of the word *trust.* When most people think of the word trust, they contrast trust against the word distrust. The thought is either you trust or you distrust someone. This is wrong. There are actually three possibilities:

- *Trust*: Assured reliance of, or confidence in, character, ability, and truth.
- *Distrust*: No trust, no assurance, or no confidence.
- *Lack of Trust*: Neither trust nor distrust. A void.

You only trust or distrust someone after repeatedly testing a relationship. While testing the relationship you have a lack of trust. After many positive tests, you develop trust; after many failed tests, you develop distrust. Thus, we see that trust is evolutionary.

Why is trust so important to establishing partnerships? Because from trust relationships grow and prosper. Consider the progression given in Figure 13.1. From trust comes respect. From this respect comes a willingness to really listen to what others are saying. From this listening grows understanding, concern, participation, and then open communications. It is open communications that lead to positive results which act as positive reinforcement for even greater trust. Therefore, without trust, there is no partnership. Neither is there the collective win-win evolution of mutual objectives, mutual strategy, mutual rewards, and mutual sharing of risk that is required to build successful partnerships.

Trust does not occur between companies, but between people. Thus, partnerships require a fundamental Revolution in relationships that occur over time as the trust between people evolves.

Figure 13.1 Trust as a Foundation for the Growth of Relationships

A Partnership Analogy

Just as a relationship between a man and a woman goes through the phases of dating, to going steady, to being engaged, and then to marriage, so too a partnership relationship evolves. The business equivalent of a couple dating is the move to a partnership with the "customer-driven" organization. Shallow sayings like "focus on the customer," "the customer is always right," "the customer comes first," and "the customer is king" is the fluff of customer service and the traditional customer/supplier interactions defined in the introduction to this chapter. In these traditional relationships, there is little real commitment between partners.

A step above dating is going steady. The partnership equivalent of going steady is invincible customer service, and although this is an important step in the beginning of the evolution of a trusting relationship (just like going steady), it is just that, a *beginning*. With invincible customer service, the relationship is stronger than the traditional relationship since there is a genuine participation in the relationship, but the relationship is still a long way from being a successful, long-term partnership. However, to move beyond this relationship, just like the step up from a couple going steady to being engaged, each of the parties must step up their commitment to one another.

The partnership equivalent of being engaged is a cooperative relationship where significant planning for partnership (marriage) occurs. The ultimate commitment of course is the marriage/partnership. Unfortunately, just like happy marriages, sometimes business partnerships result in divorce. One key result of being a Revolutionary Organization, contrary to traditional organizations, is that as long as partnerships are made with other Revolutionary Organizations, divorce will be very rare.

Table 13.1 Relationship Evolution

BETWEEN A MAN AND A WOMAN	BETWEEN PEOPLE WITHIN TWO ORGANIZATIONS
Dating	Customer-Driven Organization
Going Steady	Invincible Customer Service
Being Engaged	Cooperative Relationship Planning for Partnership
Marriage	Partnership

Although it is obvious, many organizations have not understood that, just as it takes two to be married, it takes two to create a partnership. Therefore, in each relationship we must have a supplier who is ready for partnership and a customer who is ready for partnership. An important thing to reflect on here is that every organization is the customer to some organizations and the supplier to others. So, each organization has first-hand experience in playing on both sides of potential partnership relationships. We want to learn about our fitness for partnering by understanding how we partner as a supplier and how we partner as a customer.

Japan Does 'em Right

Although I generally turn off when people start in on the "Japan is great" rhetoric, there is no better illustration of partnerships than the partnerships in Japan. In fact, consider the following quotation from the Japanese Ministry of International Trade and Industry (MITI):

> "(The) Japanese manufacturing industry owes its competitive advantage and strength to its subcontracting structure."[2]

In a study of Japan's competitive advantage by Dyer and Ouchi, they conclude that:

> "Evidence from an increasing number of industries and sources suggests that much of Japanese success can be attributed to Japanese-style business partnerships."[3]

In another study by Clark and Fujimoto, on the role of Japanese-style business partnerships during product development, they concluded that:

> "In U.S. companies, the projects in our sample were heavily influenced by the traditional system in which suppliers produced parts under short-term, arm's-length contracts and had little role in design and engineering. In the Japanese system, in contrast, suppliers are an integral part of the development process: they are involved early, assume significant responsibility, and communicate extensively and directly with product and process engineers."[4]

So, what is a Japanese-style business partnership? A Japanese-style business partnership is an exclusive supplier/customer relationship that focuses on maximizing the efficiency of the entire business system. The goal of these partnerships is to maximize quality while minimizing the total cost. The partners work to create a "see-through" business system where both partners can see costs, problems, and opportunities. Then, both partners can work together for creating Peak-to-Peak Performance. The Japanese-style business partnerships attempt to capture the synergies that would exist if the two organizations were combined under common ownership. The key characteristics of Japanese-style business partnerships include the following:

- Long-term relationships
- Frequent communications
- Mutual cooperation on creating Peak-to-Peak Performance
- Willingness to invest in the future of the partnership
- In-depth and regular sharing of technical and cost information
- Trust-building practices like owning stock, transferring employees, and flexible legal contracts
- Fewer suppliers handling more work
- Elimination of waste and true Just-In-Time

So, what can we learn from these Japanese-style business partnerships and what should be the characteristics of any Revolutionary Partnership? These characteristics of a Revolutionary Partnership are:

- The partners reject the notion that business relationships should be based on antagonism, leveraging, hammering, and negotiating.
- The partners believe in long-term relationships based on trust and a true understanding of their partner's business.
- The partners believe in the sharing of information, planning, scheduling, risk, rewards, problems, solutions, and opportunities for creating Peak-to-Peak Performance.
- The partners believe in working together toward improved performance on quality, lead times, new product development time, inventories, waste, and costs.
- The partners believe in building on each other's strengths, increasing their partner's business, and investing in the long-term partnership relationship. Due to this commitment, the partners will deal with fewer and fewer suppliers.
- The partners believe in the integration of systems and the interdependence of their organizations while still retaining their individual identities to assure innovation and creativity.
- The partners believe in frequent communications at all levels of the organization and in frequent, structured interaction on creating Peak-to-Peak Performance. Partnership proximity is, therefore, important, and will be mutually addressed.
- The partners believe in getting their partners involved early in any new innovations and working with their partners with the utmost flexibility to assure the best overall performance of the partnership.

An issue that confuses some in the discussion of Revolutionary Partnerships is that they seem to believe that this discussion only holds when dealing up the supply chain to the level below the ultimate consumer. The belief is that Revolutionary Partnerships do not include the ultimate consumer. However, to the contrary, although there will be some differences, there are many examples where a Revolutionary Partnership is formed directly with the consumer. Coke does this with their Customer Advisory Board, and Apple with their User Groups. The Lotus spreadsheet was developed when an MIT student found he couldn't use existing spreadsheets. The luggage carriers with wheels and handles that fit in airplane compartments were an idea that came from a pilot who just couldn't find any luggage that fit his needs. Mountain bikes were created by Californians who could not find bikes designed for their trails and who created the first mountain bikes by putting together components to create their own bikes. These kinds of stories are repeated over and over again.

CAUTION: IT ISN'T CLEAR THAT MOVING FORWARD IS ALWAYS GOOD

Packaged-goods manufacturers have for years wooed consumers through product innovation and advertising. This built brand-awareness and thus pleased retailers by increasing sales. Packaged-good manufacturers treated the retailers as a necessary evil and would often say with pride, "We do not sell to the retailers but through the retailers." Now, however, under the banner of partnerships, the large retail chains are trying to gain a competitive advantage by changing their relationship with manufacturers. The large retailers are demanding lower prices, better service, and customized promotions. The packaged-goods manufacturers are responding, but, in order to meet the demands, they are making major cuts in their consumer-related and advertising budgets. The pendulum has shifted to manufacturers thinking "We do not sell to consumers but to retailers."

This has cut costs, but at what cost? Many believe the loss of focus on the consumer will squelch innovation and ignore consumer needs. This leads to all brands being equal, a growth in private labels, and further pressure from the retailers for the manufacturers to cut costs. Is this a partnership? No. Is this good for the packaged-goods manufacturers? No. Is this good for the consumer? No. Is this good for the large retailers? Some say yes, some say no; time will tell. Nevertheless, it is important to realize that what is called a partnership is not always a partnership, and that what is said to be moving forward is not always good.

Revolutionary Partnerships, then, are long-term collaborative relationships based upon trust and a mutual desire to work together for the benefit of the other partner and the partnership. Revolutionary Partnerships play a key role in Organizational Revolution in general and should be pursued as soon as an organization is worthy of partnering.

Partnerships = Extraorganizational Collaboration

The best way to think about the process of creating Revolutionary Partnerships is to realize that a Revolutionary Partnership is the successful application of the collaborative process between organizations; it is *extraorganizational collaboration.* In fact, the objective of creating Revolutionary Partnerships is to create the same synergy between organizations as you create within your company through *intraorganizational collaboration.* Therefore, the process that was followed to shift an organization from individuals to teams may be used as a guide to shift two organizations from supplier/customer to partners.

Prerequisites to beginning the process of creating extraorganizational collaboration are that the individual organizations have already shifted from management to leadership and from individuals to teams. Once this has occurred, then the organizations must begin the customer/supplier to partner Revolution by throwing off the traditional customer/supplier, win/lose mind-set and adopting a win/win mind-set. The difficulty of throwing off the win/lose mind-set is at the root of most broken relationships. With the win/lose mind-set, each party is afraid the other party will gain an upper hand if they cooperate in good faith. Since they believe in win/lose, it's clear that if the other party wins, then they must lose. Unfortunately, since there is no cooperation, there is no winning for either party and in fact there is no partnership.

An evaluation of the payoff matrices given in Table 13.2 provides an interesting insight into the win/lose mind-set. In Table 13.2(a), Party A indicates that from their perspective, when either both parties cooperate or both parties don't cooperate, there is no win/lose. So although both cooperating results in a higher payoff to A (60) than both not cooperating (50), this increase is not nearly as significant as the loss incurred if Party A cooperated and Party B did not (down to 30), (win for B and a lose for A). In fact, the only big win (80) is if Party A did not cooperate and Party B did cooperate, (a win for A and a lose for B).

Table 13.2 Payoff Matrices Given a Win/Lose Mind-set

Payoff Matrix for Party A

		PARTY B:	
		Cooperate	Not Cooperate
PARTY A:	Cooperate	60	30
	Not Cooperate	80	50

Payoff Matrix for Party B

		PARTY B:	
		Cooperate	Not Cooperate
PARTY A:	Cooperate	60	80
	Not Cooperate	30	50

It is clear that the win/lose mind-set predefines anyone who cooperates as a person asking to lose. To the contrary, Table 13.3 illustrates the payoffs that exist under a win/win mind-set. For both Parties A and B, there is a loss involved when the two parties do not act in unison. Interestingly, the loss is typically still perceived as greater if you cooperate and the other party does not, than vice versa. Nevertheless, both parties are better off if you agree to not cooperate together, or much, much better off if you both cooperate. Some suggest that if you agree to *not* cooperate together you are in fact cooperating. This is true, and such are the positive thoughts you adopt with a win/win mind-set.

Table 13.3 Payoff Matrices Given a Win/Win Mind-set

Payoff Matrix for Party A

		PARTY B:	
		Cooperate	Not Cooperate
PARTY A:	Cooperate	100	30
	Not Cooperate	40	50

(continued)

Payoff Matrix for Party B

		PARTY B:	
		Cooperate	Not Cooperate
PARTY A:	Cooperate	100	40
	Not Cooperate	30	50

The win/win mind-set, when fully embraced, results in powerful relationships. A win/win mind-set supplier realizes that their growth opportunity lies in the growth of their customers. As their customers grow, so do their suppliers. Therefore, in a win/win mind-set relationship, the supplier is totally focused on the success of their customers, since it is only by their customer's achieving success that they may also succeed. The supplier will do whatever they can to bring about the success of their customers. This is at the core of a Revolutionary Partnership.

The Partner Search

Once your organization has shifted from management to leadership, shifted from individuals to teams, and adopted a win/win mind-set, then you are ready to identify potential Revolutionary Partners. Identification of potential partners can be done by the customer looking at their suppliers or by the suppliers looking at their customers. In either case, the identification of potential partners should not be based upon the sales volumes achieved in the past or projected for the future. The identification of potential partners should be based upon the opportunity for additional contributions to profit over a five-year planning horizon. Contributions to profit may be obtained by either increasing revenues or reducing costs. Factors that come into play in a potential partner's ability to contribute to additional profits include the following:

- Quality of leadership
- Quality of collaboration process
- Understanding of partnerships
- Focus on quality
- Level of innovativeness
- Understanding of time compression

- Volume of present and potential business
- Acceptance of change
- Stability of personnel
- Technical competence and creativity
- Level of information systems
- Geographical location/responsiveness
- Honesty, ethics, and trust
- Organizational consistency
- Level of distribution expertise
- Understanding of Just-In-Time philosophy
- Openness of communications
- A win/win mind-set
- Flexibility
- Desire for creating peak-to-peak performance
- Focus on value
- Product design skills
- Profitability
- Attitude towards growth
- Clarity and timeliness of decision/investment process
- Performance track record
- Willingness to experiment/take risks
- History of organizational learning
- Willingness to accept feedback
- Cultural fit
- Quality and accuracy of cost information
- Ability to run/participate in effective outreach
- Industry reputation
- Awareness of competition

These factors should be evaluated and a preliminary list of potential partners should be generated. This list of potential partners should be further refined by conducting an on-site visit with the potential partner. This visit should be positioned with the potential partner as an informal get together to understand more fully the relationship and to review future opportunities. This visit should not be positioned as the first step toward partnering. Many visits will result in decisions not to pursue a partnership and thus, not labeling the partnership concept at the outset will minimize the disruption with suppliers where it is best to retain a traditional relationship. Additionally, announcing the potential for the creation of a partnership up-front may very well scare off good potential partners much the same way that a young man would scare off a young lady if he began talking about marriage on the first date.

The on-site visit should include a plant tour, some relationship building, and a lot of discussion on the following types of issues:

- What are the keys to your success?
- Why do customers select your product?
- What changes do you see in your business?
- What do you see in the future that will change your business?
- What are you doing now to prepare for the future?
- What are the greatest opportunities for improvement?
- What is the one thing that if you could change you would like to change?
- What can we do to help you?
- What can we do to make our relationship easier?
- What can we do together to reduce costs?
- What are the cost drivers?
- What can we do together to increase revenues?
- What can we do together to increase margins?
- What can we do for each other to increase profits?
- What can we do for each other to enhance growth?

The results of some of these on-site meetings will be joint projects. The on-site meetings that do not net joint projects should not be forced to the next level of partnership. Allow these relationships to evolve at a pace with which both parties are comfortable. The on-site meetings that result in some joint projects should still be considered as potential candidates for partnership.

Every effort should be made to pursue these joint efforts while demonstrating trust, openness, and a win/win mind-set. It is important to realize that much like the Forming/Storming/Norming/Performing/ and Maturation phases of team development, the same evolution of a partnership will take place for many of the same reasons. Many successful meetings, interactions, and projects will need to take place before a relationship evolves to a partnership. Especially early in the process, the focus should be on building trust, clear communications, and creating peak-to-peak performance.

As relationships between individuals evolve, so too should the level of interaction between the potential partners. This escalation of trust, openness, and success will naturally lead to the sharing of Models of Success and strategic business plans.

Once a win/win mutual mind-set has been adopted by both parties, a Partnership Workshop should be developed. The purpose of the Partnership Workshop is to officially establish a Cooperative Relationship. The Partnership Workshop should be held off-site and should include leadership from both companies as well as the people most closely involved with the successful joint projects. The agenda for the off-site workshop should include time to share experiences, successes, and failures; to build a relationship; to establish a letter of intent for a cooperative relationship; and to establish a mutual plan toward partnership. The elements of the Cooperative Relationship Mutual Plan should include these points:

- Mutual objectives for business levels
- Mutual objectives for cost reduction
- Mutual strategies to achieve mutual objectives
- Mutual agreement on how to share risks and rewards
- Mutual agreement on a time frame for the evolution of the partnership
- Mutual agreement on the process of evolving to partnership
- Mutual agreement on the priorities to be pursued, the teams to address these priorities, and the charters of these teams
- Mutual agreement on the communications to take place between meetings and the schedule for meetings
- Mutual agreement on how to share information about the Cooperative Relationship both inside and outside of the company
- Mutual agreement on confidentiality and restrictions on business relations

The purpose of these mutual understandings is to ensure no surprises and a comfort level with what is not a natural relationship for many business people. The Cooperative Relationship should then be pursued as the relationship evolves. As this evolution occurs, many of the collaboration lessons explained earlier will be applicable.

The teams consisting of members from each of the partners will develop their own identity. The identity of suppliers/customers will become blurred, and first individuals, then teams, and then entire companies will become partners. The supplier/customer distinctions will disappear and the partners will act like one to improve, grow, and prosper while still maintaining their own corporate identities.

Figure 13.2 illustrates the process explained in this section. Please keep in mind that it is not the process but the people who make this work.

Figure 13.2 Creating a Revolutionary Partnership

PARTNERSHIPS: WINNING RELATIONSHIPS FOR PENNY PARTS AS WELL AS $300 MILLION FACILITIES

Ford Motor Company was facing the design/construction/commissioning of one of the largest automotive paint-finishing plants in the world. The 730,000 square foot, 75 car-per-hour, paint-finishing plant was to be attached to Ford's Oakville, Canada, assembly plant. This $300 million facility was to utilize leading-edge, paint-finishing technology while being built for 25 percent to 30 percent less investment than similar operations. In addition, Ford had a tight timeline and a need to significantly improve paint-finishing quality while addressing several difficult environmental challenges. Sound like an impossible task? Well, it was, and if a traditional approach had been adopted, success would not have occurred. Nevertheless, success was achieved and it all had to do with partnerships.

ABB was formed by the merger of the Swedish ASEA and the Swiss company Brown Boveri. ABB, with a market value of $11 billion, is a global electric company whose portfolio of expertise includes power generation, power transmission, power distribution, mass transportation, environmental controls, and industrial process optimization. In the mid-1980s, ABB made a commitment to pursue business with automotive companies in the design, manufacture, and commissioning of automotive paint-finishing facilities. It pursued this commitment by acquiring small companies, recruiting experienced engineers, developing and demonstrating a partnership model, and forming a construction project management partnership with Fluor Daniel. As Ford reviewed their situation, they decided to pursue a partnership with ABB/Fluor Daniel to achieve their objectives. At the core of this partnership was a deferred fixed-price contract that consisted of the following three phases:

PHASE ONE: The design of a process to establish the price and scope of the facility, the definition of a base price of 90 percent of the original ABB bid, and the exact makeup of this price. Agreement that after Phase Two each party had the right of withdrawal.

PHASE TWO: A cooperative engineering effort whereby a final scope and design was established. The sharing of the savings from the base price. The mutual improvement, innovation, and cost reduction of the facility.

PHASE THREE: The contracting for a fixed definition and cost project. ABB presented a bid for 75 percent of the original bid and Ford accepted this contract.

(continued)

The results were very, very good. Ford accomplished all of their objectives, and ABB/Fluor Daniel were able to achieve their desired profit at a significantly lower level of risk. The facility was implemented on time, at budget, and achieved all design objectives. The most interesting part of this effort lies in the Ford/ABB/Fluor Daniel relationships. Consider the following quotations from an article on these relationships:

> "ABB/Fluor Daniel and Ford managed to create a new way to conduct their business that resulted in a genuine win-win outcome."
>
> "Both the Ford/ABB and the ABB/Fluor Daniel relationships were dependent on trust."
>
> "Beyond the apparent need for a cooperative relationship, the companies created the necessary trust as a result of the process they employed for working together. They formed a governance structure that brought about repeated encounters: they used the passage of time to their advantage; they created open and simple structures for sharing financial benefits."
>
> "Only sustained relationships allow time for cross-fertilization, the compression of total project time, and the achievement of exceptionally tight schedules."
>
> "By establishing a well-defined means for dividing mutual gain, all parties were able to focus their attention on how to create that gain rather than on the distractions of claiming those gains before they were even created."
>
> "Purchasing focused more on acquiring a system rather than on acquiring component parts; more on minimizing total cost than on minimizing elemental costs; more on capturing process knowledge than on just buying hardware; more on developing meaningful relationships with a few suppliers than on enlarging the supplier base."[5]

The partnership lessons that follow from the win-win-win Ford/ABB/Fluor Daniel relationships that may be applied to all partnerships include the following:

- Acknowledge, respect, and utilize mutual strengths.
- Maintain a broad perspective and a view of the big picture.
- Use time as an ally. Do not force a contract until all factors have been resolved; mutually minimize risks.

- Structure the process of interaction around a succession of transactions. This builds trust.
- Do not negotiate price. This is a win/lose process. Establish a process that allows the development of price in a win/win context.

These lessons are applicable for partnerships buying penny screws as well as $300 million facilities. Do not overlook the potential for partnerships in any relationship. Partnerships work for all parties and are at the core of Revolutionary Organizations.

Call to Action

The synergy and benefits that result from partnerships are great. A Revolutionary Organization cannot be an island unto itself and can only be Revolutionary by partnering with other Revolutionaries. How is your organization handling partnerships? Are you an island trying to squeeze your supply chain? If so, your success can only be short-lived. To achieve long, robust success you must be a Revolutionary Partner and have Revolutionary Partnerships. Make partnerships a part of your Revolution, and enjoy the results.

14

Beginning Your Partnership Revolution

Revolution Principle #14:

A Revolution must understand the nature of a true ally relationship and be able to function within it.

I introduced the previous chapter by stating that nothing is more powerful that two Revolutionary forces working toward similar goals. That is not totally true. Actually, nothing is more powerful than two Revolutionary forces who understand *how* to work together to achieve similar goals. That is the kind of Revolution that will succeed!

I once again think of the Computer Revolution. If you think about it closely, the world was taken by two Revolutionary forces: a hardware Revolution and a software Revolution. They had the same goals, sought to reach the same people, engaged in the same learning, but were two (now hundreds on each side) totally different products, and in most cases were advanced by different companies. If we really want to get technical we could identify literally dozens of separate elements to the Computer Revolution, for example printers, monitors, accessories, computer desks, Internet providers, floppy and zip disk manufacturers, computer projectors, computer paper, and so on. Each represent a separate element in the computer world, but were all a vital part of the one Computer Revolution. When we look back on it now, we don't call it the printer Revolution, the floppy disk Revolution, or the paper Revolution; we call it the Computer Revolution. Wow! What strategy! What brilliance! This is how Extraorganizational Collaboration needs to work. However, it isn't easy. To achieve this kind of success, allies must know how to function as allies for the good of the whole.

This principle has tremendous application for your business. Do you know how to develop a partnership? Once you have a partner, do you know how to successfully function as a partner? Do you know how to position the end-user as central in the supply chain? In this chapter I will answer these and many other critical partnership questions. I hope they help you establish a Revolutionary Partnership!

Overcoming Partnership Paradigms

I said earlier that "Possibly the largest challenge in creating a successful collaboration-based organization is overcoming the existing paradigms of teams." Similarly, the largest challenge in creating successful partnerships is overcoming the existing paradigms of partnerships. In the same manner that people throw around the words consortium, acquisition, merger, strategic alliance, and joint ventures, the word partnership is used to describe many different relationships. Some of these relationships have merit and some do not. Some of these relationships work and some do not. Some of these relationships are pursued with sincerity and openness and others are just the use of the word partnership to gain some competitive advantage. Just as "Just-In-Time" has often been twisted and used as a hammer to force suppliers into a "survival of the fittest contest," so too with partnerships.

There are many documented cases where companies have used the partnership rhetoric to gain advantage over a supplier. This is why the use of the words collaboration and empowerment must be used when using the word partnership. It is critical that you not only know what you mean by the word partnership, but also that the people to whom you speak have the same understanding of the word partnership. From this perspective, it is important to understand these concepts:

- A relationship between similar companies in the same type of business who ban together to pool their resources to do research, evaluate technology, or lobby for a political position, is not a partnership. This is a *consortium.*
- A relationship between two companies where the companies lose their independence by becoming one corporate entity is not a partnership. This vertical integration is either an *acquisition* or a *merger.*
- A relationship between two companies where the companies work together to pursue a specific, single-focused business objective is not a partnership. This is a *strategic alliance.*
- A relationship between two companies where the companies form a separate entity with joint ownership to pursue a specific business objective is not a partnership. This is a *joint venture.*
- A true partnership is a long-term relationship based upon trust and a mutual desire to work together for the benefit of the other partner and the partnership.

When the Sum of Eight I's Equals One WE

In an excellent July–August 1994 *Harvard Business Review* study of relationships, Rosabeth Moss Kanter presents the following eight I's as criteria for achieving true partnerships:

- **Individual Excellence:** A win/win mentality exists between two strong partners who have something of value to contribute and gain from the partnership.
- **Importance:** The partners believe the relationship is important for their mutual long-term success and therefore they are each committed to the success of the partnership.
- **Interdependence:** The partners need each other. Neither can do alone what the two of them can do together.
- **Investment:** Both partners demonstrate their long-term commitment by devoting significant resources to the partnership.

(continued)

- **Information:** Communications are open. Partners share information with full confidence in the confidentiality and security of that which is shared.
- **Integration:** The partners develop linkages that integrate their businesses and minimize the difficulties with information and materials flowing across boundaries.
- **Institutionalization:** The relationship is formally recognized and broadly understood. The partnership encompasses all aspects of the partner's business and cannot be ended on a whim.
- **Integrity:** The partners work like a team with a focus on the continual escalation of trust. The partners honor both the spirit and the law of the relationship and practice the golden rule.[1]

Developing a Partnership

In Chapter 13, the evolution of a partnership was likened to the evolution of a relationship between a couple dating, going steady, becoming engaged, and getting married. This analogy can also be expanded to illustrate these points:

- No two relationships ever evolve in the same manner.
- The evolution of a relationship is not a cold-blooded business negotiation, but a comfortable, personal relationship between individuals.
- There exists a positive chemistry between the two halves of the relationship.
- Just as with a romance, the evolution involves the hopes, dreams, and anticipation of what the future may hold.
- A certain way to kill a relationship (either between organizations or couples) is to get third parties (lawyers, accountants, bankers, mothers-in-law, brothers-in-law, etc.) intimately involved with the evolution of the relationship.
- A key to a long-term relationship is the basic compatibility of the parties. People or organizations that come from drastically different backgrounds, that have drastically different values, or that have drastically different goals, will not be able to provide a basis for a positive long-term relationship.

- For a relationship to work, each party in the relationship must both know themselves and what they are looking for in the relationship.
- The relationship has at its very foundation the well-being of the other party as well as the relationship between the parties.
- For a relationship to progress to a successful marriage/partnership, there must not only be an acceptance by the primary parties, but the people around these parties must also accept the evolution of the relationship. With a couple, the people around the relationship may include family and friends. With two organizations, the people around the relationship may include the subordinates, stockholders, government, and other parties.
- Each party in the evolving relationship must have shared expectations of how and when the relationship will evolve. There will be no major surprises.

During the 'dating phase,' the relationship between two organizations is very traditional. The fluff of customer service is the foundation of the relationship. A typical commitment between the two organizations at this level of evolution includes the following:

- A well-defined customer quality standard.
- Quarterly review meetings between purchasing and customer service.
- Annually scheduling meetings to negotiate price and understand schedule.
- Sharing of their organization's Models of Success.

The step above the dating relationship is 'going steady,' and from an organizational relationship perspective, this is equivalent to the invincible customer service relationship. This participative relationship is the beginning of the mutual commitment between the parties in the relationship. A typical commitment between the two organizations at this level of evolution involves the following:

- The adoption of a win/win mind-set.
- A well-defined and jointly-defined quality standard.
- Monthly review meetings between purchasing and customer service.

- Semi-annual scheduling and price review meetings.
- Sharing of their organization's Models of Success, strategic business plans, and improvement initiatives.
- Annual leadership interaction.
- Annual review of business plans, forecasts, and new product plans.
- Sharing of each other's distribution requirements.
- For organizations where a partnership is viable, conducting a Partnership Workshop to further the relationship and to develop a letter of intent for a cooperative relationship and a mutual plan toward partnership.

The step above going steady is 'becoming engaged.' From an organizational relationship perspective this is equivalent to the cooperative relationship defined earlier in Chapter 14. This cooperative relationship is a significant step up in the organization's commitment and, like an engagement, indicates the intention to be married (partnership) at some future time. This level of commitment is made public and is treated with a much greater level of seriousness. This is often the point in a relationship where difficulties surface. Because there is now an awareness of the intention to be married (become partners), there are many people who step forward to speak against and, yes, even sabotage the relationship. It is important for the principal parties to remain true to their commitment, even as others voice their questions and concerns about the relationship. It is during the cooperative relationship phase where the mutual understandings of the partnership are pursued. Typical activities that occur during the cooperative relationship phase include these activities:

- The adoption of mutual improvement initiatives for all existing products.
- A mutual quality improvement process.
- Real-time review meetings between purchasing and customer service.
- Monthly scheduling and price review meetings.
- Monthly cooperative relationship progress assessments and interactions.
- Semi-annual leadership visits.
- Semi-annual review of business plans, forecasts, and new product plans.

- Joint pursuit of distribution improvements.
- Annual engineering reviews of product plans and product improvements.
- One-way Electronic Data Interchange (EDI).

The ultimate relationship is the marriage (partnership) where the parties agree to a long-term, mutually beneficial relationship. This relationship should maintain some mutually agreed to flexibility, but should nevertheless be a binding, lasting relationship that can only be ended by going through a formal divorce (dissolution of the partnership). Parties need to be aware of the fact that just as in a new marriage, the early days of a new partnership require considerable patience and understanding. Just like newlyweds, once the celebration is over, the reality of marriage sets in. As more and more people from the two organizations participate in the partnership, the positive relationships established to date may be challenged because of these factors:

- Many people within the organizations have not been involved with the partner, so although some people have developed close ties, others have no ties and so they question the relationship.
- Many people are not comfortable working with people outside of their organization, and so even though they have heard about partnering, they are not personally comfortable with the relationship.
- Many people will have a full list of internal organizational challenges and well-defined internal organizational performance criteria that do not involve the partner. So, although they may buy into the concept, they do not have adequate time to become involved with their partners.
- Some people within the organizations might not support the partnership and so openly resist being forced to participate.
- The organizations have different cultures, which sours the relationship due to differences in decision-making style, timing, documentation levels of authority, and so forth.
- Although leadership has adopted a win/win mind-set, there still exist people within the organization that have a win/lose mind-set.

- Although the cooperative relationship letter of intent was ratified, there has not been a clear understanding established over money. Leadership understands the need for flexibility depending upon the issue at hand, but others in the organizations do not understand this and confrontations over money take place.
- The organizations have different economic analysis and justification criteria and they both believe that their criteria is best. Recommendations get lost in financial confusion and frustration and resignation result.

Leadership must anticipate these challenges in their Partnership Revolution and provide an abundance of open communications to resolve these issues as they arise. After three or four months, communications should be very frequent. Typical activities that should be put in place to assure the health and evolution of the partnership include the following:

- The adoption of a mutual Peak-to-Peak Performance effort for all existing and future products.
- A real-time joint quality improvement process.
- Real-time production requirements via two-way EDI.
- Joint price setting and cost reduction goals as a result of the ongoing joint Peak-to-Peak Performance process.
- Quarterly leadership site visits to ensure partnership success.
- Quarterly review of business plans, forecasts, and new product plans.
- Joint responsibility for distribution.
- Semi-annual engineering review of product plans and product improvement.
- Annual partnership strategic retreat.

Efficient Consumer Response: A Partnership Mandate

The grocery industry consists of manufacturers who sell to wholesalers who sell to retailers who sell to consumers. The evolution over the last twenty years of how the manufacturers, wholesalers, and retailers worked together to please the customer has resulted in some very poor business practices.

At the heart of the problem in the grocery industry are the non-integrated logistics practices that have evolved. The manufacturers have taken to a never-ending promotion of their products. These promotions are done in an attempt to push products during slow seasons. To justify these promotions, the manufacturers and wholesalers called this practice *forward buying, strategic purchasing,* or *promotional selling.* What happens is the manufacturers create a super price for quantity purchases a couple of times a year, and the wholesalers load up. The wholesalers build or rent facilities to hold all this inventory and obviously won't buy more until they unload this excess inventory to the retailers and the next deal comes along. Interestingly, while waiting for the next deal, many wholesalers back-order items to the retailer which results in the retailer being out-of-stock.

Not surprisingly, the manufacturers find themselves building large inventories awaiting the announcement of the next deal. All this occurs while encountering a massive build-up in the number of items being offered. So, what happens is the manufacturer has inconstant demand as they push inventory onto the wholesalers. This inconsistency results in inefficiency and waste in their distribution of an ever-increasing number of products.

At the same time, wholesalers come to depend on the forward-buying for their profit margin, so they too built large warehouses to hold erratic ebbs and flows of ever-increasing numbers of items. The result of this practice is that the retailers have to pay more for poor service which results in them over-charging and under-servicing their customers. Then, as if this wasn't a big enough mess, the manufacturers start working promotions directly with consumers in an attempt to pull goods from the retailers who are being supplied from a wholesaler who was being pushed goods from the manufacturer.

The ultimate in stupidity results when the manufacturer pays for advertising for consumers who come to stores to buy products that are out of stock, even though the distribution costs from manufacturer and wholesaler are excessively high.

What is wrong with this picture? Well, what we have here is not a lack of synergy, but *anti-synergy*. Think about anti-synergy like this:

- *Synergy* says two plus two is six.
- *Lack-of-synergy* says two plus two is four.
- *Anti-synergy* says two plus two is zero.

The interesting thing is that everyone saw and understood this anti-synergy. The manufacturer was afraid to change because if they stopped doing deals and their competition did not, they would lose business. The wholesaler was afraid to change because the majority of their profit came from forward-buying. The retailers did not really have a choice, and so they lived with the situation and continued to over-charge and under-service the consumer. This is how it was, until the mass merchandise clubs and super-centers changed the game—until Wal-Mart, K-Mart, and others rang a loud and clear wake-up call.

The grocery industry has banded together to balance the benefits of replenishment and promotion, eliminate waste in distribution, increase consumer value, and work together as partners. The banner under which they are resolving the problems of the last 20 years is Efficient Consumer Response (ECR). ECR is defined as a grocery-industry strategy in which manufacturers and wholesalers are committed to working together to bring about better value to the grocery consumer. ECR obtains results by having the customer and supplier jointly focusing on the efficiency of the total grocery supply system, rather than the efficiency of individual components. ECR reduces total system costs while improving the consumer's choice of high quality, fresh grocery products. The ultimate goal of ECR is a responsive, synthesized supply chain in which manufacturers and wholesalers work together as partners to maximize consumer satisfaction at a minimal systems cost. Interestingly, the four core initiatives of ECR include these points:

- *Continuous Replenishment Inventory Systems*: The capturing of Point-Of-Sale (POS) data and the transmission of this data on a daily basis via Electronic Data Interchange (EDI) to the wholesaler to bring supply in-line with demand.
- *Flow-Through Distribution Systems*: The increased efficiency of handling products from the manufacturers to the wholesalers and to the retailers. Transportation and warehouse management systems to eliminate waste and speed the product flow through distribution.
- *Pipeline Logistics Organizations*: The creation of more integrated manufacturing organizations, wholesaler and retailer organizations, and the adoption of a broader total supply chain view.
- *Pipeline Performance Measures*: The development of performance measures that focus on costs and service across the supply chain and the application of management techniques that take into account the total supply chain performance.

Now this all sounds fine, but is ECR missing something? Here are a few thoughts from around the grocery industry:

> "One stumbling block is that many wholesalers and retailers question the motives of manufacturers in pushing ECR."

> "Mentally, wholesalers and retailers need to come to grips with being partners more than they have historically."

> "We are having a terrible time getting ECR down through the system. Everybody talks fine at industry meetings. But when we get back home and talk to manufacturer's reps, they don't know what we are talking about."

> "The industry has studied the retailer backward and forward on stores and distribution. We hear we are inefficient, but we don't know about the manufacturer's efficiency. This lack of trust on allowances can destroy ECR before it starts. How about a study of the manufacturers?"

> "I read in the *Wall Street Journal* that manufacturers who have moved to continuous replenishment are posting earnings up 15% and 20%, but then I pick up *Supermarket News* to find that supermarkets are just making ends meet. Something's not right."

> "ECR is about creating a true system of teamwork through alliances among grocery industry trading partners. But who, I wonder, makes the first move? Manufacturers? Retailers? Or wholesalers?"

> "Even if we buy the idea that we are going to create a system of teamwork through alliances among grocery industry trading partners, the question is, do I give up my margin? Do you give up your margin? Or do we both give up some of our margin?"

> "The problem of getting it done is leadership. The technology is easy, the culture is hard. Without leadership, this cannot be done. ECR comes with obstacles and pain."

> "The primary challenge is not big investments in technology, like EDI, rather, it is the human commitment to change business practices."

The challenge in making ECR a reality is the challenge of becoming a Revolutionary Organization. The technology of ECR is fine, but before ECR can even begin to pay a true dividend, there must be a Revolution from management to leadership, then a Revolution from individual to team, and then a Revolution from the traditional supplier/customer (manufacturer/wholesaler/retailer) relationship to a partnership. If this is not done, ECR will never work. An organization cannot partner until they become collaboration-based, and an organization cannot be collaboration-based until after they have become leadership-driven. Manufacturers, wholesalers, and/or retailers cannot make ECR work until after they have first adopted an internal culture of creating Peak-to-Peak Performance so that they may then adopt an external culture of creating Peak-to-Peak Performance. This external culture of creating Peak-to-Peak Performance is the essence of a partnership and is a prerequisite for success with ECR.

Integrated, Linked, Boundaryless, Seamless, and Synthesized

So far I have focused on ECR, but it would have been just as easy to talk about Quick Response (QR), Fluid Distribution (FD), Continuous Flow Distribution (CFD), and so on. The essence of all of these outreaches are the same—the real-time capture of information on demand so that supply may be fully responsive to the needs of the market place while minimizing the total system costs. All of these have at their core both a technology component and a partnership component. The technology component is well-defined, and given the proper expertise, is not a major problem. The partnership component requires a Revolution from the traditional supplier/customer relationship to a Revolutionary Partnership, and is a major hurdle for most organizations.

For organizations to meld together, to have success with ECR, QR, FD, or CFD, it is critical that they truly understand partnerships. All of the talk about *virtual organizations* and *virtual enterprises*, that, although they do not really exist, act as if they do, is absolutely impossible without Revolutionary Partnerships. For ECR, QR, FD, CFD, and all other virtual-enterprise type solutions to achieve their potential, the following must occur:

- All partners must shift from management to leadership.
- All partners must shift from individuals to teams.
- All partners must fully embrace and implement the reality of partnerships to become:
  1. *Integrated*: Where the partners trust, understand, and are compatible with each other and are mutually working towards the same objectives. Where both partners are focused on the well-being of their partners and the partnership.
  2. *Linked*: The partners are both interdependent but still independent. Interdependent in that the partners need each other, have good relationships, and share a win/win mind-set. Independent in that they do their job well, do valuable work, maintain their own identity, and are independently creative and innovative.
  3. *Boundaryless*: The partners have open, frequent communications, totally shared information, and see-through business. The partners see the same costs, problems, and opportunities.
  4. *Seamless*: The partners have mutual participation in creating Peak-to-Peak Performance and a joint relationship that is based upon synergy. The partnership is flexible and free from interfering rules or bureaucracy.
  5. *Synthesized*: The partners, through high levels of tolerance and interface, unify and reorder to achieve new levels of integration. The links of the supply chain melt, allowing a new entity to emerge that seeks ultimate customer satisfaction.[2]

Call to Action

This was a brass tacks chapter on partnerships. My call to action is a call to understanding. As a Revolutionary Leader, leading a Revolutionary Organization into Revolutionary Partnerships, you need to thoroughly understand the partnership process. This is a chapter you should read over and over until its way of thinking and vocabulary becomes your way of thinking and vocabulary. A robust understanding of partnerships will help you avoid the confusion so many others have fallen into, and will help you be successful in your pursuit.

Part IV

The following pages could perhaps be the most challenging pages in this book. We come to the subject of the way we compensate and recognize those within our organization. This is always a volatile subject, but it is absolutely essential to the success of the Organizational Revolution you are trying to lead. If it weren't, I would not include it as a chapter in this book, not to mention as a whole section.

It is important as you begin to read this section to understand that within most organizations today, the compensation system is broken. What is needed is not a refinement of the traditional compensation plans, but a Revolution toward a whole new approach to compensation. This section charts out how can we lead a Compensation Revolution.

A key thing to remember with respect to Compensation Revolution is the reality that there will never be two compensation plans that are alike. One size does not fit all. Therefore it is critical that organizations understand the process whereby they can design their own unique compensation plan. It is by this participative process that great performance will be rewarded, that all employees will believe there is a balance between their contribution and their compensation, and that companies will prosper.

In short, this final section answers the question, "What's in it for me?" Once managers have become leaders, through the Revolution process outlined in this book, once individuals and organizations begin to collaborate, then Peak-to-Peak Performance will result; which when rewarded and recognized by Revolutionary Compensation will drive even greater performance, which will merit even greater rewards and recognition by Revolutionary Compensation, which will. . .

It's a wonderful story: Peak-to-Peak Performance created by a leadership-driven, collaborative process, and driven to even higher peaks by rewards and recognition. Once you understand Part 4, you will fully understand how to keep the Revolution process and Peak-to-Peak Performance going.

15

You Get What You Pay For

Revolution Principle #15:

Revolutionary Leaders must be skilled in the science and psychology of rewards and recognition.

Few individuals will participate in a Revolution for reasons other than personal reward of some kind. After all, reward is the primary reason for starting a Revolution of any kind. The Industrial Revolution had economic rewards, the American Revolution had freedom as its reward, the Computer Revolution has cultural advancement for its reward. Every Revolution in history has had some kind of reward as its motivation. It's interesting to me to observe that each Revolution has a primary reward and many other sub-rewards. The Industrial Revolution also advanced the culture, the American Revolution also had great economic reward, and the Computer Revolution is rewarding people with a new kind of freedom and autonomy.

Revolution Leaders must understand the immense power of rewards and recognition. If people will rally around a cause and pledge their allegiance to a Revolutionary movement, it will be primarily because of the reward that is offered to them. It is logical, then, that the more significant the reward—the more it is defined and communicated up front—the greater the allegiance and alignment will be. This is why it is critical that Revolution leaders be skilled in the science and psychology of rewards and recognition, because it has more potential to build a committed Revolutionary force than anything else.

Business leaders have much to learn here. Often they expect unprecedented performance from their employees, and may even now be attempting to start an Organizational Revolution. But if they are not skilled in the science and psychology of rewards and recognition, they probably aren't rewarding and recognizing well, and therefore they are probably not seeing the performance they desire. As much as we would like to think that people work above and beyond what and how we pay them, the fact is it isn't true. If you are not properly rewarding and recognizing your people, I would wager that you are probably dissatisfied with performance.

Because Organizational Revolution is concerned with Peak-to-Peak Performance, I want to give you all that is necessary to be skilled in the science and psychology of rewards and recognition. As you read this and the following chapters, I hope you will keep *your* rewards and recognition practices in mind, and compare them to what I describe. I know it's difficult, but you are probably going to see areas that need to be changed in your practice. But that's okay; it is just another part of the Revolution process. This chapter shows you how to begin a Compensation Revolution.

I have showed you how to have Revolutionary Leadership, Revolutionary Collaboration, and Revolutionary Partnerships in your organization. Is there any doubt that these Revolutions naturally require Revolutionary Compensation? Once the above Revolutions have begun to take hold, isn't it common sense that without a Compensation Revolution, the impacts of the prior Revolutions will be dampened? The result of organizational Revolution improves the situation of the entire organization. Improved compensation demonstrates the reality that Revolution does reward the individual. Without a Revolution in compensation, the prior Revolutions cannot be expected to be sustained because individuals will still be driven by the traditional individual compensation system. The confusion will surface with comments like these:

"You ask why I am not working on my team assignment? Well, let me tell you; my raise depends not on our team but on how well I do on the performance appraisal, and secondly, my boss doesn't have a clue what I am doing on the team. Do teams really matter?"

"My boss has asked me to devote my energy to a partnership with our supplier on our new product X, but my bonus is still based on the budget conformance of my old department. What am I to do?"

"They asked me to work on a team, but my efforts on teams are not even on my performance appraisal. Believe me, if they wanted me to really support teams, it would be on my appraisal too."

The Compensation Revolution or lack thereof can have a major impact on the reinforcement or negation of the Leadership, Collaboration, and Partnership Revolution.

To Change or Not to Change?

In many organizations, the compensation plan has not been significantly changed in the last twenty years. With the exception of the addition of some form of retirement plan, the rewards, recognition, and performance appraisals in most organizations are the same today as they have been for years. Often employees do not understand the compensation structure but are more than happy to be critical of how it functions.

Even though there has been and continues to be study after study of compensation, little changes; no one is willing to change something as fundamental as how people are compensated. So, companies continue with a traditional compensation structure that is ineffective but similar to what others are doing. There has been little innovation and the focus tends to be more on how to refine our methodology of doing the wrong things rather than shifting to do the right things. Isn't this amazing? Compensation is a key area in all companies, and what we have settled for and continue to settle for are compensation practices that try to minimize employee dissatisfaction while keeping our costs in line. We don't need a new approach to the traditional compensation practices. We need new, innovative approaches to compensation. For the most part, today's compensation practices will not support an Organizational Revolution. Revolutionary Organizations require Revolutionary Compensation.

The title of this chapter, for better or worse, is true. Companies do get what they pay for. For example, Sears used to pay their automobile mechanics based upon the volume of repairs done by the mechanics. In 1992, the attorneys general in 41 states alleged that Sears mechanics were repairing things that were not broken. Sears settled the charges for $15 million and eliminated commissions for mechanics.

In this chapter, I want to take a look at what we have been paying for. I also want to provide an overview of the conflicting psychological views of compensation. My goal is to get you thinking good and hard about the compensation system in your organization, and whether or not it supports the Revolution you are seeking.

Traditional Compensation

Traditional compensation consists of a pay scale and little or no recognition. The pay scale may be based on incentive pay or merit pay. Merit pay may be an hourly rate or a salary, both of which are initially tied to the base pay for a specific job that is then adjusted in accordance with seniority and/or a performance appraisal. Let's look at incentive pay, merit pay, and performance appraisals in further detail.

Incentive Pay

The ultimate pay-for-performance plan is incentive pay. Incentive pay is when the employee is paid a given piece-rate for each piece they produce. The essence of an incentive pay plan has to do with a task being so boring, repetitive, simple, and routine that there is no intrinsic motivation in continuing to perform the task. Since the task is paced by the employee, the external motivation of paying a certain amount of money per piece keeps employee productivity high.

In the 1920s, 1930s, and 1940s, incentive pay was the most common approach for compensation. Since the 1950s, however, fewer and fewer companies have used incentive pay plans, and today most have been eliminated. The demise of incentive pay plans has to do with the increased talents of the workers, the unbearable hassle with the plans, and the changing work environment.

Unfortunately, the increased talents of workers were not used to contribute to the well-being of the company but rather to outsmart, beat, and cheat the incentive pay system. Everyone associated with incentive plans can tell stories about the way workers work together to beat the system. To try and catch the outsmarting, beating, and cheating, large staffs were employed to control, monitor, update, fight grievances, and administer the incentive pay plan. Adversarial relationships developed between workers and management as the fights over piece-rates continued. As for productivity, the incentive plan did not increase it, it limited productivity. All the workers agreed to the level at which they all would produce so as to protect their jobs and their pay.

In today's work environment of high quality, mass customization, highly skilled work force, and collaboration-based participation, incentive pay really does not fit in the incentive plan. Although some companies still successfully use incentive pay, it is not the approach of Revolutionary Organizations.

Merit Pay

In theory, traditional merit pay plans are also pay-for-performance plans. The essence of a merit pay plan lies in a job-based pay table, a performance measurement system, and an increase in pay based on merit.

The job-based pay table is a series of pay ranges for different levels of jobs. These pay ranges may be salary ranges or hourly wage ranges. Job-based pay tables are typically the result of a job evaluation system that consists of a job description, job factors, the allocation of points to jobs based on the factors, and job point scores which are then translated into pay ranges. The pay received by a person on a job will be within the pay range for the job and will be determined by a combination of past merit, seniority, and recent merit. A person will then be evaluated for their recent merit (typically within the last year), and an increase in their pay will be defined.

There are five problems with traditional merit pay that will eventually lead to fewer and fewer firms using this approach:

1. *There are fairness, credibility, and accuracy problems with the performance measurement system most companies use and upon which merit increases are based.* The reviews that result from the performance measurement system do not accurately assess performance, so the basis for merit increases are wrong.
2. *The performance measurement system is used to evaluate individuals, not teams, but organizations want to encourage teams.* Giving merit increases to individuals based upon a review of their individual efforts is counter to the objectives of teams.

3. *Due to the first two problems with merit pay, the difference in merit pay increases from the worst to the best employee are small.* It would not be unusual for the best employee to receive a 4 percent pay increase and the worst to receive a 2 percent pay increase. Is this small difference supposed to be a motivation?
4. *Since in a merit pay plan the past merit increases become a part of the person's new base pay, this past performance becomes an annuity.* This results in a system that is supposed to pay on merit, but in which the people who are really performing the best are rarely paid the best. In fact, in most merit pay plans, rarely do the top performers receive the top pay.
5. *Due to the pay ranges for specific jobs, individuals will reach a point where they will hit the upper limit of pay for that job.* When this occurs, there will be no potential for pay increases until the pay ranges are adjusted. Unfortunately, when an individual hits the upper limit, often, to give this person further merit increases, they are promoted. Thus, the reason for the promotion is not because the person should be promoted, but because this is the only way to increase the person's salary. This is a problem, since often the wrong person is promoted.

Most organizations will relate and agree with these five problems. For this reason, even though traditional merit pay is the most popular approach to compensation today, to achieve the objectives of Organizational Revolution, this approach must be significantly altered.

A BROKEN PAY PLAN, SAD STORY NUMBER 3,268

The ten-year-old California company had grown quickly and had not been consistent with human resource issues. There were pay problems. What a person got paid had more to do with when they were hired than what they did or how well they did it. During their fast growth period, the company had to pay some pretty high wages just to get people in the door. There were no real quantifiable goals or performance criteria applied. A new pay plan was needed, so a compensation expert was hired to do this. Well, after everyone took tests, filled out forms and sat through interviews, the day of the pay raises arrived. Everyone had talked about this for weeks. Everyone had told their spouses about the pay raises and the whole company was braced for a celebration. But it was not a happy day. Some people got no

(continued)

raise at all. Some people were told they make more money than they should. Some people got very small raises, some got good raises, and some got great raises. All the people in the test department came out very well. All the people in assembly got nothing. The average pay in test was higher than the highest pay in assembly! Everyone was told these were not pay increases, but adjustments. The pay raises would be done in December and would be based on merit, but that these adjustments were not done on merit, just based upon the pay ranges for the point totals for each job. To get a feel for this situation, look at this snapshot of the company two weeks after the big day:

President: "We give out over $600,000 in annual pay increases and I have the most unhappy people in the world."

Human Resource Manager: "This has not gone well. I can't believe the compensation expert let me down like this."

Vice President of Operations: "I can't even walk out on the floor or go to the cafeteria without getting beat up over this pay thing."

Assembly Person: "They think I will accept this? I am looking for another job and as soon as I find one I am gone."

Test Person: "It is not fair that I got such a big raise and many others got nothing. I am embarrassed to even talk to the people in production. This is not good!"

What went wrong? Consider the following list:

- People were allowed to have expectations of a big pay increase. Although this was never said, this is what people *heard*.
- There was no participation by the workers in the design, refinement, or implementation of the plan.
- The new plan was poorly implemented. There were no phases in the plan.
- The people did not understand what was done, why it was done, or where the plan went from here.
- People felt betrayed. People felt manipulated. People were now being rewarded or punished based upon assignments that were arbitrarily made when people were first hired.

What happened? The plan was eliminated, the company ate crow, all pay increases were left in place, all people who did not get a significant pay raise were given one, the Human Resources Manager was fired, and as of today, there is no plan in place to manage compensation. Isn't this sad? I guess what is even worse is that this story is repeated, repeated, and repeated. Let's quit playing with this stuff and Revolutionize our compensation instead!

Performance Appraisal

A good starting point for a discussion on traditional performance appraisals is for us each to think back in our career to the performance appraisals we have received. How did you feel about these appraisals? Most of us were not happy. At the core of our lack of happiness is a problem with the objectives of the performance appraisals. Isn't it obvious that if the objectives of the organization, the appraiser, and the appraisee are different, that the performance appraisal will not be a success? Well, what are the objectives of a performance appraisal? Here are a few:

- Career guidance and counseling
- Improving job performance
- Improving motivation
- Improving alignment with company
- Clarifying present job requirements
- Improving appraiser and appraisee communications
- Skill enhancement
- Defining training needs
- Defining performance-for-pay purposes
- Creating a complete human resources file on the individual

Not included in this list are the many unspoken objectives such as getting even, showing who is in control, fulfilling an order from my boss that I do this, straightening out a troublemaker, telling someone in authority how underpaid I am, trying to get some action on a problem that has not been resolved, speaking up for my co-workers, and so on. To combat the lack of success of performance appraisals, organizations are continually revising the performance appraisal system. A normal cycle is:

Year 1: Begin developing a new performance appraisal system. Revise the old system by adding or eliminating categories and other cosmetic things.

Year 2: Implement new system and debug.

Year 3: Obtain feedback that the new system has problems and that people are not happy with their performance appraisals. Go back to Year 1 while still using the last system for one more year.

The problem is not in the cosmetics of the performance appraisal system, but at a much more basic level. The issues that need to be addressed but are not include the following:

1. What are the objectives of the performance appraisal? Do both the appraiser and appraisee share this objective?
2. What should the frequency of performance appraisals be?
3. Are the people doing the performance appraisals comfortable doing them? Do they support the process?
4. What lasting impacts on communications, relationships, and egos will result from the appraisal?
5. What are the legal implications of performance appraisals?
6. How much time should be allocated to preparing and presenting performance appraisals? Is this time available?
7. What is the role of teams in performance appraisals?
8. What should the level of participation by the appraisee before, during, and after the appraisal be?
9. Should appraisers be forced to a predefined distribution of appraisal results? How should the halo effect be handled?
10. What form should be used? Are the rating factors subjective or objective? Do the appraisers have a choice or input on the forms used?

These issues are typically not addressed successfully, thus the problems with traditional performance appraisals. Performance appraisals are a key feedback mechanism, but for the appraisals to accomplish the objectives of a true performance appraisal, a significantly different approach must be taken from the approach traditionally used.

WRITE YOUR OWN SIDEBAR

A few days after I finished each chapter, I went back and read the chapter and at that time wrote these little sidebars to illustrate a key point or topic. It is fun doing these sidebars.

Well, as I got to this point in this chapter about twenty sidebars immediately jumped into my mind. So, needing to make a decision on which one

(continued)

to include, I decided on one and wrote it. It was good. I liked it. However, that night in bed, I decided, "No, I need to do a sidebar on this other experience." This went on and on. I think I could write a whole book of sidebars on performance appraisal. As I reflected on this, I thought that you may be in a similar position. So, to resolve my problem, I decided to prepare the following generic performance appraisal sidebar into which you may insert your own story.

I remember it well. I had been with ______ about ______ years when my boss called me in for my annual performance appraisal. Things had been going well. I really didn't see my boss much, since he had always said he would leave me alone as long as I was getting the job done. Well, was I in for a surprise. First, when I get there for the review, he was very cold. Then he lays this form on me that I have never seen. He starts off, and from what he says implies that I was lucky I was not being fired. What a jerk! This guy wouldn't know a good operation if he fell on one. Then, did you see what it says on the form next to the factor _______. Well, I lost all respect for this guy. Then, he gets around to money and he says I get a ________ raise. I can't believe I work so hard for these turkeys and then they say ______ about me and give me a _______ raise. At the end, he asks if I have any questions. Well, I had a bunch, but I wasn't going to talk then since I was so mad, I might have said something that would cost me later. As I sit here now two weeks later, I see everyone else feeling just about like me. On the one hand, I want to do a good job but to tell you the truth, I am not sure what my boss wants. On the other hand, I don't want to think about this any more since it just gets me mad all over again. Can you believe what it said on my form? Unbelievable.

Traditional Gainsharing

Traditional gainsharing is a reward system that allows employees to share in a bonus based upon increases in productivity. Gainsharing has existed for over 60 years and has typically been used in manufacturing organizations. Over the last ten years, with the shift to teams, many organizations have switched to gainsharing. Unfortunately, the organizations that have pursued traditional gainsharing plans have not been successful.

All traditional gainsharing plans require that a historical standard of expected labor be computed, and then any improvement in labor performance nets a gain which creates the bonus that is shared. Most gainsharing applications split the bonus, half to the company and half to everyone involved in increasing the productivity. The three most popular traditional gainsharing plans are the Scanlon plan, the Rucker plan, and Improshare.

The Scanlon plan is based upon an allowable payroll cost as a percent of the value of production (where value of production is sales minus returns plus increases or decreases in inventory). For example, consider a company that in the last period spent $1.8 million on payroll and has an allowable payroll cost of 20 percent. Given that the value of production last period was $10 million, the allowable payroll cost would be $2 million. Given the labor cost of only $1.8 million, a labor savings of $200,000 existed last period and a bonus percentage of 11.1 percent ($200,000/$1,800,000) would be available to be split between the company and all eligible employees.

The Rucker plan is similar to the Scanlon plan except instead of utilizing the value of production, which includes work done by outside organizations, the Rucker plan only considers the value added by their own organization. So, in the example used for the Scanlon plan, let's say the allowable payroll cost of the value-added was historically 40 percent. Then, given the $10.0 million in sales and the actual payroll cost of $1.8 million with a cost of outside purchases of:

Materials and Supplies	$3.2 million
Other Outside Purchases	$1.6 million
Total	$4.8 million

The value added would be $5.2 million and the allowable payroll cost would be $1.92 million ($4.8 million x .4). Given the labor cost of $1.8 million, a labor savings of $120,000 existed last period and a bonus percentage of 6.7 percent ($120,000/$1,800,000) would be available to be split between the company and all eligible employees.

Improshare is an improvement on the Scanlon and Rucker plans since it takes shifts in product mix into consideration. The factors required to calculate the bonus percentage available via Improshare are the base productivity factor, the labor standards for each product, and the performance for the period. As an example, let's assume a base productivity factor of two (this says for each hour of direct labor, there is one hour of indirect labor). Then, if the labor standards for Product A were one hour/unit, and for Product B were two hours/unit, and 100 of each were made, the hours earned would be:

Product A: (100 x 1 x 2) = 200 hours

Product B: (100 x 2 x 2) = 400 hours

for a total hours earned of 600 hours. Then, if the actual hours worked were 550 hours, the 50 hours savings would translate into a 9 percent (50/550) bonus percentage, to be split between the company and all eligible employees.

The difficulties with the productivity-based traditional gainsharing programs are their concentration on labor and assumption that employees can increase productivity by working harder. In many manufacturing organizations today, direct labor is ten percent or less of the total cost of manufacturing, so the focus of the gainsharing plan on labor is inappropriate. Additionally, contrary to incentive pay where employees can increase their personal productivity by working harder, it is not clear that this will work for entire organizations. Although traditional gainsharing plans refer to cooperation and involvement, the plans do not include a collaboration-based process to make or allow this to happen. For these reasons, Revolutionary Organizations do not find traditional gainsharing plans useful in defining a Revolutionary Compensation structure.

NICE TRY, BUT NO CIGAR

The company is located in New Jersey and they have just hired a new president. Their problems are numerous, but highest on the list are quality, morale, and market share. The new president spends time talking to the workers and concludes that the quality and market share problems are a result of the morale problems, and that at the heart of the morale problems is a lack of pay increases.

With the exception of a few random merit increases and promotions, people have not had an increase in three years. The new president does not have the funds for a pay increase so he turns to a gainsharing plan. The plan selected is a Rucker plan and the plan is installed with a lot of fanfare and a big speech by the new president about how gainsharing will allow everyone to gain. After several periods of little gainsharing understanding, no process to create the gainsharing gains, and no pay-out from the plan,

(continued)

a single large order is responsible for a small bonus being paid at the end of the fifth period. Employees are not excited with what they call "coffee money," but there is an increased interest in attending the gainsharing meetings.

The new president has also been working on several large projects which begin to bear fruit. Knowing the company needs a shot in the arm, he implements a $1 per hour pay increase for everyone on the floor who had been with the company more than six months. The company business level is up. In fact, some overtime is needed. There still has been no process installed to make gainsharing work, and now with the pay increases and the overtime being worked, the Rucker plan goes negative and stays negative. The employees appreciate the pay increase and are happy about the overtime, but as each weekly gainsharing chart is posted and each four-week period is ended, the employees feel worse and worse about gainsharing.

A quote from the president's big gainsharing kickoff speech where he said "As the company grows, you grow; as the company gains productivity and quality, you gain money" echoes through the shop. The employees know the company has grown. They see the numbers up almost 30 percent. The employees know productivity is up; they are shipping 20 percent more but have only added about 4 percent new workers, and look at the quality charts. Everything is great, except, no gainsharing payout.

What is the president to do? He decides to eliminate gainsharing just a little over a year after gainsharing is installed. So he holds a plant-wide meeting and says that gainsharing was a mistake, the meetings are a waste of time, and so "there will be no more gainsharing." To support his positions, he asks the Chief Financial Officer to make a presentation as to why gainsharing could not be made to work with today's wages and overtime. The employees did not understand much of what the financial guy said except that "because the people on the floor were making so much money that there is no way the company could have gains to share."

The employees went bananas. Morale hit an all-time low. This impacted both quality and productivity. More overtime was needed to get out the new work, but with the quality problems, they began to lose orders. Two years after taking the job, the new president was fired. The company profits, level of business, market share, and quality were all lower than when he was hired. Morale was shot; there was no trust.

As the new president became the old president, his thoughts were, "I did everything right except for gainsharing and look where it got me." Well, what did he expect? If you do everything right but then lie to the people about their gainsharing check, do you think everything will be fine? No, I think not. We need to be careful. We need to understand that gainsharing , like everything else, can be done well or can be done poorly. In this case, a big time mistake. To the now old president, "Nice try, but no cigar."

The Psychology of Rewards and Recognition

Well, which do you feel more like—a rat, a pigeon, a dog, a patient in a psychiatric hospital, a child, or an African tribe? There are psychological studies done based upon experiments with all of these subjects which supposedly explain how you and I act. The thing I find most funny is when one psychologist who experiments with patients in a psychiatric hospital questions the work of another psychologist because their work is based on experiments with rats. Personally, I am not overly impressed with Pavlov's dog, rats in mazes, or how three-year-old children respond. In fact, my in-depth research has allowed me to gather sufficient psychological background to prove just about any position I desire on rewards and recognition. Take any position and there is an experiment somewhere that can prove your point. It is not my fault that your position is only strongly endorsed by pigeons who like unsalted peanuts.

Psychology boils down to three basic positions:

Behaviorism: With B. F. Skinner as their visionary, behaviorists believe that human behavior can be modified and performance improved by rewarding acceptable behavior. Behaviorists believe in pay for performance and that rewards motivate people. Behaviorists may be summarized with the slogan "What gets rewarded gets done."

Humanism: With Abraham Maslow as their visionary, humanists believe that what will impact human behavior depends upon the individual's level on a hierarchy of human needs. The five levels of human need are first food, then shelter, then belonging, then self-respect, and lastly self-actualization. Humanists believe you must understand each person as an individual and their level of development before you can determine what will motivate them. Humanism may be summarized by the slogan "It depends."

Anti-Behaviorism: With Alfie Kohn as their visionary, anti-behaviorists believe that rewards punish and that behaviorists are wrong. They believe rewards are given in an effort to control people and that this is bad. Anti-behaviorists are not sure how people should be paid but that what motivates people is not rewards but the inner satisfaction of doing a job well. Anti-behaviorists may be summarized with the slogan "What is rewarding gets done."

Much of the psychological discussion has to do with extrinsic and intrinsic motivation. Extrinsic motivation relates to being stimulated by external sources like recognition and rewards. Intrinsic motivation has to do with being stimulated internally and performing because of the challenge, satisfaction, and enjoyment of making a contribution. Behaviorists believe that extrinsic motivation works and don't have much to say about intrinsic motivation (how do you ask a rat if he ran the maze for the treat or just because he enjoyed running the maze?). Anti-behaviorists believe extrinsic motivation doesn't work (all rewards are just bribes) and the utilization of rewards will result, in the long term, in a degradation of performance. Anti-behaviorists believe work needs to be redesigned to ensure intrinsic motivation exists. Humanists have a belief in both extrinsic and intrinsic motivation and feel that which one will have the biggest impact depends upon the individual's personal development. So, what we have is two extremes—the behaviorist and the anti-behaviorist, with the humanist in the middle. To fully understand the dichotomy between the behaviorist and the anti-behaviorist, it is useful to review the following six-point framework of why the anti-behaviorist thinks the behaviorist is wrong:

1. *Pay is not a motivator.* Too little pay is a demotivator but increasing pay is not a motivator.
2. *Rewards punish.* Rewards have a punitive effect because just like punishment, they are manipulative. The reward statement "Do this and you'll get that" is not really very different from "Do this or here's what will happen to you."
3. *Rewards rupture relationships.* Competition for rewards will result in a few winners and many losers.
4. *Rewards ignore reasons.* When managers focus on rewards to get results, they lose sight of the things that need to be done to get the results.
5. *Rewards discourage risk-taking.* So as not to lose a reward, individuals will shy away from taking a risk and will play it safe and play by the rules so as not to lose out on the reward.
6. *Rewards undermine interest.* The more a manager stresses what an employee can earn for good work, the less interested that employee is in the work itself.

It is good that I am not a psychologist. If I were, I would have to take a position and then try to prove to you that I am right. It is a shame that behaviorists and anti-behaviorists are so adamant over their positions. If they really listened to each other, they could both probably learn something. Nevertheless, this all has value, and it is here, against this psychological backdrop, that I present what all this means. Here is my view of all that is known about the psychology of rewards and recognition, which will help you in your Compensation Revolution:

- *Pay should be related to performance.* This performance should include all aspects of a person's job as the person works to move an organization toward the organization's Model of Success. Only desirable performance should be rewarded.
- *Rewards and recognition can be done well or they can be done poorly.* If the person being rewarded feels manipulated, this is bad. If the person being rewarded feels respected, honored, and enthusiastic about even greater performance, then the reward is good.
- *Rewards and recognition should not be exclusionary.* When one person receives a reward, this should not limit other people from receiving a reward. Since teams and whole organizations receive rewards, rewards should be well-understood and well-justified.
- *Individuals and teams should participate in designing rewards and recognition.* Once the reward program is designed, performance measured against this reward should be reviewed, but the focus should be on the performance, not on the reward.
- *Leadership must utilize the collaborative process to help organizations improve the intrinsic motivation of all jobs and all employees.* Rewards and recognition are just one part of this many-part equation.
- *Performance feedback must be frequent and not viewed as an opportunity to be critical of anyone, but to be critical of unacceptable performance.* The objective is to define solutions that will result in improved performance and advancement.
- *Leadership must encourage and reward risk-taking.* Everyone must understand that creating Peak-to-Peak Performance is at the heart of a Revolutionary Organization and that there will be no rewards for anyone if all we do is continue doing what we have already done. There should be no loss of rewards for trying something that does not work.

- *Leaders should not focus on rewards and recognition but on Revolution and Peak-to-Peak Performance.*
- *Motivation of individuals is a delicate topic.* All people are different and there is no one approach that will successfully motivate all people. The safest approach is to involve people in the design of their rewards and environment to ensure their motivation. It is important, independent of what the rats, dogs, pigeons, or psychologists say, to understand that one size does not fit all. Many of the traditional approaches to rewards and recognition are flawed, but this does not mean that rewards and recognition are unimportant. At the same time, it is a mistake to think the upgrade of rewards and recognition will solve all problems. Revolutionary Organizations must focus on the three Revolutions—leadership, collaboration, and compensation. Any one or two Revolutions will not work—all three Revolutions must take place.
- *Rewards and recognition are a source of celebration.* It is critical that these celebrations be positive, reinforcing, and inspiring times for all involved.

Call to Action

I realize that asking you to consider changing the way you compensate your employees is asking a lot. But I believe it is central to your pursuit of Revolution. Remember, the second principle of Revolution is *change for improvement's sake.* In most organizations compensation must be improved. You have probably already attempted to revamp compensation in your organization, and, if you're like so many others, have probably not seen much success. However, I ask you to try again, this time bringing a broader, more scientific understanding of rewards and recognition with you. That, together with the implementation of the compensation principles in this book, is what will make your Compensation Revolution a success.

16

Learning to Fish

Revolution Principle #16:

Every Revolution must have a custom system of rewards and recognition to directly reinforce the cause.

What motivates one group of Revolutionaries may unmotivate another group. Think back to the three Revolutions I talked about in the previous chapter: the Industrial Revolution, the American Revolution, and the Computer Revolution. Freedom would not have been a viable reward for the Industrial Revolution as it was in the American Revolution. Cultural advancement would not have motivated the American Revolutionaries to secede from England. And freedom in itself was not a motivating factor for the Computer Revolution, although now it is giving people more independence than they have ever known.

Every Revolution must have its own plan for rewards and recognition. There is no pre-fabricated reward that will instantly motivate a group of people into Revolution. The reward is based on history, present context, and future possibilities. In every Revolution those factors will differ. A Revolution must do the hard work of analyzing these three factors in the beginning, and based on their analysis, seek to offer their Revolutionaries rewards that are appropriate. Revolution Leaders have found that even if they reward people well, if it is the wrong kind of reward, or the method by which the reward is granted is faulty, they still see poor performance. So a Revolution must be concerned with not only rewarding *well* but rewarding *correctly*.

What is true about rewards in a Revolution in general is even more true about rewards in an Organizational Revolution. Every company requires a compensation plan that is custom to their situation based on history, present context, and future possibilities. Most likely your compensation plan needs to be improved, but how to improve it in your context is the real challenge. This chapter is written to guide you through the process of changing the Rewards and Recognition plan in your organization to reinforce the Revolution you are seeking. This is so vital to your success; I can't emphasize its importance enough. Your ability to achieve Peak-to-Peak Performance is directly linked to how and when you apply this chapter. Let's get started.

I Thought I Taught Them to Fish

For ten days, I lectured nine hours a day to over 100 manufacturing executives from all over China. I found the executives very hungry students. I adjusted to everyone jumping to their feet when I entered or left the room. I started to get used to simultaneous translation difficulties. But I was not ready for the eleventh and last day of my lecture services in Zheng-Zhou, China.

I had planned a two-hour session on manufacturing maintenance, then questions and answers, then a round-robin discussion on computerized applications, and then a one-hour closing on the future of manufacturing. I was told the TV crews would be there at 4:00 p.m. and that they wanted to film the end of my lecture and an awards ceremony. Well, I did the two-hour session on manufacturing maintenance. The executives liked this material since they had not focused on this topic as a key element of their success.

After a short break, I asked for questions. Well, I got questions. In fact, the questions did not end until after 6:00 p.m. Each of the 147 executives had several written questions. Unfortunately, all of the questions and all of the follow-up questions were of the same nature. Every question, and I mean *every* question, stated a set of conditions, then asked me for a solution. Here I had spent ten days teaching how to plan their business, design their operations, create Peak-to-Peak Performance, and run efficient and effective manufacturing organizations, and these executives were not asking how to apply the tools they had learned, but rather for a specific solution to a specific—and I suspect, real—problem. My goal was not to give these professionals a fish but to teach them how to fish.

So here I was on the eleventh day of the world's greatest fishing lecture and my students had little interest in fishing—but they sure were hungry for me to give them a fish. Well, I was disappointed, to say the least. The more I tried to draw them into the thought process of addressing their own questions, the more I realized I was fighting a losing battle. These executives were managers, not leaders; and they were more interested in eating fish than in understanding how to catch fish. What did I do? I served them fish.

I tell you this story because I have learned that whenever we are faced with a challenge that we believe is bigger than we can handle, our tendency is to ask for someone else to grab the pole and catch the fish for us. This chapter may offer such a challenge to you. How do you achieve Revolutionary Compensation? How do you address recognition and rewards? These are huge challenges, and we face an almost unlimited number of paradigms and preconceived notions. This makes me think about the old saying about "talk about anything you want except politics and religion." I guess I would say "change anything you want in an organization, but do not touch a person's compensation."

So, what you would like me to do in this chapter is tell you the answer to Revolutionary Compensation, to lay it all out, leaving you to simply implement it. By me giving you this fish, you would be absolved of all responsibility. Well, I have worked, and worked, and worked to be able to do this for you. But unfortunately, here again, "one size does not fit all." There is no one correct answer to compensation. The correct answer for you is different from the correct answer for another organization. The correct answer depends upon your organization's past compensation practices; your present approach to compensation; your organization's satisfaction with the present approach; the agreements, contracts, or guidelines for compensation; and the objectives to be accomplished through compensation. This is why I presented the background and psychological views on recognition and rewards in the previous chapter—to provide the framework and overall architecture of Revolutionary Compensation, which I will present in this chapter. This framework does not tell you the answer to Revolutionary Compensation, but when combined with all the background material, will allow your organization to achieve a Revolutionary approach to compensation. Whether or not there will be fish for dinner depends upon you. Happy fishing.

The Framework for Revolutionary Compensation

Revolutionary Compensation consists of a recognition element and a rewards element. The recognition element consists of a formal individual goal assessment portion and an ongoing, informal, emotional recognition portion. The rewards element consists of the following components:

1. Base Pay
2. Pay-for-Skill
3. Individual Bonus
4. Goalsharing

Figure 16.1 illustrates these components of Revolutionary Compensation. Although each of these components needs to be customized for each organization, the remainder of this chapter presents guidelines for each of these components.

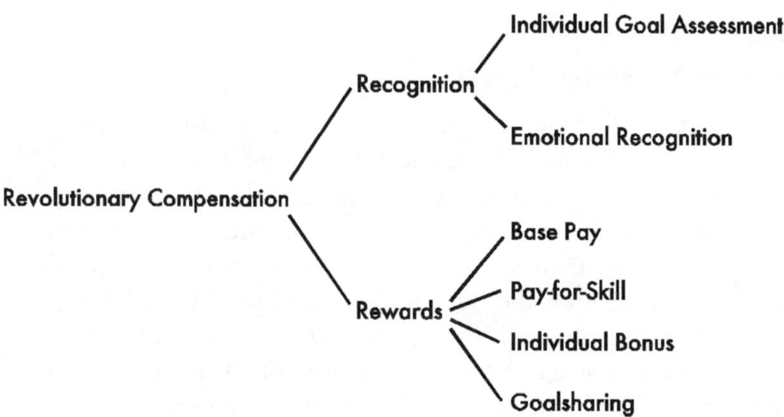

Figure 16.1 Revolutionary Compensation

Revolutionary Recognition

A key to the success of Revolutionary Compensation is realizing that there is an intimate link between recognition and rewards. What works from a recognition point of view depends upon the rewards, and vice versa. Not only does recognition have an impact on rewards, but the rewards also have an impact on recognition.

Another key to the success of recognition is the proper allocation and understanding of time. Many supervisors, managers, and leaders complain that the whole recognition process takes too much time. True; recognition is very time-consuming. It is also true, however, that this time is very, very well spent. Recognition requires daily involvement from an emotional-recognition perspective and weekly, monthly, or quarterly involvement from an individual goal-assessment perspective

A final thought on the big picture of recognition is the need to be reminded of what we learned from the humanists in Chapter 16: All individuals are unique. There is no single approach to recognition that will be effective on different people. Revolution Leaders must understand that in order to bring out the best in each individual, they will need a unique, customized approach to each person.

Emotional Recognition

The basic guideline for how Revolution Leaders should treat people is to say thank you—truly appreciate people helping you. A Revolution Leader will say thank you many, many times every day. The need for emotional support and emotional recognition is a part of every person and requires constant attention. A basketball coach does not sit quietly on the sidelines waiting for the game to be over to provide feedback. A basketball coach is involved with the game and provides emotional support and recognition on each and every play. The Revolution Leader will write notes of appreciation, verbally recognize employees in private and in public, and recognize achievement via certificates, plaques, and other tangible gifts, demonstrating their genuine appreciation for the work done by individuals and teams.

However, emotional recognition can be done incorrectly. You might ask, "How can you recognize someone incorrectly?" Well, here are some common ways:

- *Recognition lacks genuine appreciation or sincerity.* A real challenge with emotional recognition evolves from the philosophy "Catch people doing something right and praise them for it," or the poster seen in many schools, "Praise every child every day." When recognition lacks spontaneity, a genuine excitement for something done, it will be viewed as phony and will undercut the value of all other recognition. People will see through and resent a strategy of complimenting every person every day. When recognition is used as a gimmick, people will receive the recognition as manipulative and as a demotivator.
- *Recognition is not specific.* We all have met the person who had a wonderful spouse, a wonderful family, a wonderful job, worked for a wonderful company and a wonderful boss. Blah! Phony, phony, phony. For recognition to be of value, it has to be specific.
- *Recognition based on the person or team and not the action done by the person or team.* We all have learned that when correcting or disciplining it is necessary that we do it in private, and we should not be critical of the person but of the person's actions. Well, guess what? The same is true for recognition. Don't say that a person is a good person, say that they really do a great job in

planning marketing outreaches. Don't take the comment about "in private" to mean that public recognition is bad. To the contrary, public recognition is fine, if handled well. What you should understand from this is that you should never recognize something in public that you have not previously recognized in private. Handling recognition in this way will be much more rewarding for the person.

- *Recognition creates a win/lose situation.* Recognition should never be done by comparing someone to somebody else. Do not recognize anyone by saying "Here is Sue, my best salesperson." By definition, every other salesperson who hears this comment will then believe they are below the best. Therefore, recognition needs to be wholly positive. Try instead "Here is Sue, the salesperson who had a sales volume of over $1,000,000 last year."
- *Recognition has bad motives.* Who is going to benefit most from the recognition? If the answer is anyone other than the person receiving it, do not give the recognition. The person giving the recognition needs to make sure they are not receiving the benefit. For example, the following recognition is better off not said: "I am really excited about Bob's performance since he has come around to my way of thinking."
- *Recognition focuses on people's normal routine.* Such recognition is accepted as being condescending. The person receiving the recognition does not feel like they are being recognized but rather put down. For example, "I would like to congratulate Bob here who turned in his expense account on time every month last year." Don't recognize people when doing so indicates that you have low expectations of the individual's performance.
- *Recognition focuses on something that has yet to occur.* For example, "Tiffany, I really appreciate the work you are doing on that great new video you are working on." What this recognition has done is place a level of expectation on Tiffany which may be unfair and, in fact, may undercut the potential for success.

At the same time, not providing emotional recognition is also a major mistake. Therefore, Revolution Leaders must do the following:

- Continually provide positive reinforcement to recognize Peak-to-Peak Performance.

- Allow their spontaneity and genuine excitement for Peak-to-Peak Performance to surface.
- Make a regular habit of saying "Thank you."
- Provide specific recognition in a real-time mode.
- Recognize both individuals and teams for great performance.
- Be aware of and sensitive to the feelings of both the person or team being recognized, as well as the feelings of others.
- Always recognize first in private and then in public.
- Encourage others to recognize Peak-to-Peak Performance.
- Be consistent and genuine in recognizing Peak-to-Peak Performance.
- Be natural, be yourself, and have fun while providing recognition.

MARY KAY ENTHUSIASM: THE POWER OF RECOGNITION

In 1963, Mary Kay sold $198,000 in cosmetics. By 1993, the sales were over $600 million and the Mary Kay sales force was over 300,000 people. Even more impressive, over 6,000 beauty consultants are driving complimentary pink Cadillacs and other cars worth over $90 million, and each summer over 30,000 Mary Kay beauty consultants travel to Dallas, Texas, and pay to attend *seminar*. What is seminar? Three days of nonstop recognition. There are minks, diamonds, color-coded suits, sashes, badges, crowns, emblems, flowers, jewelry, kisses, hugs, holding hands, tears, and stories of amazing success. The emotional compensation is the secret of seminar success and the success of Mary Kay. Beauty consultants can immediately see by inspecting one another what they have accomplished. Nothing is subtle or hidden here. Sales people come to seminar for recognition and it is recognition they get. Between annual seminars, Mary Kay recognizes top performers with five-star vacations, which Mary Kay Ash often attends herself to get to know her "daughters" better and to develop lifelong relationships with them.

Possibly, some think this works for Mary Kay consultants but has little to do with the world of business. Well, think again. Two-thirds of the beauty consultants have full-time jobs in addition to selling Mary

Kay products. Several beauty consultants are lawyers; there are also pediatricians, and even a Harvard MBA. When considering the issue of when the Mary Kay reward-by-recognition will become mainstream, John Kotter, the Konosoke Matsushita Professor of Leadership at Harvard Business School, says, "The genius of great leaders is that they understand money is only one of the things that make people light up."[1] Applause, prizes, and peer recognition are very, very powerful. It is likely that Mary Kay and Mary Kay Ash are way ahead of the rest of us. Cash is a secondary benefit. Recognition is the emotional compensation that brings the enthusiasm that creates success.

Individual Goal Assessment

W. Edwards Deming declared war on performance appraisals. He felt appraisals were the number one problem in American management. Deming felt that performance appraisals should be eliminated because they were destructive, and actually resulted in declines in performance. He felt the average employee took six months to get back on track after a performance appraisal.

I believe Deming was partially correct. I believe poorly designed performance appraisals should be eliminated. I believe any performance appraisal that deflates the person being appraised should be eliminated. However, I also believe that if the objectives of the performance appraisals are clear, if the goals upon which the performance appraisal are based are clear, and the outcome to flow from the performance appraisal are predictable and understood by both the appraiser and the appraisee, that performance appraisals are powerful tools for Peak-to-Peak Performance. In fact, they are at the very foundation of Peak-to-Peak Performance.

I can understand why Deming felt as he did. Let's face it, in Japan they do not have annual appraisals. Instead they have daily feedback and things work well. In America, performance appraisals are done poorly. As I said earlier, most of us are not happy with the performance appraisals we have received, but let's not throw out the baby with the bath water! Just because most companies do a lousy job of performance appraisals does not mean we should not have them. What we need to do is to take a different approach to them.

As a starting point, I believe we need to eliminate the words *performance appraisal* because these words have a negative connotation to us all.

Instead, what we need is to divide performance appraisals into the two separate elements that people think of when they think of performance appraisals, treating the two separate elements individually. The two elements are *individual goal assessment* and *career guidance*. These two elements should be undertaken at different times, in different ways, by different people, and should be kept separate. In fact, I do not believe career guidance should even be a portion of compensation or recognition. I view career guidance as a benefit, or a training or development issue. At the same time, career guidance is often thought to be a portion of performance appraisals, so it makes sense to at least touch on the subject here.

Careers in business today are not necessarily linear, logical progressions, for example, from engineer to project engineer to senior engineer to engineering manager to vice president of engineering. With today's flatter organizations, the traditional upward climb up the corporate ladder is unlikely. More often than not one's career is much more likely to take a zig-zag route. With creating Peak-to-Peak Performance as a motivator, career paths will appear disjointed, but this diversity of background is what results in perpetual growth for both the individuals and the organization. For this to occur, the following career guidance principles should be understood and practiced:

1. *Career guidance is not the responsibility of the organization but the individual.* Nevertheless, with the individual taking the lead, the Revolutionary Organization will actively support the career guidance of the individual.
2. *Career guidance support will only rarely be done by a person's supervisor.* In today's rapidly changing environment, it would not be surprising if an individual had five different supervisors over a five-year period. It is impractical to think about an individual receiving career guidance from five different people over a five-year period. Career guidance support may come from a mentor, a senior person within the organization, a senior person outside the organization, or from human resources.
3. *Career guidance has no impact on rewards.* Career guidance is separate and should be handled separately from individual goal assessment.
4. *The timing of career guidance will vary tremendously depending upon the individual whose career is being guided.* Although your organization should encourage people to think about their career

and offer people the opportunity to learn about career planning, the timing for career guidance should be in the hands of the individual. For young employees, maybe a career guidance session would be warranted every six months, whereas a 50-year-old executive may handle their own career guidance. Revolutionary Organizations should make it clear whom to turn to for career guidance.

The success of individual goal assessment is based upon people knowing what is expected—feedback about performance measured against expectation and financial rewards based upon meeting or exceeding expectations. The following guidelines should be considered when ensuring that people know what is expected and providing feedback about performance measurements against expectations.

1. *Each person's individual goals and individual goal assessment is a highly personalized thing.* Bureaucracy should be minimized and no attempt should be made to force the individual goals or the assessment of these goals into a rigid format.
2. *Individual goals and the assessment of these individual goals should be done to ensure alignment with the organization's Model of Success and the Evidence of Success for all teams in which the individual is a member.* Individual goals should be consistent and supportive of the organization's and the team's path. A portion of an individual's goals should be based upon how well the individual contributes to the organization and the team's success, as well as the overall success of the organization and these teams.
3. *Establishing individual goals and assessing performance against these goals should be highly participative.* The assessor and the assessee should interact frequently while both establishing and assessing of individual goals. A format that works is as follows:
   a. Supervisor defines categories and performance criteria for which goals will be established.
   b. Supervisor and employee discuss categories and performance criteria and reach mutual understanding.
   c. Employee sets goals for agreed-to performance criteria and submits these to supervisor.
   d. Supervisor and employee discuss goals and reach mutual agreement on goals and review schedule.

e. In accordance with review schedule, employee performs a self-assessment and submits it to the supervisor.

f. Supervisor and employee discuss self-assessment and reach mutual agreement on goal assessment.

g. Steps E and F are repeated until it is time to return to A.

4. *Individual goals should always be objective, observable, and verifiable.* These goals can be either numerical or descriptive. With numerical goals, the issue of objective, observable, and verifiable is straightforward. For example, a goal for an author to publish three articles this year can be clearly measured, observed, and can be verified objectively. With descriptive goals to ensure objective, observable, and verifiable assessment, three factors must be defined:

   - Who makes the assessment?
   - Factors to be assessed.
   - Description of what meeting expectations are.

   For example, a goal of being actively involved with company publications may be objective, observable, and verifiable given the following:

   - Who makes the assessment: Rhonda Jones
   - Factors to be assessed: Responsiveness on editing; meeting of deadlines; good, thought-provoking titles; unique, provocative materials.
   - Description of what constitutes "meeting expectations": Good communication, no surprises, on time, editors who like material, and success in getting published.

   Goals which should be avoided are those that are subjective or have to do with traits such as attitude, reliability, friendliness, and so on. These traits typically result in problems with communications. For example, the term *reliability* is vague and emotionally difficult. No one wants to be thought of as unreliable. Traits should be translated into behaviors, such as "meets deadlines" or "good attendance," for reliability, and so on.

5. *The result of an appraisal for each factor must be a rating.* These ratings should fall into four to six categories. For example, at Tompkins Associates, Inc., we have Exceptional, Commendable, Satisfactory, Needs Improvement, and Unsatisfactory. Expecta-

tion levels should be mutually agreed upon for each of these ratings at the outset. This is easiest with numerical goals. For example, with the previously given illustration of articles being published, the following scale may be used:

Exceptional: Five articles published per year

Commendable: Four articles published per year

Satisfactory: Three articles published per year

Needs Improvement: Five articles submitted for publication but less than three published

Unsatisfactory: Less than five article submitted or less than two published

6. *Although an annual overall goal assessment cycle is typical, the review schedule depends upon the individual being assessed.* New employees are reviewed much more frequently than established employees. Lower level employees are reviewed much more frequently than higher level employees. For example, a review schedule that may be used looks like this:

	Duration of Employment		
Employee Classification	**6 Months or Less**	**6 to 18 Months**	**18 Months or Longer**
Hourly	Weekly	Weekly	Monthly
Supervision	Weekly	Monthly	Monthly
Middle Management	Monthly	Monthly	Quarterly
Upper Management	Monthly	Quarterly	Annually

7. *It is important to maintain flexibility with individual goals when circumstances change.* For example, if a person needed to sell 20,000 books and direct mail was one of the avenues for selling the books, and then the direct mail budget was cut by 50 percent, it would be fair to change the goal of 20,000. To the contrary, if the direct mail was done and response rates were low, the goal of 20,000 books should not be changed. Although it is important to be flexible, it is also important not to change goals just because things are not working out.

8. *Although it should be obvious, mutual agreement on individual goals should be reached prior to the beginning of the period covered by the goals.* Basic as this may seem, I have seen goals that were not established until after the assessment period was over or nearly over. This is unacceptable. It is not difficult to predict who will win a football game when the score is 42 to 0 with only 30 seconds remaining. Without prior agreement to individual goals, there will always be difficulties.

Revolutionary Rewards

Just as it is critical for Revolutionary Organizations to upgrade their approach to recognition, it is also critical that they upgrade their approach to rewards. A Revolutionary Organization must have both Revolutionary Recognition and Revolutionary Rewards. Revolutionary Rewards require innovative approaches to the following four reward components:

1. Base Pay
2. Pay-for-Skill
3. Individual Bonus
4. Goalsharing

The following four subsections present an approach to each of these components.

Base Pay

Base pay in a Revolutionary Organization will be very straightforward. There is just one decision to be made: Should base pay be the same for everyone doing a job, or should base pay have three to five steps based upon seniority, or should some hybrid of these two exist? These base pay rates should be published and there should be no secrets about them. When base pay is not disclosed, speculation is rampant. If the disclosure of base pay would be an embarrassment, then whatever is the cause of the embarrassment should be rectified and the base pay then disclosed. Table 16.1 illustrates a base pay table for a manufacturing organization.

Base pay should be reviewed annually, and adjusted in accordance with the market.

Table 16.1 Base Pay Table

Position	Fixed	>1 Yr Tenure	1–5 Yrs Tenure	6–10 Yrs Tenure	11–20 Yrs Tenure	>20 Yrs Tenure
President	$250,000*					
Executive Vice Pres.	$175,000*					
Vice Pres.	$150,000*					
Director	$125,000*					
General Manager	$100,000*					
Manager		$60,000*	$65,000*	$70,000*	$75,000*	$80,000*
Supervisor		$30,000*	$34,000*	$38,000*	$42,000*	$46,000*
Level III		$15.00	$16.00	$17.00	$18.00	$19.00
Level II		$11.00	$12.00	$13.00	$14.00	$15.00
Level I		$7.00	$8.00	$9.00	$10.00	$11.00

Annually*

Pay-for-Skill

Pay-for-skill, also known as *skill-based pay,* or *pay-for-knowledge,* is a reward and development program to increase a nonmanager's base pay based upon the individual's demonstrated capability to perform a variety of skills. Pay-for-skill programs utilize a series of base pay increases based upon increases in skill proficiency. The method for increasing and documenting skill proficiency is called *competency-based development* or *skill-based training.*

Competency-based development is based on the principle of demonstrated capability. Either an individual does or does not have the skills required to perform a given task. By giving an individual a test, we may determine if the individual has the required skills, or if further training, or on-the-job experience is needed. If further training or experience is needed, the results of the test will target the specific needs to increase the individual's competence.

Figure 16.2 presents the process of competency-based development. The first activity, job analysis, identifies the required tasks to successfully perform a given job. The second activity requires that the skills required for each task be identified. These skills are then used to develop the competency evaluation criteria. The evaluation criteria describe what would be measured or how an individual should perform to demonstrate competence. Often, this evaluation criteria will be categorized by the level of competence demonstrated, for example, neophyte, operator, or expert.

Using this evaluation criteria, a test can be developed to check the competence levels of an individual and the quality of their development. Based on this test, individual weaknesses can be identified. Specific training or experience can then be delivered to address these weaknesses. Individuals can then be retested and trained, retested and trained, and so on, until the individual can be certified as competent and eligible for the pay-for-skill increase consistent with the level of competence demonstrated. For example, building upon the base pay rates given in Table 16.1, Table 16.2 illustrates how the pay-for-skill approach would increase base pay given different levels of competence.

Figure 16.2 The Pursuit of Competency-Based Development

Table 16.2 Increase In Base Hourly Pay For Demonstrated Competence

Position	Operator in 1 Area	Expert in 1 Area	Expert in 1 Area/ Operator in 1 Area	Expert in 2 Areas	Expert in 2 Areas/ Operator in 1 Area	Expert in 3 Areas
Level III	$.25	$.50	$.75	$1.00		
Level II	$.25	$.50	$.75	$1.00	$1.25	
Level I	$.25	$.50	$.75	$1.00	$1.25	$1.50

The most significant benefit that results from the pay-for-skill approach is the increased skill levels of the work force. Further benefits that result from this method include:

1. Increased work force flexibility
2. Increased work force competence
3. Increased productivity
4. Improved customer service
5. Increased organizational commitment
6. Decision making can be pushed to the lowest appropriate level
7. Reduced turnover and absenteeism
8. Increased work force participation
9. Increased work force self-esteem
10. Increased work force motivation

Individual Bonus

At the same time that individual goals are established for a person, the bonus-for-performance schedule or formula should also be established. The individual bonus should be based upon performance measured against the individual's goals. It is the combination of the individual goals and the individual bonus plan that should be mutually agreed upon prior to the start of the performance period. These should then be signed by the supervisor and the employee to form the "contract" for the performance period. The bonus-for-performance may be very simple, for example:

- $10,000 for an Exceptional assessment
- $6,000 for a Commendable assessment

- $3,000 for a Satisfactory assessment
- $0 for a Needs Improvement assessment
- $0 for an Unsatisfactory assessment

Or the bonus-for-performance may be a variable percentage of one's salary or profits, such as:

- 20 percent of annual salary for an Exceptional assessment
- 10 percent of annual salary for a Commendable assessment
- 5 percent of annual salary for a Satisfactory assessment
- 0 percent of annual salary for a Needs Improvement assessment
- 0 percent of annual salary for an Unsatisfactory assessment

Or the bonus-for-performance may be some combined formula based upon the assessment, overall company profitability, base salary, and so on. Often the best bonus-for-performance is a hybrid of a couple of different approaches. Prior to the creation of the individual bonus plan, an organization must establish guidelines on the range of funds available for bonuses and the payout method for bonuses. It would not be unusual for there to be a couple of ranges of bonus, depending upon one's level in the organization. For example, a range of 0 to 40 percent, for upper management, 0 to 30 percent, for middle management and 0 to 20 percent of base pay for all others.

The method of bonus payment is typically not just one lump sum. Some organizations pay 40 percent of the bonus at the end of the performance period and then 20 percent at the end of the first, second, and third quarters. Other organizations pay 12 percent of the bonus at the end of the performance period and then 8 percent at the end of the next eleven months. A requirement in place in many organizations is that a person must complete one year of employment prior to participating in individual bonuses. Another rule often employed is that a condition of receiving a bonus is that the person must still be employed. An individual's bonus payout ends at the same time as their base pay, should they terminate their employment.

The individual bonus eliminates the problem of the built-in annuity of the traditional merit pay plans. This results in a fairer overall compensation plan, since individuals are paid based upon their current performance. This allows new employees who are performing at a high level to receive a high bonus, and requires all employees to maintain performance at a high level to continue receiving a high bonus.

Goalsharing

Goalsharing is a type of gainsharing, but it is so different from traditional gainsharing that, when discussing gainsharing, care must be demonstrated so that the negative gainsharing feelings do not affect the understanding of goalsharing. The basic concept of goalsharing is the same as the basic concept of individual goals and individual bonuses. The only difference is that goalsharing is based upon the total organization's performance and individuals' rewards; not on their individual performance but on the performance of the organization as a whole. Goalsharing is a rewards program that rewards team performance and accordingly has at its foundation the organization's Model of Success.

For example, consider an organization whose Model of Success indicates a need to increase productivity, reduce scrap, and improve customer satisfaction. For a particular time frame, the following goals and rewards might be established:

Goal #1: Productivity
Level 1: If increase of productivity 0–5%, a 1% bonus
Level 2: If increase of productivity 5.1–10%, a 2% bonus
Level 3: If increase of productivity 10.1–15%, a 3% bonus
Level 4: If increase of productivity greater than 15.1%, a 4% bonus

Goal #2: Scrap
Level 1: If scrap is between 1.5% and 1%, a 1% bonus
Level 2: If scrap is between .99% and .5%, a 2% bonus
Level 3: If scrap is between .49 and 0%, a 3% bonus

Goal #3: Customer Service
Level 1: If a customer satisfaction rating of 95%–96%, a 0.5% bonus
Level 2: If a customer satisfaction rating of 96.1%–97%, a 1% bonus
Level 3: If a customer satisfaction rating of 97.1%–98%, a 1.5 bonus
Level 4: If a customer satisfaction rating of 98.1%–99%, a 2% bonus
Level 5: If a customer satisfaction rating of 99.1%–100%, a 3% bonus

Then, at the end of each period, performance is assessed and a bonus is paid accordingly. For the example above, a period of the following would result in an overall bonus of 6 percent of base pay to all employees:

Goal #1:	Productivity up 9%	results in 2% bonus
Goal #2:	Scrap at .76%	results in 2% bonus
Goal #3:	Customer Service at 98.3%	results in 2% bonus
		Total: 6% bonus

In this manner, teams and teamwork are the basis of an ongoing, organization-wide reward for performance enhancement, in the direction of the organization's Model of Success.

VOLVO'S KALMAR PLANT ANSWERS QUESTION: "WHAT IS IN IT FOR ME?"

In the late 1970s, the Volvo assembly plant in Kalmar, Sweden, was brought on-line with a collaboration approach linked with Automated Guided Vehicles (AGVs). Participative management and a team-based culture were the drivers of this successful forerunner of the Revolutionary Organization. The 1,800 employees were divided into 125 work teams who had responsibilities to lay out the work area, make work assignments, and design jobs. Communications were open and, on the whole, results were good. However, by the mid 1980s, the motivation for Peak-to-Peak Performance was low and employees did not see the benefits of improving.

In 1987, a goalsharing program was installed that answered the question being asked by many people at Kalmar: "What is in it for me?" The goalsharing plan was based upon the following six factors:

1. Quality
2. Spoilage and Adjustments
3. Consumption of Materials and Suppliers
4. Consumption of Added Materials
5. Man-Hours per Car
6. Capital Costs for Total Inventories and Other Costs

At the same time the goalsharing plan was installed, all employees in the shop were given the same hourly wage. The performance against the goals were calculated and communicated every 14 days.

An in-depth series of surveys and studies of Kalmar have indicated the following:

1. The tremendous success of the goalsharing plan as a tool to improve key performance indicators.
2. Positive motivation through rewarding the teams for their performance.
3. A problem for some in the leveling all wages. This leveling would have been satisfactory if an individual bonus plan had been a portion of the total compensation.
4. A need to reward people who increase their ability to contribute. This would be totally resolved at Volvo had they implemented a pay-for-skill portion to the compensation plan.

(continued)

The Volvo Kalmar facility has pioneered many innovative concepts and continues to do so. In this case, they have done well in realizing the need to shift compensation to ensure the continuous pursuit of Peak-to-Peak Performances. We have learned and continue to learn from this illustration. However, let's not only learn from what they have done, but let's also learn from what they have yet to do. In this way, your Revolutionary Organization will move well beyond Volvo.

Call to Action

Well, are you ready to fish? I realize that you probably have several very specific questions concerning your specific rewards and recognition situation. My hope is that I have given you the insight to think through them on your own. Rewards and recognition must not be underestimated in your Revolutionary activity. If you do them right and do them well, you will experience tremendous levels of success, alignment, morale, and excitement. This is what I want for you; not frustration and failure. As you pursue your Compensation Revolution, be very careful. Keep this book by your side, and refer to it constantly. Happy Fishing!

17

Starting Your Compensation Revolution

Revolution Principle #17:

Revolutionaries must have the opportunity to participate in and agree upon the development of the rewards and recognition.

This final principle is one that most Revolutions completely miss, yet it is essential. Revolutionaries must be rewarded according to what *they* feel is fair and motivational, not according to what the leader feels is fair and motivational. This principle will be repulsive to a Revolution that is merely an extension of the leader's ego and not a true Revolution concerned with the betterment of the general population.

But if a leader really desires to improve the life of the general population and to see the Revolutionary goals attained, then this principle must be applied.

If a leader wishes to start a Revolution to overthrow an oppressive and abusive government, they must consult with representatives of the general population to determine what they feel would be a viable reward for their participation. Would a viable reward be simply a new abusive dictator? Would a viable reward be a non-abusive dictator, but who didn't lower their taxes? Or would a viable reward be a new democratic government, that lowered taxes and put the power of government in the hands of the people? Who knows. But before a leader even thinks about trying to rally a Revolutionary force, they had better find out.

The greatest Revolutionaries are always those who stick closest to the general population. This is a trait of great leadership in general. But this characteristic is especially important when determining how a Revolutionary force will be rewarded. It is a simple philosophy: If a Revolutionary force develops their own rewards they will sense ownership of the movement. That sense is worth more than anything we could pay to get it, because it is this sense of ownership to which performance is attached.

As you consider Revolutionizing the rewards and recognition in your organization, heed this principle. Don't do it alone, separate from your employees. Don't go off to some seminar, then come back and implement a new pay system. Don't even read this book, then go and instantly change your pay system. This chapter will give you what I believe is the absolute best path forward for your Compensation Revolution, which is to allow your employees to participate in its development and implementation.

Let my People Participate

A key objective of compensation is to balance each person's contribution with their compensation. If this balance doesn't exist, you will have unhappy people who won't make their maximum contribution to the overall performance of the organization. The balance that must be pursued, however, is not an organizational balance, but rather an individual balance. Each individual must feel that their own compensation is balanced with their own contribution.

At the same time, leaders understand that if they design the compensation plan, they will be held accountable for it. Obviously, the compensation plan is a highly emotional and important issue that, if designed by leadership, will result in leadership being judged on the fairness of the compensation plan. I believe that leadership will never be viewed as fair because each person has their own definition of what constitutes fair compensation. Thus, what is needed for your Compensation Revolution is a highly participative design process. Participation in the design process will accomplish the following:

- Significantly contribute to effective implementation
- Build understanding of the whole compensation topic
- Result in a higher-quality compensation plan

It is based upon these thoughts that many compensation experts recommend putting together a "diagonal slice" group, team, or task force to design the compensation plan. However, the use of teams may be a major problem with the National Labor Relations Board (NLRB). Although many compensation experts recommend and utilize a cross-functional, salary, and hourly compensation design team to develop an organization's compensation plan, this may be viewed by the NLRB as unlawful. The two-part test used by NLRB to determine if management exerts an unlawful domination of a labor organization are:

1. Is the entity a labor organization?
   - Do employees participate?
   - Does the team have authority to make decisions without management influence?
   - Does the team deal with wages and bonus plans?
   - Do team members represent others, or do they just represent themselves?
2. Is the entity unlawfully dominated by management?
   - Does the entity obtain financial support?
   - Are members paid for meetings?
   - Are supplies and meeting places provided?
   - Does management select members and control voting procedures?
   - Does management set agendas, lead meetings, or participate?
   - Did management conceive the idea for the entity?

Interestingly, the "diagonal slice" compensation design team, as recommended by many compensation experts, earns a "Yes" in all of these questions and, therefore, according to the NLRB, is unlawful. Obviously, this path must not be pursued. Rather, to obtain beneficial participation in the compensation design, an approach other than a collaborative approach must be pursued. In union organizations, the desired approach is to work with the union on the design of the compensation plan. If the union refuses to enter into such a design effort, an agreement should be reached on the process to be pursued and the role the union would like to play in the design process. If either the union does not want to be involved or if there is no union, the design of the compensation plan should be created by the organization's leadership, while obtaining significant input and participation from everyone in the company via meetings and surveys where each individual addresses their own viewpoint and does not in any way represent or speak for others. This chapter presents the process which might be adapted to either a union or non-union environment to allow an organization to Revolutionize its compensation.

The Process of Revolutionizing Your Company's Compensation

The process of Revolutionizing your company's compensation is made up of the following 10 steps:

1. *Lay a foundation for the Compensation Revolution.* The person on the Steering Team most familiar with your company's present compensation plan should accept the role of point person for laying the foundation for the Compensation Revolution. This point person should organize a half-day education session for the Steering Team and the Leadership Team that covers the present compensation plan, the information presented in Chapters 16, 17, and 18 of this book, and an open discussion of opportunities for improvement. The organization's Model of Success should be used as a focal point during these discussions in aligning the organization and the organization's compensation plan.

After the education session, the Leadership Team should charter a strategy team of salary personnel to design the compensation plan. If a union exists, the charter for this design team should reflect the role, participation, and interface that should exist between the Design Team and the union. If a union does not exist, the requirements of the NLRB should be included in the charter. As a portion of the kickoff of the Revolutionary Compensation Plan Strategy Design Team, this team should be given the same education session as the Steering Team and Leadership Team received.

2. *Define the overall compensation plan structure*. The Revolutionary Compensation Plan Strategy Design Team should define the overall structure of the plan. This structure should include factors such as:
   - Base pay will be the same for all people doing the same job except for a seniority graduation.
   - A pay-for-skill system will be put in place based upon competency-based development.
   - An individual bonus will be in place based upon individual goal assessment.
   - A goalshare plan will be in place based upon overall organization performance.
   - The structure should not include:
     — Specific base pay rates
     — Specific pay-for-skill compensation levels or methodology for Competency-Based Development
     — Specific bonus levels or procedures for individual goal setting or assessing
     — Specific bonus numbers or criteria to be included

At this point in the development of the Revolutionary Compensation Plan, what is needed is the overall structure of the plan, not the details. Determining factors in designing this structure include:

- Problems with the present compensation plan
- Ensuring fairness and balance between contribution and compensation

- Providing proper motivation
- Providing for alignment with the organization's Model of Success
- Assuming simplicity of understanding while still providing responsiveness to market conditions

3. Obtain an assessment of the present compensation plan, input on the structure of the Revolutionary plan, and feelings on compensation ranges for the Revolutionary plan. A one-to-two-hour session should be held either with the union and then all employees or with all employees. The background on the present compensation plan should be presented as well as the structure of the Revolutionary Compensation Plan. The utmost care must be demonstrated at this point to be certain false expectations about pay increases are not generated. The last portion of the session should be the completion of a compensation survey. This survey should include an assessment of the present compensation plan and of the Revolutionary Compensation Plan structure, and a series of questions documenting feelings on specific base rates, compensation levels, bonus levels, or bonus numbers. There should be an opportunity for people to provide comments on the survey as well as ask questions at the session. It is very important at this point of the Revolutionary Compensation Plan design that all input be solicited.
4. *Refine structure and establish next level of detail.* Based upon the inputs received from the survey, the Revolutionary Compensation Plan Strategy Design Team should refine the plan structure. The other survey inputs on base rates, compensation levels, bonus levels, and bonus numbers should also be summarized. The Strategy Design Team should then charter a series of teams to develop the Revolutionary Compensation Plan at the next level of detail. These teams should all be made up of salaried employees and may include:
   - Individual Goal Setting and Assessing Design Team
   - Emotional Recognition Design Team
   - Base Pay and Pay-for-Skill Rate Design Team
   - Competency-Based Development Design Team
   - Individual Bonus Design Team
   - Goalshare Design Team

5. *Develop an implementation plan and a communication plan.* As the detailed level of the Revolutionary Compensation Plan is being developed, the Compensation Plan Strategy Design Team should be developing an implementation plan and a communication plan. The implementation plan is typically quite easy to develop. It consists of the timing for the following events:
   - System refinement
   - System communication
   - System start-up
   - System debug
   - System improvement

   By contrast, the communication plan is anything but easy. At the heart of the challenge with the communication plan is the issue of compensation secrecy. Probably more than any one other single topic, the control over compensation information reflects the traditional power of the authoritarian organization. In some organizations, people can be fired for disclosing their compensation. Unfortunately, this secrecy does much more harm than good. The fact of the matter is that when compensation information is kept a secret, rarely is it truly a secret. When secrecy is maintained, the rumors and gossip are pervasive. Although there may be some merit in not disclosing individual compensation information, what is the problem with defining the compensation information for the categories of jobs? Some organizations answer this question by saying that the secrecy is needed because the compensation plan has many inconsistencies. Well, why not clear up the inconsistencies? In fact, a good reason to end compensation secrecy is to eliminate the inconsistencies. Other reasons to maintain compensation secrecy are based on deception, lack of openness, politics, and maintaining old paradigms.

   In short, there are no good reasons to maintain secrecy and from a motivation, honesty, openness, and feedback perspective, there are many good reasons to make compensation by category public information. This having been said, it is interesting to note that most organizations today still employ compensation secrecy, and therefore we must all be patient while this practice is updated. Once the secrecy issue is resolved, the communication plan should be developed to specifically define in what time frames specific information is to be shared. It is from the combination of the implementation plan and the communication plan that the following types of information should be presented:

- When are individual goals to be established, and for what time period?
- When will the new base pay rates be announced? When will they become effective? When will they be adjusted again? What about future adjustments?
- When will the individual goal assessments be done and when will the individual bonuses begin?
- When will the competency-based development effort begin? How about pay-for-skill? What is the timing for competency certification and does this have an expiration date?
- When will goalsharing begin? What is the base goalsharing period? When will the employees be eligible for goalsharing bonuses? How will employees learn about goalsharing performance? When?
- What is the method of appealing an individual goal assessment?
- How do I gain more understanding about the compensation system?

6. *Conduct information exchange meetings and refine the compensation plan.* Given all the detailed information that results from the teams established in Step 4 and the Implementation Plan and the Communication Plan from Step 5, a series of information exchange meetings should take place where all employees have the opportunity to understand and provide feedback on the draft of the Revolutionary Compensation Plan. An open-ended survey should be completed by all employees attending the meetings. The results of the survey should be used to refine both the compensation system and the presentation of the compensation system. A final compensation plan manual and presentation should be created.
7. *Communicate Revolutionary Compensation Plan to each employee.* A training program should be developed to teach coordinators how to present the Revolutionary Compensation Plan. This program should include a detailed review of the compensation plan

manual and presentation, as well as an in-depth understanding of the plan. Once trained, the coordinators should conduct a series of one-on-one meetings with employees to ensure their understanding of the system. All questions and concerns about the system should be captured and feedback given to the Strategy Design Team.

8. *Initiate the Revolutionary Compensation Plan.* Although relatively minor, further refinements may be made at this point based upon the feedback obtained in Step 7's survey and feedback. Then, in accordance with the Implementation Plan and the Communication Plan, the Revolutionary Compensation Plan should be implemented. This will involve team and individual meetings. The individual meetings between coordinators and employees are very important to ensure understanding, awareness, and acceptance of the Revolutionary Compensation Plan. The importance of these sessions must be stressed to the coordinators to differentiate the Revolutionary Compensation Plan from the traditional compensation plan.

   Often at this point, there will only be adjustments in compensation to bring people in-line with base pay guidelines. The individual bonus, pay-for-skill, and goalsharing portions of the compensation plan won't result in increased compensation, but just in the initiation of the individual goal, competency-based development, and goalsharing processes. The team meeting will present the opportunities available to everyone to pursue competency-based development, and the encouragement of teams to establish specific plans to use continuous improvement to achieve goalsharing goals.

9. *Debug the Revolutionary Compensation Plan.* Even though the design of the system has been very participatory, there will be problems with the implementation of the system. There will be mistakes and disagreements on things as straightforward as seniority. Built into the Revolutionary Compensation Plan should be an appeal process where any individual at any time can, without negative repercussions, appeal any part of their personal compensation. Early in the implementation, this appeal process will be tested and must be handled efficiently and effectively. In fact, employees should be encouraged to probe and question to maximize understanding and minimize uncertainty.

10. *Improve the Revolutionary Compensation Plan.* The Revolutionary Compensation Plan Strategy Design Team and the Design Teams reporting to this strategy team should be terminated. The design is now complete. However, the Revolutionary Compensation Plan is not in its final form. In fact, the Revolutionary Compensation Plan will never be in its final form. As the organization and individuals evolve, so too must the compensation plan. For this reason, a Revolutionary Compensation Plan Improvement Team must be established. In a union environment, this improvement team should consist of salaried people and union people. Unfortunately, in a non-union environment, involving hourly people may create NLRB problems, so the team must consist only of salaried people. The Leadership Team should charter the Revolutionary Compensation Plan Improvement Team and this team should proceed just like all other teams. Often it is this team that handles appeals. Certainly, this team is involved with working with the Communication Team in reporting results, making suggestions to the Leadership Team, altering the Revolutionary Compensation Plan, making policy interpretations, ensuring all portions of the organization are properly following the system in a timely manner, and educating new employees on the functioning of the system.

It is by following these steps that an organization may succesfully Revolutionize its compensation system. Although these steps will be the same for all organizations, and for some organizations even the components of Revolutionary Compensation will be the same, the Revolutionary Compensation Plan that flows from this process will be unique for each organization.

Expectations Can Undermine Results

When my second daughter was in high school, we had a problem. She was a quiet, sweet, and active young woman who enjoyed life, but who had unreasonable expectations of ordinary events. It did not matter if it was a school dance, a date, a vacation, a church outing, or just a meal at a nice restaurant. This young woman would anticipate and mentally rehearse the upcoming event to such an extent that when the event took place, it never quite lived up to her expectations. The bad news is that this made many really super events disappointing. The good news is that she grew out of this phase, and we no longer have to brace ourselves for the backlash after an event.

What does this have to do with compensation? A lot. No matter how clearly and how often you explain Revolutionary Compensation to people, there are some who build up their expectations about increases in compensation. This often results in these individuals going shopping for a new car, new living room furniture, a new dress, and so on. Then, when Revolutionary Compensation is implemented, and there is either no pot of gold or the pot is smaller than they expected, there is a lot of disappointment, maybe even hostility, and a feeling of being cheated. It is for this reason that the design of each company's Revolutionary Compensation Plan must be done in a very participative environment and with clear and open communications. Leadership must avoid elevating expectations, and every effort must be made to underestimate and under-promise the results of Revolutionary Compensation, so that when the Revolutionary Compensation Plan is implemented, there is no disappointment or let down.

Implementing Competency-Based Development

Here is the process that should be followed to implement Competency-Based Development as a part of your Compensation Revolution:

1. *Lay a foundation for implementing Competency-Based Development*: The person on the Revolutionary Compensation Plan Strategy Design Team most familiar with employee training should develop a presentation that describes all task-specific training that has been done by the organization. This presentation should be made to the Revolutionary Compensation Plan Strategy Design Team who should then charter the Competency-Based Development Design Team. The charter for the Competency-Based Development Design Team should require this design team to work closely with the Revolutionary Compensation Plan Strategy Design Team as it develops the specific application of competency-based development.

2. *Enhance awareness and understanding of Competency-Based Development*: The same presentation that was provided to the Revolutionary Compensation Plan Strategy Design Team (or the task-specific training done by the organization) should be given to the Competency-Based Development Design Team. In addition, the following topics should be presented by the Revolutionary Compensation Plan Strategy Design Team to the Competency-Based Development Design Team:
   - Relationship of Competency-Based Development to Pay-for-Skill.
   - Integration of Competency-Based Development implementation to the implementation of the overall Revolutionary Compensation Plan.
   - The Competency-Based Development design process defined in this book.
3. *Establish a Competency Level Skill Requirements Matrix*: The three-step process to define the Competency Level Skill Requirements Matrix is:
   1. Define all job classifications.
   2. Define the functional tasks required by all of the job classifications.
   3. Define the skill level of each functional task for each job and record these skill levels in a Competency Level Skill Requirements Matrix.

   For example, the job classifications that exist in a warehouse include the following:
   - Lift truck driver
   - Lead operator
   - Supervisor
   - Traffic manager
   - Customer service representative
   - Scheduling
   - Clerical
   - Rework
   - Quality assurance

The functional tasks in this warehouse include the following:

- Receiving
- Putaway
- Picking
- Shipping
- Inventory management
- Re-warehousing
- Traffic
- Order administration
- System administration

The skill levels include:

- Level I, beginner
- Level II, user
- Level III, expert

Then the Competency Level Skill Requirements Matrix can be designed as shown in Table 17.1.

4. *Develop Competency-Based Development Functional Tests for each skill level for each functional task*: The person on the Competency-Based Development Design Team most familiar with each functional task area should take responsibility for the development questions for each skill level found for the functional tasks in the Competency Level Skill Requirements Matrix. These questions should be multiple choice–type questions. These questions should be reviewed by the team for their clarity, relevance, and proper definition by skill level. A functional test for each job classification may then be developed by combining the questions at the appropriate skill level for each of the functional tasks.

   For example, for the job classification *lift truck driver* in Table 17.1, the competency-based test would consist of expert knowledge (Level III) of receiving, putaway, picking, shipping, and re-warehousing; user knowledge (Level II) for inventory management; and beginner knowledge (Level I) for traffic, order administration, and system administration.

Table 17.1 An Example of a Competency Level Skill Requirements Matrix for a Warehouse (I = Beginner, II = User, III = Expert, NA = Not Applicable)

	FUNCTIONAL TASKS								
JOB CLASSIFACTIONS	**Receiving**	**Putaway**	**Picking**	**Shipping**	**Inventory Mgmt.**	**Re-warehousing**	**Traffic**	**Order Admin.**	**System Admin.**
Lift Truck Operator	III	III	III	III	II	III	I	I	I
Lead Operator	III	III	III	III	III	III	II	III	II
Supervisor	III	III	III	III	III	III	III	III	III
Traffic Manager	N/A	N/A	N/A	I	N/A	N/A	III	III	I
Customer Service	I	N/A	N/A	I	II	N/A	I	III	I
Scheduling	I	N/A	N/A	N/A	III	N/A	N/A	III	I
Clerical	II	I	I	II	III	N/A	II	III	III
Rework	N/A	III	III	N/A	III	III	N/A	V	I
Quality Assurance	I	N/A	N/A	N/A	II	N/A	N/A	N/A	I

5. *Refine functional tests*: A standard test review questionnaire should be developed to collect information from qualified employees in each job classification. This questionnaire, along with the test for each job classification, should be given to two to four people who are recognized as fully qualified for the job. The purpose of these trial tests and the questionnaire is to identify poorly worded questions and questions where there might be more than one correct answer. The people who take the trial test should be encouraged to provide feedback on all questions and to suggest additional questions as appropriate. The questions with problems should be refined, new questions added and, if necessary, additional trial tests performed. This should be continued until valid tests are developed for all job classifications.
6. *Develop Competency-Based Development scenario tests for each job classification*: A scenario test is a 10 to 20 minute test that requires the employee to act out or simulate an answer. Two or three scenarios should be developed for each job classification. For example, for a lift truck driver classification, tests may include the following:
   - You are traveling down an aisle and a pallet is out in the aisle. What do you do?
   - You are instructed to pick a product from a given location. The location contains another product. What do you do?
   - You are doing a cycle count and you discover damaged product. What do you do?

   These scenarios and the answers to the scenarios should be reviewed by the Competency-Based Development Design Team for their clarity, relevance, and proper definition by skill level. A scenario test for each job classification might then be developed by using any combination of the developed scenarios.
7. *Refine scenario tests*: This step is the same as Step 5, except here the scenarios are refined, instead of the questions.
8. *Train people to train people to be competent in each job classification*: Develop training materials for each skill level for each functional task. Combine these training materials to obtain a

training manual for each job classification. The Competency-Based Training Design Team should use these materials to train the trainers. The trainers should then administer both the functional test and the scenario test for the job classifications they are to train. Any questions missed should result in either a change in the test or a change in the training materials.

9. *Train a test group*: Each trainer should train a small test group of employees. This is important not only to test the materials but also to test the effectiveness of the trainer. Both the functional test and the scenario test should be given to the employees who were trained by the trainers. Any problems identified with the trainers should be addressed.
10. *Develop Competency-Based Development policies on using Competency-Based Development skills, retraining, and retesting*: A difficulty that occurs in some organizations is that people are trained, tested, and certified for certain job classifications; receive the appropriate pay-for-skill pay rate; but then never utilize the increased skills they have obtained. The Competency-Based Development Design Team should develop policies on the utilization of job classification skills and the retesting of employees to both update employees and to ensure the paying for skills that still exist. A policy for retraining employees who are no longer competent should also be developed by the Competency-Based Development Design Team.
11. *Implement Competency-Based Development*: Integrate competency-based development with the Pay-for-Skill Rate Design Team results and implement them along with the other elements of the Revolutionary Compensation Plan. Follow the process as presented in Step 8 of the overall implementation of Revolutionary Compensation. Individuals should be encouraged to pursue competence in different job classifications to broaden their expertise and ability to support the increased performance of the organization.
12. *Debug and participate in the Revolutionary Compensation Improvement Team*: As people receive training and take the Competency-Based Development tests, the Competency-Based Development

Design Team should review the results and provide whatever additional support is needed to ensure the success of Competency-Based Development and pay-for-skill. As the start-up difficulties of Competency-Based Development are resolved, the Competency-Based Development Design Team should be terminated. At least one member from this design team, however, should be placed on the Revolutionary Compensation Plan Improvement Team to help this improvement team accomplish these tasks:

- Update and/or upgrade Competency-Based Development tests and training materials as appropriate.
- Create new Competency-Based Development tests and training materials as appropriate.
- Encourage people to enhance their value to the organization and their pay rate by pursuing Competency-Based Development.
- Oversee the competency-based development policies for the utilization, retest, and recertification of skills.

Implementing Goalsharing

The process that should be followed to implement goalsharing as a part of the shift to Revolutionary Compensation is:

1. *Lay a foundation for implementing goalsharing*: As a portion of the overall shift from traditional compensation to Revolutionary Compensation, the Steering Team, the Leadership Team, and the Revolutionary Compensation Plan Strategy Design Team have all participated in an education session that included an overview of goalsharing. Based upon this framework, the Revolutionary Compensation Plan Strategy Design Team should charter a Goalshare Design Team with the task of designing the specific application of goalsharing. This Goalshare Design Team should report to the Revolutionary Compensation Plan Strategy Design Team, but will also directly communicate with the Steering Team and the Leadership Team and shall obtain approval of the recommended goalsharing plan from the Steering Team.

2. *Enhance awareness and understanding of goalsharing*: Either the Revolutionary Compensation Plan Strategy Design Team or a consultant should be given the task of developing and presenting a three-to-four-hour discussion on goalsharing. Topics to be included are:
   - The relationship of goalsharing to traditional gainsharing.
   - The integration of goalsharing implementation to the implementation of the overall Revolutionary Compensation Plan.
3. *Goalshare Design Team Designs Goalsharing Plan Structure.* The Goalshare Design Team should collect history on the goal factors and do a historical simulation of the bonuses that would be paid if various goals had been in place.
4. *Goalshare Design Team gets input on Goalsharing Structure.* The Goalshare Design Team should present the goalshare structure and historical simulation to the Steering Team, the Leadership Team, and the Revolutionary Compensation Plan Strategy Design Team. The people on these teams should provide input via comment and survey. This input should be used to refine the goalshare structure and the presentation of the goalshare plan.
5. *Goalshare Design Team defines specific goals and bonuses.* The result of Step 4 will be a refined goalshare structure and feedback on the historical simulations. Based on this input, the Goalshare Design Team should establish the specifics of the goals and bonuses for the first year of the goalsharing plan. These specific goals and bonuses should be presented to the Steering Team along with a simulation of the range of potential results for the Steering Team's feedback, refinement, and approval.
6. *Goalshare Design Team defines Goalshare Implementation Plan.* In concert with the Revolutionary Compensation Implementation Plan, the timing for the implementation of the Goalshare Plan should be established. This Implementation Plan should include the date for the Goalshare Plan initiation, the payout periods, and the dates for bonus distribution.
7. *Develop a Goalshare Policy Document.* This four-to-six-page document should explain the why, what, how, and when of goalsharing for the company. This document will be integrated with the materials from other teams to form the basis for the

information exchange meetings. The survey information on goalsharing obtained at these exchanged meetings should be passed to the Goalshare Design Team to further refine the goalsharing plan. These refinements should be made to the goalshare policy document and the goalshare presentation package.

8. *Support the communication of the Revolutionary Compensation Plan to each employee.* Step 7 of the implementation plan for Revolutionary Compensation involves the training of coordinators and a series of one-on-one meetings with employees. The Goalshare Design Team should be an active participant in developing goalshare training materials and in helping coordinators and employees understand the mechanics, procedures, and benefits of the goalsharing plan. The Goalshare Design Team should be a strong advocate in the Revolutionary Compensation transformation for the organization's team-based process. The Goalshare Design Team should be a loud voice in support of using the team-based process to achieve the goals and obtain the bonuses available from goalsharing. Minor refinement of the goalsharing plan might be made at this point based upon feedback received from employees.
9. *Implement goalsharing.* As a part of Step 8 in the implementation of Revolutionary Compensation, goalsharing will be implemented. At the outset, team meetings should be held with each team to emphasize the goalsharing plan and the opportunity for teams to create Peak-to-Peak Performance to work toward achieving goals. Teams should be encouraged to define their role in achieving the goalsharing goals and to set their own team goals in concert with the goalsharing goals. It is critical to recognize that in addition to the individual attention people will be getting with the implementation of Revolutionary Compensation, goalsharing must be proactively used to continue to focus people's attention on the team-based process.
10. *Debug and participate in the Revolutionary Compensation Improvement Team*: As the first goalsharing reports and the first goalsharing checks are issued, there will be many questions and concerns. The Goalsharing Design Team should provide whatever support is necessary at this time to ensure understanding of the

goalsharing plan. As the initial implementation concerns pass, the Goalsharing Design Team should be terminated, but like the overall design of Revolutionary Compensation, the job is never completely done. At least one member from the Goalsharing Design Team should be placed on the Revolutionary Compensation Plan Improvement Team. It is this team that will perform these tasks:

- Report to the Communication Team on the performance of goalsharing.
- Oversee the proper interpretation and application of the goalsharing plan.
- Define new factors and interface with the Steering Team to set goals and bonuses for the next year.
- Continue to stress to all teams the impact of their team efforts on the goalsharing goals and to encourage team goal setting and achievement in concert with the goalsharing goals.

Revolutionary Compensation Success Factors

I once again turn to the issue of success. I really want your Compensation Revolution to be successful. Here are the ten most important factors that support the success of a Compensation Revolution:

1. *Leadership Commitment.* The Revolution from traditional compensation to Revolutionary Compensation only works after there has been a Revolution from management to leadership, from individuals to teams, and from traditional supplier/customer relationships to partnerships. Leadership must drive the organization to become a team-based organization focused on creating peak-to-peak performance, and then must be dedicated to the philosophy of paying-for-performance, paying-for-skill performance, paying-for-skill, and rewarding team initiatives for achieving goals. This dedication must be a long-term commitment and not a passing fancy. All employees must understand and observe this leadership dedication. Leadership must be enthusiastic and consistent in their support of the team-based

process, partnerships, and Revolutionary Compensation.

2. *Model of Success.* Everyone in the organization must understand that the Model of Success is the navigation system for the company's Revolution. Revolutionary Compensation must support and reinforce the commitment to the Model of Success.
3. *Quality Communications.* The Revolutionary Compensation Plan Strategy Design Team, the Revolutionary Compensation Plan Improvement Team, and the Communication Team must be persistent and consistent in presenting the Revolutionary Compensation message. Communication requirements are ongoing. Each week there will be new questions and new issues that must be addressed. All employees need to be kept up-to-date on the continuous evolution of Revolutionary Compensation. Quality communications demand calculation accuracy, responsiveness to problems, and clarity of all Revolutionary Compensation communications.
4. *Trust.* Without trust, there cannot be a successful buy-in to Revolutionary Compensation. Attempting to use Revolutionary Compensation to overcome cultural problems, lack of leadership, non-functioning teams, or any other problem will not work. Revolutionary Compensation must not be viewed as a bribe to overcome problems, but rather as a reward to celebrate peak-to-peak performance.
5. *Peak-to-Peak Performance.* Revolutionary Compensation is the rewards portion of Peak-to-Peak Performance. Without Peak-to-Peak Performance in leadership, collaboration, and partnerships, there are no rewards for Revolutionary Compensation to distribute. Without Peak-to-Peak Performance, there is no emotional recognition, no pay-for-skill, no individual bonus, and no goalsharing bonus. Peak-to-Peak Performance is the driver behind Revolutionary Compensation.
6. *Equitability and Understandability.* The success of Revolutionary Compensation depends upon everyone understanding Revolutionary Compensation, and that everyone understands the balance between contribution and compensation. Revolutionary Compensation must not only be fair to all employees, but also to the organization, and be sufficiently flexible so that Revolutionary Compensation adapts as conditions change, to maintain equitability.

7. *Employee Participation.* Revolutionary Compensation must be respectful of NLRB requirements but must also allow significant employee involvement so that all employees own, accept, and are enthusiastic about Revolutionary Compensation. There should be no barriers to employees providing feedback, having information, or participating in the design and continuous improvement of Revolutionary Compensation.
8. *Employees must connect Peak-to-Peak Performance with increased compensation.* Employees must understand that when they perform well, both individually and as a part of a team, that this is the basis of Revolutionary Compensation and increased compensation. At the same time, when the organization does not perform well as individuals or as teams, Revolutionary Compensation will not result in increased compensation.
9. *Flexibility.* All successful Revolutionary Compensation Plans are custom-designed for the organization. Revolutionary Compensation must be consistent with and reinforce the organization's Model of Success and the team-based process. It is important that the entire organization understand that Revolutionary Compensation must be fluid and that it will continuously improve and evolve just as the organization will. It is the responsibility of the Revolutionary Compensation Plan Improvement Team to be certain that Revolutionary Compensation is up-to-date and properly reflects the priorities of the organization.
10. *Revolutionary Compensation success.* At the end of the day, the true measure of Revolutionary Compensation success has to do with whether the organization is better off and whether the employees are better off. If for whatever reason the company is not more profitable and the employees are not better compensated, then Revolutionary Compensation has not been a success. Therefore, the company must re-learn the shift from manager to leader, from individuals to teams, and from the traditional supplier/customer relationship to partnerships, and this will bring about Peak-to-Peak Performance that results in the success of Revolutionary Compensation that leads to more Peak-to-Peak Performance and on, and on, and on, continuously getting better and better.

Call to Action

I realize this chapter threw a lot at you. But a thorough understanding of the issues I have presented is what will make your Compensation Revolution successful. My call to action is simple—implement. Take what you have read and put it to work. I have done all I can do to give you a clear road map to success. Don't let these words sit in this book one more day. Implement them, and then enjoy the success, for that is why I wrote this book.

Conclusion

How do you like a movie to end? Some movies end with the good guys defeating evil and everyone living happily ever after. Other movies don't end; they just kind of stop. For days on end, my wife and I will discuss who really did it? What would happen next? Did the couple get back together or not? What did she mean when she said, "I am really anxious to see you"? The movie did not end, it just stopped.

How about the books you read? How do you like them to end? Some non-fiction books end with the *plan*—the seven steps you should follow to do whatever it was the book promised you could do. Other books don't end but just kind of stop. Now, I know you want your seven-step plan. Unfortunately, this book is not really a seven-step plan type of book, because what you need to do next depends upon where you start.

Two stories come to mind. The first from *Alice in Wonderland*, where Alice, lost in the woods and faced with a fork in the road, asks the cat which way to go. The cat says the path selection depends on where Alice wants to go. Alice does not know where she wants to go, so the cat replies, "Then it matters not which path you take." The other story is credited to Yogi Berra. When asked what to do when facing a decision such as Alice's, Yogi is reported to have said, "When you come to a fork in the road, take it." You see, what you should do next depends on where you are and the status of your organization. I think we should learn from Alice and begin our path forward by trying to understand both where we are now and where we are trying to go. I think we should learn from Yogi and realize that it is not as important for us to decide which path as it is for us to do something. To make something happen! To take some direction! To act! Nevertheless, I know you still want your seven-step plan, so here goes:

STEP 1: Share this book with others.

STEP 2: Determine your organization's status on the Revolution from management to leadership. Define a path forward. Do it.

STEP 3: Determine your organization's status on the Revolution from individuals to collaboration. Define a path forward. Do it.

STEP 4: Determine your organization's status on the Revolution from traditional customer/supplier relationships to partnerships. Define a path forward. Do it.

STEP 5: Determine your organization's status on the Revolution from traditional compensation to Revolutionary Compensation. Define a path forward. Do it.

STEP 6: Determine your organization's status on becoming a Revolutionary Organization. Define a path forward. Do it.

STEP 7: Return to Step 2 with enthusiasm.

A COMPANY BECOMES A REVOLUTIONARY ORGANIZATION: TWICE

The pursuit of becoming a Revolutionary Organization began in 1990. By early 1991, management had become leadership, the organization was collaborative, and compensation had been upgraded. Things were good. Sales were up, profits were up, salaries were up, and quality was up. Everything was great. By early 1992, the growth forced the company to pursue an Organizational Design Team and to restructure responsibilities. Growth continued, profits continued to grow, things were good. When the firm reached a point of twice the size it had been two years earlier, it began

(continued)

to lose control. Because of the level of business, leadership shifted to management, and the collaborative process fell into disrepair. Many new people were hired and the culture became one of static consistency. Innovation and improvements ceased and most people focused on simply getting through. By 1994, the company was no longer a Revolutionary Organization.

The process was reinstalled in the summer of 1994. Leadership went back to being leaders. Individuals went back to collaborating, and the team-based compensation plan began paying bonuses again. The second attempt at becoming a Revolutionary Organization was more difficult, since many had watched the company succeed and then fail. The second attempt at becoming a a Revolutionary Organization was easier, since many knew it worked, liked the process of renewal, and understood where they went wrong. The reinstallation of the process took place over a three-month period, and today the organization is once again a Revolutionary Organization. Guess what? Sales are way up, profits are way up, quality is way up, salaries are way up. In this case, it was not only proven that a Revolutionary Organization works, but that it can be made to work twice in the same organization.

Yes, But . . .

Many have read this book, many have heard me explain Organizational Revolution, and many have pursued the process. The process works and is fundamental to business success. Nevertheless, skepticism exists and needs to be addressed. I do not view skepticism as negative, but rather as a desire to more fully understand how the process of becoming a Revolutionary Organization really works. This is great. Allow me to respond to the five questions/concerns I am most often asked:

QUESTION 1: *I am not in a position in my organization where I can make the decision to become a Revolutionary Organization. What should I do?* This is a good question, since the pursuit of becoming a Revolutionary Organization is a leadership-driven pursuit, and this question indicates an awareness of the role of leadership. At the same time, it is important to understand the level of leadership that is required. For example, a plant manager who has 300 people under their leadership may not be able to make the shift in compensation, but would certainly be positioned to begin the process of becoming a Revolutionary Organization.

Similarly, a distribution center manager who has 40 people under their leadership may not be able to make the Revolution to partnerships or in compensation, but would certainly be positioned to begin the process of becoming a Revolutionary Organization. By contrast, a branch manager of a bank having 12 employees or a department manager in a hospital having 80 employees would not be properly positioned to pursue the organization becoming a Revolutionary Organization.

The issue has less to do with size of staff and more to do with the ability of the leader to define a Model of Success, transform culture, and pursue a team-based environment. If a leader is positioned to accomplish these things, then this is the level of leadership needed to begin the pursuit of becoming a Revolutionary Organization. If this level of leadership is not on board, the next step is to get this level on board. Give these people a copy of this book and help them understand how and why the organization should pursue becoming a Revolutionary Organization.

QUESTION 2: *I am the right level in the organization and we wish to become a Revolutionary Organization. What should I do?* There are two different ways to answer this question correctly. The first way is to begin by involving people. Give them a copy of this book. Hold a meeting. Host a presentation on the process of becoming a Revolutionary Organization. Begin by involving people and having people define the path forward. Maybe even follow the seven-step plan. The second way to answer the question is not only a good answer, but also helps explain why the first answer works.

The second answer to the question is that it does not matter what you do first as long as you are willing to learn from whatever you decide to do. If you do something that moves the organization closer to becoming a Revolutionary Organization, great. Do it some more. If you do something that does not move the organization closer to becoming a Revolutionary Organization, this is also okay. Learn from this mistake; do not do it again, but try something else. You see, it does not matter what you do, what matters is that you are doing something and that you are learning from your actions. This is the true pursuit of a Revolutionary Organization and no matter what it is that was done, it will allow you to learn and thus be on the path to becoming a Revolutionary Organization.

QUESTION 3: *What are the costs of becoming a Revolutionary Organization?* Once again, there are two correct answers to this question. The first answer may be viewed as being somewhat sarcastic because it answers a question with a question, but is not meant to be sarcastic. The first answer is, what is the cost of NOT becoming a Revolutionary Organization? In a *Fortune* article entitled "Burned-Out Bosses," it said that "Work no longer energizes; it drains." As companies have downsized and re-engineered, this results in overworked and under-motivated workers who are not trying to improve anything but rather just hanging on. This results in poor performance, unsatisfactory profits, which leads to more layoffs, more overworked staff, less performance, less profits, more layoffs, and so on. Without the transformation of becoming a Revolutionary Organization, there is no evolution of success and therefore, the cost of not pursuing the process of a Revolutionary Organization is huge. Without the movement to becoming a Revolutionary Organization, all is lost; the company will eventually be history.

On the other hand, the more direct answer to the question of what it will cost to be a Revolutionary Organization is that it will cost somewhere between a few days to a few weeks payroll for the people contained within the organization to be transformed into a Revolutionary Organization. For an advanced organization with a leadership-driven team-based process in place, the cost will be a few days of payroll. For a traditional organization with a dinosaur culture and no team-based process, the investment could be as much as four weeks of payroll of the people impacted.

At the same time, the bottom line benefits of becoming a Revolutionary Organization are very large. For an advanced organization, the payback of becoming a Revolutionary Organization will take somewhere between four and eight weeks. For a traditional organization, the payback could take much longer, but in no case ever more than six months. Yes, there is seed money that is required to jump start the process of becoming a Revolutionary Organization, but this seed money will be returned many, many times over from the benefits that will result from being a Revolutionary Organization.

QUESTION 4: *How long does it take to become a Revolutionary Organization?* Please excuse what appears to be a flip answer here, but the truth is that it takes about 10 percent longer than what leadership estimates it will take to become a Revolutionary Organization. If leadership estimates it will take 10 weeks, it will probably take 11 weeks; if leadership estimates it will take 10 months, it will probably take 11 months; and if leadership estimates it will take 10 years, it will probably take 11 years. The reality is that the time leadership projects more often than not will become a self-fulfilling prophecy. The rate at which an organization is transformed depends upon how much time an organization believes it has to be transformed. An organization that is in financial trouble and on the verge of going out of business, if it can be transformed, will be transformed in a few weeks. An organization who believes that all is well and that there is no urgency to be transformed can easily take years to become a Revolutionary Organization. The one thing that is clear is that it is easier to do it quickly. Good advice is to start quickly and then keep accelerating. Becoming a Revolutionary Organization quickly creates a sense of urgency, excitement, energy, and confidence. I can think of no reason to not start quickly and then keep accelerating.

QUESTION 5: *What are the risks of trying to become a Revolutionary Organization and failing?* The only way to fail at becoming a Revolutionary Organization is to quit. Sure, there will be disappointments, setbacks, and problems while becoming a Revolutionary Organization, but these difficulties are not failures, they are opportunities to grow, learn, progress, and improve. Therefore, the only risk of trying to become a Revolutionary Organization is the risk associated with the level of commitment by leadership. If leadership is not committed for the long term, there is a significant risk since once the organizational transformation begins, it is very difficult to reverse. Once leaders begin to lead and once the transformation from individuals to teams begins, the organization will be very unhappy and uncomfortable with any attempt to return the organization to its original status. Oliver Wendell Holmes said this best when he said, "Man's mind, stretched to a new idea, never goes back to its original dimensions."

So, the only risk leadership is exposed to in the pursuit of becoming a Revolutionary Organization is the risk of not maintaining their commitment and enthusiasm for becoming a Revolutionary Organization. If leadership is uncomfortable with this risk, then they should not pursue becoming a Revolutionary Organization. Otherwise, let's begin, let's do something.

Call to Action

An alternative title for this book could be: "How Are You Gonna Get To Where You Gotta Go." I ask, if you are *not* going to pursue the Revolution from management to leadership, from individuals to collaboration, from traditional customer/supplier relationships to partnerships, and from traditional compensation to Revolutionary Compensation, "How are you gonna get to where you gotta go?" You see, I believe you have no choice. I know the process presented in this book works. I know the process is appropriate for where your organization is today and where it will be in five years. This process itself is not static, but within your organization will evolve, grow, and improve. For your organization to achieve its full potential, you must become a Revolutionary Organization. The next step is yours. You need to do something. You need to start quickly and then keep accelerating. The sense of momentum that will occur from your quick start will pull people into the process. This involvement, while following the process and learning as you go, will result in the synergy needed to create Peak-to-Peak Performance, which will encourage others to be involved. You must take responsibility for making something happen, for doing something now, for starting your Organizational Revolution. My recommendation? Go, Go, Go!

End Notes

Chapter 1
Continuous Process

Notes:

[1] P. Riley, *The Winner Within: A Life Plan for Team Players* (New York: G.P. Putnam's Sons, 1993), 161

[2] *ibid.,* p. 211

[3] *ibid.,* p.154

[4] *ibid.,* p. 45

[5] *ibid.,* p. 45

[6] *ibid.,* p.139

[7] C.J. Loomis, "Dinosaurs," Fortune (3 May 1993), 36-42.

Other Works Consulted:

Blumenthal, B., and P. Haspeslagh. "Toward a Definition of Corporate Transformations." *Sloan Management Review*, Spring 1994.

Dessler, G. *Winning Commitment: How to Build and Keep a Competitive Work Force*. New York: McGraw-Hill, 1993.

Gordon J. "Into the Dark: Rough Ride Ahead for American Workers." *Training*, July 1993.

Goss, T., R. Pascale, and A. Athos. "The Reinvention Roller Coaster: Risking the Present for a Powerful Future." *Harvard Business Review,* November-December 1993.

Huey, J. "The New Post-Heroic Leadership." *Fortune,* 21 February 1994.

Loomis C.J. "Dinosaurs." *Fortune*, 3 May 1993.

Johnson, H.J. *Relevance Regained: From Top-Down Control to Bottom-Up Empowerment.* New York: The Free Press, 1992.

Pritchett, P. *Culture Shift.* Dallas: Pritchett Publishing Company, 1993.

Pritchett, P. *Firing Up Commitment During Organizational Change.* Dallas: Pritchett Publishing Company, 1994.

Smith, L. "Burned-Out Bosses." *Fortune*, 25 July 1994.

Stewart, T.A. "Welcome to the Revolution." *Fortune*, 13 December 1993.

Stewart, T.A. "The Information Age in Charts." *Fortune*, 4 April 1994.

Chapter Two

None.

Chapter 3
Follow the Leader

Notes:

[1] G. Gschwandtner, "Margaret Thatcher Leads You to Success," *Personal Selling Power* (October, 1993).

[2] G. Gschwandter, *Superachievers* (Prentice Hall: New York, 1984), 149.

[3] R. Emerson, *Essays and Poems* (London: The Everyman Library, 1992), 146-52.

[4] W. Bennis, *On Becoming a Leader* (Phoenix: Perseus, 1994), 151.

[5] A.J. Zaremba, *Management in a New Key: Communication In The Modern Organization* (Norcross: IIE, 1989), 4-5

[6] Ibid., 13-129.

[7] G. Gschwandter, *Superechievers* (Prentice Hall: New York, 1984),

[8] D.J. Phillips, *Lincoln on Leadership* (New York, Warner Books, 1992), 154, 161, 169.

[9] M.K. Fleschner II and Mike Ditka, "Winning With Teamwork the Bears Way," *Personal Selling Power* (April, 1992).

Other Works Consulted:

Stratford, S. "A Master Class in Radical Change." *Fortune,* December 1993.

Belasco, J. A. and R. C. Stayer. *Flight of the Buffalo: Soaring to Excellence, Learning to Let Employees Lead.* New York: Warner Books, 1993.

Brown, T. and Joel Barker. "New Thoughts on Paradigms." *Industry Week,* 18 May 1982.

Deutschman, A. "The CEO's Secret of Managing Time." *Fortune,* 1 June 1992.

Dock, J. D. "Managing Change: The Art of Balancing." *Harvard Business Review,* November/December 1993.

Falvey, J. "Selling to the Sales Force." *Sales and Marketing Management,* April 1992.

Huey, J. "Sam Walton in His Own Words." *Fortune,* 29 July 1992.

Kotter, J. P. *A Force for Change.* New York: The Free Press, 1990.

Kouzes, J. M. and B.Z. Posner. *The Leadership Challenge.* San Francisco: Jossey-Bass, 1987.

Lebow, R. *A Journey into the Heroic Environment.* Rocklin: Prima Publishing, 1992.

Maynard, B. "Winning Organizations in the 90s." *TeleProfessional,* April 1993.

Neusch, D. R. and A.F. Siebenaler. *The High Performance Enterprise.* Essex Junction: Oliver Wight Publications, 1993.

Tompkins, J. A. "Project Leadership." *Industrial Product-Bulletin*, January 1990.

Tompkins, J. A. "Team-Based Continuous Improvement: How to Make the Pace of Change Work for You and Your Company." *Material Handling Engineering,* February, 1993.

Tompkins, J. A. *Winning Manufacturing: The How-to-Book of Successful Manufacturing.* Norcross: IIE, 1989.

Waitley, D. *10 Seeds of Greatness.* Old Tappan: Fleming H. Revell Company, 1983.

Wick, C. W. and L.S. Leon. *The Learning Edge.* New York: McGraw-Hill, 1993.

Chapter 4
Cultural Revolution

Notes:

1 L. Iacocca and W. Novak, *Iacocca: An Autobiography* (New York: Bantam Books, 1984), 165.

2 Ibid., 280.

3 J.P. Kotter and J. L. Heshett, *Corporate Culture and Performance* (New York: The Free Press, 1992), 84.

4 N.M. Tichy, "Revolutionize Your Company," *Fortune* (13 December 1993).

Other Works Consulted:

Kotter, J. P. *A Force for Change: How Leadership Differs From Management.* New York: The Free Press, 990.

Kouzes, J. M. and B.Z. Posner, B.Z. *The Leadership Challenge.* San Francisco: Jossey-Bass Publishers, 1991.

Ott, J. S. *The Organizational Culture Perspective.* Pacific Grove: Brooks/Cole Publishing Company, 1989.

Tompkins, J. A. *Winning Manufacturing: The How-to Book of Successful Manufacturing,* Norcross: IIE, 1989.

Tompkins, J. A. "Dinosaurs and Crocodiles: How-to Grow Your Business." *Network for Material Handling,* November 1992.

Westbrook, J. D. "Organizational Culture and its Relationship to TQM." *Industrial Management,* January/February, 1993.

Chapter 5
The Vision Thing

Notes:

1 J.M. Kouzes and B.Z. Posner, *The Leadership Challenge* (San Francisco: Jossey-Bass Publishers, 1991), 81.

2 W. Bennis, *On Becoming a Leader* (Phoenix: Perseus, 1994), 186.

3 B. Nanus, *Visionary Leadership* (San Francisco: Jossey-Bass Publishers, 1992), 3.

4 J.A. Belasco and R.C. Stayler, *Flight of the Buffalo: Soaring to Excellence, Learning to Let Employees Lead* (New York: Warner Books, 1993), 90.

5 S. Stratford, "A Master Class in Radical Change," *Fortune* (13 December 1993).

6 D.J. Phillips, *Lincoln on Leadership* (New York: Warner Books, 1992), 162.

7 P.M. Senge, *The Fifth Discipline: The Art and Practice of the Learning Organization* (New York: Doubleday Currency, 1990), 9.

8 J.M. Kouzes and B.Z. Posner, *The Leadership Challenge* (San Francisco: Jossey-Bass Publishers, 1991), 85.

9 J.A. Belasco and R.C. Stayler, *Flight of the Buffalo: Soaring to Excellence, Learning to Let Employees Lead* (New York: Warner Books, 1993), 43.

10 D. Lavin, "Robert Eaton Thinks 'Vision' is Overrated and He's Not Alone," *The Wall Street Journal* (4 October 4 1993), A1.

11 Ibid., A1.

12 Ibid., A1

13 D. Schaff, *Total Quality: One Hundred and One Logical Ways to Improve Quality for Your Customers (Without Hiring a Guru or Spending Thousands)* (Lakewoods Publications, 1992).

14 T. Peters, *Thriving on Chaos* (New York: Alfred A. Knopf, 1992), 398-408.

15 T. Peters, *Liberation Management* (New York: Alfred A. Knopf, 1992), 616-17.

16 B. Nanus, *Visionary Leadership* (San Francisco, Josey-Bass, 1992), 134-56.

17 Ibid., 28-29.

18 J. Madden with D. Anderson, *Hey, Wait A Minute, I Wrote a Book* (New York, Ballentine, 1985), 225-26.

19 George Labovitz and Victor Rosansky, *The Power of Alignment* (New York: John Wiley and Sons, 1997), 4-5

20 Ibid., 5

21 Ibid., 6-7

Other Works Consulted:

Brown, T. "Is Your Company Vision-Driven?" *Industry Week*, 18 May 1992.

Dessler, G. *Winning Commitment.* New York: McGraw-Hill, 1993.

Farnham, A. "State Your Values, Hold the Hot Air." *Fortune*, 19 April 1993.

Fuchsberg, G. "Visionary Missions Becomes Its Own Mission." *The Wall Street Journal*, 7 January 1994.

Johnson, H.T. *Relevance Regained.* New York: The Free Press, 1992.

Kaplan, R.S. and D.P. Norton. "Putting the Balance Scorecard to Work." *Harvard Business Review*, September/October 1993.

Kotter, J.P. *A Force for Change.* New York: The Free Press, 1990.

Kotter, J.P. *The Leadership Factor.* New York: The Free Press, 1988.

Lee, C. "The Vision Thing." *Training*, February 1993.

Nelton, S. "Put Your Purpose in Writing." *Nation's Business*, February 1994.

Neusch, D.R. and A.F. Siebenaler. *The High Performance Enterprise.* Essex Junction, Oliver Wight Publications, 1993.

Quigley, J.V. *Vision: How Leaders Develop it, Share it, and Sustain it.* New York: McGraw-Hill, 1993.

Sayles, L.R. *The Working Leader.* New York: The Free Press, 1993.

Tompkins, J.A. "Team-Based Continuous Improvement." *Material Handling Engineering*, March 1993.

Wick, C.W. and L.S. Leon. *The Learning Edge.* New York: McGraw-Hill, 1993.

Chapter 6
Leadership is a Verb

Notes:

[1] D. Kirkpatrick, "Intel Goes for Broke," *Fortune* (16 May 1994), 62-68.

Other Works Consulted:

Belasco, J.A. and R.C. Stayer, *Flight of the Buffalo: Soaring to Excellence, Learning to Let Employees Lead.* New York: Warner Books, 1993.

Dumaine, B. "The New Non-Manager Managers." *Fortune*, 22 February 1993.

Huey, J. "The New Post-Heroic Leadership." *Fortune*, 21 February 1994.

Huey, J. "The Leadership Industry." *Fortune*, 21 February 1994.

Kotter, J.P. *A Force for Change: How Leadership Differs From Management.* New York: The Free Press, 1990.

Kotter, J.P. *Corporate Culture and Performance,* New York: The Free Press, 1988.

Kotter, J.P. *The Leadership Factor.* New York: The Free Press, 1988.

Kouzes, J.M. and B.Z. Posner. *The Leadership Challenge.* San Francisco: Jossey-Bass Publishers, 1991.

Nanus, B. *Visionary Leadership.* San Francisco: Jossey-Bass Publishers, 1992.

Pell, A.R. "Effective Leadership Means Empowerment." *The Wholesaler,* December 1993.

Tapscott, D. and A. Caston. *Paradigm Shift.* New York: McGraw-Hill, 1993.

Chapter 7
The Power of Collaboration

Notes:

1 G. Hall, J. Rosenthal, and J. Wade, "How to Make Reengineering Really Work," *Harvard Business Review* (November/December 1993), 119.

[2] M. Hammer and J. Champy, *Reengineering the Corporation* (New York: Harper Business, 1993), 200.

[3] J.V. Owen, "Concurrent Engineering," *Manufacturing Engineering* (November 1992), 72.

[4] C. Power et al., "Flops: Too Many New Products Fail. Here's Why and How to do Better," *Business Week* (16 August 1993), 77.

[5] M. Herquet, "Worker Involvement Lights Up Neon," *Training* (June 1994), 22.

Other Works Consulted:

Belbin, R.M. *Management Teams: Why They Succeed or Fail.* London: Butterworth Heinemann, 1981.

Caggiano, C. "The Profit-Promoting Daily Scorecard." *Inc,* March 1994.

Davenport, T.H. and N. Nohric. "Case Management and the Integration of Labor." *Sloan Management Review* (Winter 1994).

Drucker, P.F. "There's More than One Kind of Team." *Wall Street Journal,* 11 February 1992.

Gordon, J. "Work Teams: How Far Have They Come?" *Training,* October 1992.

Johnson, H.T. *Relevance Regained: From Top-Down Control to Bottom-Up Empowerment.* New York: The Free Press, 1992.

Kaeter, M. "Reporting Mature Work Teams." *Teams,* April 1994.

Kaplan, R.S. and D.P Norton. "Putting the Balanced Scorecard to Work." *Harvard Business Review*, September/October 1993.

Katzenbach, I.R. and D.K. Smith. *The Wisdom of Teams.* Boston: Harvard Business School Press, 1993.

Kleiner, B.M. "Managing Communication Successfully in Your Management System." *Industrial Management*, September/October 1993.

Kouzes, J.M. and B.Z. Posner. *The Leaderships Challenge.* San Francisco: Jossey-Bass, 1991.

Maguire, B. "Integrate Performance Measures to Focus Every Employee on What Matters." *Institute of Industrial Engineering Conference Procedures*. Norcross: IIE, 1994.

Meyer, C. "How the Right Measures Help Teams Excel." *Harvard Business Review,* May/June 1994.

Navarre, L. "Wolfpack: Reengineering An Organization for Global Competition." *Industrial Institute Annual Conference.* Norcross, 1994.

Neusch, D.R. and A.F. Siebenaler. *The High Performance Enterprise.* Essex Junction: Oliver Wight Publications, 1993.

Ott, J.S. *The Organization Culture Perspective*. Pacific Grove: Brooks/Cole Publishing Company, 1989.

Paulser, K.M. "Total Employee Involvement-Why are You Waiting?" *Industrial Engineering,* February 1994.

Peters, T. *Thriving on Chaos.* New York: Alfred A. Knopf, 1987.

Provost, L. and S. Leddich. "How to Take Multiple Measures to Get a Complete Picture of Organizational Performance." *National Product Review*; Autumn 1993.

Sayles, L.R. *The Working Leader.* New York: The Free Press, 1993.

Tapscott, D. and A. Caston. *Paradigm Shift.* New York: McGraw-Hill, 1993.

Templin, N. "Auto Plants, Hiring Again, are Demanding Higher-Skilled Labor." *Wall Street Journal,* 11 March 1994.

VanAken, E.M. and D.S. Sink. "Addressing Problems and Implementation Issues of Self-Managing Teams." Norcross: *International Industrial Engineering Conference Proceedings*, 1992.

Wellirs, R. and J. Workler. "The Philadelphia Story." *Training,* March 1994.

Zarembra, A.J. *Management in a New Key.* Norcross: Industrial Engineering and Management Press, 1989.

Zemke, R. "Rethinking the Rush to Team Up." *Training,* November 1993.

Chapter 8
Team Anatomy

Works Consulted:

Moran, L. and K. Hurson. "Mastering the New Role of Team Leadership." Milwaukee: *48th Annual Quality Congress Proceedings* ASQC, 1994.

Niles, J.L. and N.J. Salz,. "Why Teams Poop Out," Milwaukee: *48th Annual Quality Congress Proceedings,* ASQC, 1994.

Carson, N. "The Trouble With Teams." *Training,* August 1992.

Chapter 9
Demystifying the "E" Word

Notes:

1 B. Geber, "Guerrilla Teams: Friend or Foe," *Training* (June 1994).

2 J.C. Hyatt, "GE Chairman's Annual Letter Notes Strides by 'Stretch' of the Imagination," *Wall Street Journal (*7 March 1994), 1A.

Other Works Consulted:

Belasco, J.A. and R.C. Stayer. *Flight of the Buffalo: Soaring to Excellence, Learning to Let Employees Lead.* New York: Warner Books, 1993.

Holpp, L. "Applied Empowerment." *Training*, February 1994.

Kouzes, J.M. and B. Posner. *The Leadership Challenge.* San Francisco: Jossey-Bass Publishers, 1991.

Landes, L. "The Myth and Misdirection of Employee Empowerment." *Training*, March 1994.

Parsons, N.E. "Employee Empowerment: A Tactical Approach." *Quality*, February 1994.

Stewart, T.A. "Brainpower." *Fortune*, 3 June 1991.

Tompkins, J.A. "Team-Based Continuous Improvement." *Job Shop Technology*, March 1993.

________. "Team-Based Continuous Improvement: How to Make the Pace of Change Work for You and Your Company." *Material Handling Engineering*, January, February, March, April 1993.

________. "Teams." *Industrial Product Bulletin*, October/ November 1992, January, February, March 1993.

Vogt., J.F. and K.L. Murrell. *Empowerment in Organizations.* San Diego: Pferffer, 1990.

Chapter 10
What Do You Know?

Notes:

[1] D.A. Garvin, "Building a Learning Organization," *Harvard Business Review* (July/August 1993), 78.

[2] P.A. Galagan, "How to Get Your TQM Training on Track," *Nations Business* (October 1992), 24.

[3] D.H. Kim, "The Link Between Individual and Organizational Learning," *Sloan Management Review* (Fall 1993), 37.

[4] D.A. Kolb, *Experimental Learning: Experience as the Source of Learning and Development* (New York: Prentice-Hall, 1984), 41.

[5] D.H. Kim, "The Link Between Individual and Organizational Learning," *Sloan Management Review* (Fall 1993), 37.

[6] D.A. Garvin, "Building a Learning Organization," *Harvard Business Review* (July/August 1993), 78.

[7] C. Argyris and D. Schon, *Organizational Learning: A Theory of Action Perspective* (Reading: Addison-Wesley, 1978), 6.

[7] D.A. Garvin, "Building a Learning Organization," *Harvard Business Review* (July/August 1993), 78.

[9] C.W. Wick and L.S. Leon, *The Learning Edge: How Smart Manager and Smart Companies Stay Ahead* (New York: McGraw-Hill, 1993), 124.

[10] P.M. Senge, *The Fifth Discipline: The Art and Practice of the Learning Organization* (New York: Doubleday Currency, 1990), 3.

[11] Ibid., 10.

[12] Ibid., 235.

[13] D.H. Kim, "The Link Between Individual and Organizational Learning," *Sloan Management Review* (Fall 1993), 37.

Other Works Consulted:

Bennett, J.K. and M.J. O'Brien. "The Building Blocks of the Learning Organization." *Training*, June 1994.

Galagan, P.A. "How to Get Your TQM Training on Track." *Nations Business*, October 1992.

Kelly, K. "Motorola: Training for the Millennium." *Business Week*, 28 March 1994.

Kolb, D.A. *Experimental Learning: Experience as the Source of Learning and Development.* New York: Prentice-Hall, 1984.

Popoff, F. "The Seven Deadly Sins of Process Improvement." *Chief Executive*, June 1994.

Tapscott, D. and A. Caston. *Paradigm Shift: The New Promise of Information Technology.* New York: McGraw-Hill, 1993.

Chapter 11
Applied Science

Works Consulted:

Belasco, J.A. and R.C. Stayer. *Flight of the Buffalo: Soaring to Excellence, Learning to Let Employees Lead.* New York: Warner Books, 1993.

Belbin, R.M. *Management Teams.* Oxford: Butterworth-Heinemann, 1981.

Bennis, W. and B. Nanus. *Leaders: The Strategies for Taking Charge.* New York: Harper & Row Publishers, 1985.

Gerber, B. "From Manager into Coach." *Training*, February 1992.

Holpp, L. "5 Ways to Sink Self-Managed Teams." *Training*, September 1993.

Katzenbach, J.R. and D.K. Smith. *The Wisdom of Teams.* Boston: Harvard Business School Press, 1993.

Kouzes, J.M. and B.Z. Posner. *The Leadership Challenge: How to Get Extraordinary Things Done in Organizations.* San Francisco: Jossey-Bass Publishers, 1991.

Neusch, D.R. and A.F. Sienbenaler. *The High Performance Enterprise.* Essex Junction: Oliver Wight Publications, 1994.

Popoff, F. "The Seven Deadly Sins of Process Improvement." *Chief Executive*, June 1994.

Sayles, L.R. *The Working Leader, The Triumph of High Performance Over Conventional Management Principles.* New York: The Free Press, 1993.

Schaffer, R.H. and H.A. Thomson. "Successful Charge Programs Begin With Results." *Harvard Business Review*, January-February, 1992.

Tapscott, D. and A. Caston. *Paradigm Shift: The New Promise of Information Technology.* New York: McGraw-Hill, 1993.

Tompkins, J.A. "Team-Based Continuous Improvement: How to Make the Pace of Change Work for You and Your Company - Part 3." *Material Handling Engineering*, March 1993.

Tompkins, J.A. "Team-Based Continuous Improvement: How to Make the Pace of Change Work for You and Your Company - Part 4." *Material Handling Engineering*, April 1993.

Van Aker, E.M. and Sink. D.S. "Addressing Problems and Implementation Issues." *International Industrial Engineering Conference Proceedings. Institute of Industrial Engineers.* Norcross, 1992.

Chapter 12
Customer Service Isn't Enough

Works Consulted:

Belasco, J.A. and R.L. Stayer. *Flight of the Buffalo: Soaring to Excellence, Learning to Let Employees Lead.* New York: Warner Books, 1993.

Davidou, W.H. and B. Uttal. *Total Customer Service.* New York: Harper and Row Publishers, 1989.

Denton, D.K. "Total Customer Satisfaction: The Next Step." *Industrial Management*, November/December 1993.

Kaeter, M. "Customer Training: More Than a Sales Tool." *Training*, March 1994.

Lane, D.A. "Customer Service is not a Department." *APICS: The Performance Advantages,* February 1994.

Reichheld, F.F. "Loyalty-based Management." *Harvard Business Review*, March/April 1993.

Tompkins, J.A. "Team-based Continuous Improvement: How to Make the Pace of Change Work for You and Your Company, Part 7." *Material Handling Engineering*, October 1993.

Tompkins, J.A. *Winning Manufacturing: The How-to-Book of Successful Manufacturing.* Norcross: IIE, 1989.

Chapter 13
I Choose You

Notes:

[1] T. Peters, "The Boundaries of Business Partners - The Rhetoric and Reality," *Harvard Business Review* (October, 1991).
[2] J.H. Dyer and W.G. Ouchi, "Japanese Style Partnerships: Giving Companies a Competitive Edge," *Sloan Management Review* (Fall, 1993), 51.
[3] Ibid., 51.
[4] K.B. Clark and T. Fujimoto, *Product Development Performance* (Boston: Harvard Business School Press, 1991).
[5] S.C. Frey and M.M. Schlosser, "ABB and Ford: Creating Value Through Cooperation," *Sloan Management Review* (Fall 1993), 65-71.

Other Works Consulted:

Belasco, J.A. and R.C. Stayer. *Flight of the Buffalo: Soaring to Excellence, Learning to Let Employees Lead.* New York: Warner Books, 1993.

Conway, B. "Partnering for Quality Improvement." *Quality*, April 1994.

Gulat, R., T. Khanna, and N. Nohria. "Unilateral Commitments and the Importance of Process in Alliances." *Sloan Management Review*, Spring 1994.

Hanan, M. *Growth Partnering: How to Build Your Company's Profits by Building Customer Profits.* New York: Amacom, 1992.

Hillman, G.P. "Partnering in Practice." *ASQC 48th Annual Quality Congress Proceedings,* 1994.

Johnson, H.T. *Relevance Regained: From Top-Down to Bottom-Up Empowerment.* New York: Free Press, 1992.

Moody, P.E. *Breakthrough Partnering: Creating a Collective Enterprise Advantage.* Essex Junction: Oliver Wight Publications, 1993.

O'Brien, J.M. "Are Consumers Being Jilted?" *Direct*, July 1994.

Remich, N.C. "Big Time Partnering." *Appliance Manufacturer*, June 1994.

Stein, M. "The Customer-Driven Organization." *Corporate Meetings and Inventories*, May 1994.

Tapscott, D. and A. Caston. *Paradigm Shift: The New Promise of Information Technology*. New York: McGraw-Hill, 1993.

Tompkins, J.A. *Winning Manufacturing: The How-to Book of Successful Manufacturing*. Norcross: IIE, 1989.

Urban, G.L. "How Partnering With Lead Users can Impact Product Development." *The Planning Forum Network*, April 1994.

Williams, G. and L. Reid. "Enhancing Customer-Supplier Relationships." *Quality*, April 1994.

Chapter 14
Beginning Your Partnership Revolution

Notes:

1 Kanter, R.M. "Collaborative Advantage: The Art of Alliances," *Harvard Business Review* (July/August 1994), 100.

2 This definition of synthesis is drawn from Jerry Hirshberg, *The Creative Priority* (New York: Harperbusiness, 1998).

Other Works Consulted:

Brooker, D. "Faster Food: How Just-In-Time Techniques Can Cut Supermarket Distribution Costs." *Materials Management and Distribution*, May 1993.

Herlitz, A. "Partnering May not be All it Seems." *U.S. Distribution Journal*, October 1993.

Lipnack, J. and J. Stamps. "The Best of Both Worlds." *Inc.*, March 1994.

Mathews, R. "ECR Initiatives Threatening Margins Unacceptable to Wholesalers." *Grocery Marketing*, November 1993.

Mathews, R. "ECR Opens Door to New Era of Supplier/Distribution Interface." *Grocery Marketing*, October 1993.

Messing, A. "What it Takes to be a Virtual Enterprise." *U.S. Distribution Journal*, 15 October 1993.

Nannery, M. "Forging Relationships: Retailers and Manufacturers are Allying Themselves in the Pursuit of ECR's Goals." *Supermarket News*, 17 January 1994.

Sansolo, M. "Formula for Success." *Progressive Grocer*, November 1993.

Tichy, N.M. "Revolutionize Your Company." *Fortune*, 13 December 1993.

Tompkins, J.A. and D. Harmelink. *The Distribution Management Handbook.* New York: McGraw-Hill, 1994.

Weinstein, S. "Small Firms Need Help." *Progressive Grocer*, February 1994.

Chapter 15
You Get What You Pay For

Works Consulted:

Banerjee, N. "Rebounding Earnings Star Old Debate on Productivity's Tie to Profit-Sharing." *Wall Street Journal*, April 1994.

Fierman, J. "The Perilous New World of Fair Pay." *Fortune*, 13 June 1994.

Keenan, W., Jr. "Breaking With Tradition." *Sales and Marketing Management*, June 1994.

Kohn, A. "Why Incentive Plans Cannot Work." *Harvard Business Review*, September/October 1993.

________. *Punished by Rewards.* New York: Houghton Mifflin Company, 1993.

Kouzes, J. M. and B.Z Posner. *The Leadership Challenge.* San Francisco: Jossey-Bass Publishers, 1991.

Lawler, E., III. *Strategic Pay: Aligning Organizational Strategies and Pay Systems.* San Francisco: Jossey-Bass Publishers, 1990.

McGrath, T. C. "Tapping the Groove in Human Productivity." *Industrial Engineering*, May 1994.

Moore, B. G. and T.L. Ross. *Gainsharing: Plans for Improving Performance.* Washington D.C.: The Bureau of National Affairs, Inc, 1990.

Muller, P. "Employee Monetary Systems: The Past or Future in Employee Motivation." *IM*, November/December 1993.

Zigon, J. "Making Performance Appraisal Work for Teams." *Training*, June 1994.

Chapter 16
Learning to Fish

Notes:

1 J.P. Kotter, *A Force for Change* (New York: Macmillan, 1990), 61.

Other Works Consulted:

Caggiano, C. "What Workers Want." *Inc.,* November 1992.

Ehrenfeld, T. "The Productivity-Boosting Gainsharing Report." *Inc.*, August 1993.

Farnham, A. "Mary Kay's Lessons in Leadership." *Fortune*, 20 September 1993.

Fenn, D. "Skill-Based Pay Takes Off." *CFO*, January 1993.

Fierman, J. "The Perilous New World of Fair Pay." *Fortune*, 13 June, 1994.

Hauch, W. and T.L. Ross. "Expanded Teamwork at Volvo Through Performance Gainsharing." *Industrial Management*, July/August 1988.

Jackson, W.M. "Gainsharing for High Productivity." *Profit*, January/ February 1994.

Kohn, A. *Punished by Rewards*. New York: Houghton Mifflin Company, 1993.

Kouzes, J.M. and B.Z Posner. *The Leadership Challenge: How to Get Extraordinary Things Done in Organizations.* San Francisco: Jossey-Bass Publishers, 1991.

Lawler, E.E. III. *Strategic Pay: Aligning Organizational Strategies and Pay Systems*. San Francisco: Jossey-Bass Publishers, 1990.

McGrath, T.C. "Gainsharing: Tapping the Groove in Human Productivity." *Industrial Engineering*, May 1994.

Peters, T. *Liberation Management*. New York: Alfred A. Knopf, 1992.

Peters, T. *Thriving on Chaos: Handbook for a Management Resolution.* New York: Alfred A. Knopf, 1987.

Rountree, D and J. Yorkutat. "Reward-Results Linkages." *1994 Industrial Engineering Conference Proceedings, Institute of Industrial Engineers*, Norcross, 1994.

Tompkins, J.A. "Gainsharing 1-6." *Industrial Product Bulletin,* September, October, November, December 1993, and January, February 1994.

Tompkins, J.A. "Team-Based Continuous Improvement: How to Make the Pace of Change Work for You and Your Company." *Material Handling Engineering*, August 1993.

Tully, S. "Your Paycheck Gets Exciting." *Fortune*, 1 November, 1993.

Zigon, J. "Making Performance Appraisals Work for Teams." *Training*, June 1994.

Chapter 17
Starting Your Compensation Revolution

Work Consulted:

Belasco, J.A. and R.C. Stayer. *Flight of the Buffalo: Soaring to Excellence, Learning to Let Employees Lead.* New York: Warner Books, 1993.

Day, M. "Employee Involvement and Gainsharing in the Retailing Industry." *International Industrial Engineering Conference Proceedings.* Norcross: IIE, 1990.

Fierman, J. "The Perilous New World of Fair Pay." *Fortune,* 13 June 1994.

Graham-Moore, B. and T.L. Ross. *Gainsharing: Plans for Improving Performance.* Washington D.C.: The Bureau of National Affairs, 1990.

Hart, J.G. "Gainsharing: The Double-barreled Solution to Low Morale." *Business Leader,* March 1994.

Lawler, E.E. III. *Strategic Pay: Aligning Organizational Strategies and Pay Systems.* San Francisco: Jossey-Bass Publishers, 1990.

Neusch, D.R. and A.F. Siebenaler. *The High Performance Enterprise.* Essex Junction: Oliver Wight Publications, 1993.

Peters, E. "A New Approach to Systems Training." *Automatic ID News,* July 1994.

Schmid, R.O. "Structuring Gainsharing for Success." *Industrial Engineering,* July 1994.

Conclusion

Works Consulted:

Belasco, J.A. and R.C. Stayer. *Flight of the Buffalo: Soaring to Excellence, Learning to Let Employees Lead.* New York: Warner Books, 1993.

Index

A

B

M

T